Women in Public

THE JOHNS
HOPKINS
SYMPOSIA IN
COMPARATIVE
HISTORY

The Johns Hopkins Symposia in Comparative History are occasional volumes sponsored by the Department of History at the Johns Hopkins University and the Johns Hopkins University Press comprising original essays by leading scholars in the United States and other countries. Each volume considers, from a comparative perspective, an important topic of current historical interest. The present volume is the fifteenth. Its preparation has been assisted by the James S. Schouler Lecture Fund.

Women in Public

Between Banners and Ballots, 1825–1880

Mary P. Ryan

The Johns Hopkins University Press
Baltimore and London

The Johns Hopkins University Press
701 West 40th Street Baltimore, Maryland 21211
The Johns Hopkins Press Ltd., London

The paper used in this publication meets the minimum requirements of
American National Standard for Information Sciences—Permanence of Paper
for Printed Library Materials, ANSI Z39.48–1984.

LIBRARY OF CONGRESS CATALOGING-IN-PUBLICATION DATA

Ryan, Mary P.
    Women in public : between banners and ballots, 1825–1880 / Mary P. Ryan.
        p.   cm.—(The Johns Hopkins symposia in comparative history; 15th)
    Bibliography: p.
    Includes index.
    ISBN 0-8018-3908-4 (alk. paper)
    1. Women in public life—Louisiana—New Orleans—History—19th century.
2. Women in public life—California—San Francisco—History—19th century.
3. Women in public life—New York (N.Y.)—History—19th century.   I. Title.
II. Series.
HQ1391.U5R9   1990
305.4′2′0973—dc20   89-32863
                                                                         CIP

For Rick

Contents

Preface and Acknowledgments

The first reckless steps that led to this book were taken half-consciously and quite a number of years ago. Motivated by questions left in suspension by my previous work, which focused on the family context of women's history, and by a certain impatience with developments in American social history, I formulated a hopelessly ambitious research agenda, to search out the meaning of "the public" in the last century. The inestimable value of the new social history—its inclusion of neglected populations, its cultivation of local sites of social life, its revelation of social processes once veiled in privacy—had inevitably created lacunae in the transformed historical landscape: uncharted relationships between different social groups, gaps between insulated communities, unmapped pathways between social life and political institutions. The concept of the public harbored promises of linking the dispersed elements of social history and bringing its powerful but diffused insights into contact with one another on the plane of politics.

I had no intention of jettisoning the concerns or the methods of social history. My goal was to bring the substance of social history—its attention to the formation of and relationships between social groups, its sensitivity to social change and social stratification, its respect for social differences—to a larger and centering plane of both behavior and analysis. Most certainly I did not intend to retreat from the history of women, but rather to bring female subjects and the representation of gender into the center of a social history of the public. This goal of placing gender in the public domain rested awkwardly within my comprehensive and pluralistic formulation of the history of the public. The uneasy historical relationship between women and the public presented too many complications, quandaries, and mystifications for women to be swiftly and smoothly incorporated into a narrative of public life. This relationship required concerted, central attention in its own right and on its own terms.

I was delivered from this scholarly predicament by the invitation from the Johns Hopkins University to deliver the James S. Schouler lectures. The Schouler lectures offered me the freedom to write a speculative version of the second book that resided so uncomfortably in my original and foolishly ambitious project. This may well be a perversely backwards approach: to insert women and gender into the historical space of "the public," whose overall contours have yet to be mapped. Although I find a certain perverse attraction in a procedure that inverts the customary order of historiography by starting with women and then proceeding on to what is usually perceived as the center and the whole, I put these essays before you in a spirit of exploration. The formality of my prose and the covers of a book should not disguise my speculative posture, my intention to plod on toward my original quixotic goal, and my confidence that even as I write others are clarifying and correcting this tentative picture of women in public.

The serpentine path of my explorations has rambled across the country and left a trail of intellectual and personal debts. It started on the coast of California, first at the University of California, Irvine, where the world's best colleagues fed me ideas and encouragement while the university and the American Council of Learned Societies financed the first stages of the research. My movement northward began with a fellowship at the Center for Advanced Study in the Behavioral Sciences in Stanford (financed in part by the National Endowment for the Humanities). The combination of quiet and conversation and the luxurious library services at the Center made my research possible and pleasant.

With my move to the University of California, Berkeley, in 1986, my debts mounted up. The university supplied essential funds for the completion of the manuscript, and graduate assistants Sharon Ullman and Lisa Cody perfected my text and footnotes with energy, intelligence, and good-humored tolerance of the author's scatter-brained work habits. The brunt of my absent-mindedness was borne by the staff of the Berkeley's Women's Studies Program, Eli Coppola, Sara Luria, and Carla Atkins. To Carla I owe nothing less than my sanity, preserved by her constant efficiency and the warm ripples of her laughter. I am especially indebted to the scores of Women's Studies faculty who for three years have given me unfailing support as director of that program. In our countless hours of working together we rarely had the time to discuss our own research, yet they fed me an uninterrupted stream of ideas and inspiration. These women and men, too numerous to list here, are responsible for the tone of optimism that infuses these essays: their energy and intelligence prove that in the public university we can work together through our differences toward common feminist goals.

The trail of my scholarly debts also wends its way to the south and the east, first to archivists at the New Orleans Public Library's Louisiana Collection, the Louisiana State Museum, the Historic New Orleans Collection, and the University of New Orleans, and then on to New York's Municipal Archives and the New-York Historical Society. My hosts in these prized cities deserve special acknowledgment. Joe Logsdon was the perfect traveler's guide to New Orleans past and present, and Judy and Danny Walkowitz provided, as they have for over a decade, the finest movable seminars, over morning coffee in Manhattan. It was in Baltimore and at Johns Hopkins that the first products of my work were exposed to public view and where I encountered especially helpful and trenchant criticism from faculty and students. I would like in particular to thank Cathy Kerr for provoking me to create Chapter 3. The productivity and pleasure of my stay in Baltimore owes much to the hospitality of John Russell-Wood. At the Johns Hopkins University Press I incurred major debts to Henry Tom and Carol Ehrlich for their skills, patience, and congeniality.

The essays that follow were written in dialogue with a legion of scholars who read early drafts and provoked countless revisions. Thomas Laqueur and Catherine Gallagher provided shrewd guidance at critical points in their formulation. Joseph Logsdon and Michael Wallace alerted me to critical sources and spared me major mistakes. Four scholars provided such perceptive and detailed readings that they fundamentally shaped the manuscript. I wish to especially acknowledge and deeply thank Nancy Fraser, Linda Kerber, Michael Rogin, and Ronald Walters. I only wish that I could have met the high standard of their criticism more fully. The wide-ranging subject of these essays has made me especially dependent on other scholars who can be acknowledged only in the footnotes, but I wish to credit in particular the many young historians whose dissertations I have mined unmercifully. Timothy Gilfoyle and Peggy Pascoe are specially deserving of thanks for showing me manuscripts that contributed essential information and sharp insights about my subject matter.

Finally, my acknowledgments take me home, to Richard Busacca and Anne Busacca-Ryan. Annie was conceived at about the same time as this project, and has grown more robustly and in blissful counterpoint to it. She is a "pleasure and a privilege and a heavenly delight." Rick sustained me through these years with his superb homemaking, his unsurpassed understanding of social and political theory, and the example of his political engagement. To my partner in the pleasures of the public and the private, thanks, in equal measure, for the social theory and the *salsa caliente!*

Women in Public

INFAMOUS!

VIDE LORD PALMERSTON'S SPEECH.

HEAD-QUARTERS, DEPT OF THE GULF.
NEW ORLEANS: *May 15, 1862.*

As the OFFICERS and SOLDIERS of the UNITED STATES have been subjected to REPEATED INSULTS from the WOMEN, calling themselves 'LADIES,' of NEW ORLEANS, in return for the most scrupulous NON-INTERFERENCE and COURTESY on our part, it is ordered that hereafter when any female shall by word, gesture, or movement, insult or show contempt for any OFFICER or PRIVATE of the UNITED STATES she shall be regarded and held liable to be TREATED as

A WOMAN OF THE TOWN
PLYING HER VOCATION.

By command of
Maj.-Gen. BUTLER

Introduction

In Search of the Public

On May 15, 1862, Major General Benjamin Butler, commander of the Union forces in New Orleans, issued General Order Number 28, which read as follows: "As the officers and soldiers of the United States have been subject to repeated insults from the women (calling themselves ladies) of New Orleans, in return for the most scrupulous non-interference and courtesy on our part, it is ordered that hereafter when any female shall, by word, gesture or movement, insult or show contempt for any officer or soldier of the United States, she shall be regarded and held liable to be treated as a woman of the town plying her vocation."[1] All the themes of the essays that follow come together in this single document, a bizarre dramatization of the place of women in public life a century ago. General Butler's edict proves that the attempt to search out women in public is not futile. Contrary to common assumptions that women's place in nineteenth-century America was in the home, it is not difficult to locate Victorian women, even Southern ladies, in the public arena. The beleaguered general of an occupied city learned, much to his chagrin, that the women of New Orleans laid claim to the public in at least four ways, each the subject of one of these exploratory essays. First, women were conscripted into a code of public conduct which prescribed that they present themselves as "ladies" outside the home. Second, they occupied public space, the streets and squares where they so brashly defied the authority of Union soldiers. Third, women became the subjects of public policy, provoking a military order aimed at controlling the behavior of one sex. Finally, women were central actors in public discourse about the most consequential issues, lending their voices to the fratricidal politics of the Civil War.

Yet despite these multiple points of entry into the public life of this nineteenth-century city, women hardly found a commodious, legitimate, or powerful place in the polity. When the women of New Orleans abused the privileges of the public, they were labeled prostitutes and thereby rudely exiled to the most ignominious ranks of the citizenry. This episode also speaks volumes about the public man of the nineteenth century, who, personified by Benjamin Butler and challenged by women in public, was reduced to slinging sexual epithets at the "weaker sex." When, in Chapter 4, I examine this strange encounter between General Butler and the women of New Orleans in more detail, it should become clear that this episode is not a curiosity of local history but one telling example of the consequential and contradictory position of women in American public life.

To search for women in public is to subvert a longstanding tenet of the modern Western gender system, the presumption that social space is divided between the public and the private and that men claim the former while women are confined to the latter. This investigation is not premised on a perverse inclination to defy conventional wisdom but rather is an obvious step in the progression of feminist scholarship and women's history. The feminist theory and the women's studies scholarship produced in the last twenty years provide a direct incentive to defy the rigid classifications of male/public and female/private. These paired dualisms, highly useful guideposts to feminist scholars early in the 1970s, had become objects of suspicion by the end of the decade and are now prime candidates for extinction at the hands of deconstructionists. But before these concepts and the gender relationships imputed to them are simply excised from the feminist vocabulary, one alternative strategy might prove useful. That strategy, and the premise of this exploration, is to retain the concept of the public but shun its gender correlate; that is, to go defiantly in search of women in public. The object of my search is simultaneously women as subjects and gender as both a linguistic construction and a set of social relationships.

The concept of the public entered forcefully into the vocabulary of feminist theory in the now-classic essay published in 1974 by Michelle Rosaldo, "Woman, Culture, and Society: A Theoretical Overview." Casting over the first tide of cross-cultural evidence about women's status, which issued from the new wave of feminism, Rosaldo proposed a structural explanation for the seemingly universal subordination of women. The baseline of sexual inequality, she argued, was a pervasive association of women with private spaces and domestic functions and their parallel underrepresentation in the public realms where men spoke and acted authoritatively for the whole community. Rosaldo's thesis understandably had wide appeal to feminists. It seemed broad enough to explain a pervasive pattern of inequity without recourse to reductionist biological causes; it was not women's reproductive biology nor men's reputedly superior physical strength, but the social and cultural process of assigning the sexes to public or private space that underpinned sexual inequality. Because social constructions are amenable to human intervention, Rosaldo's thesis also provided theoretical ballast for feminist attempts at social change.[2]

The concepts of the public and the private also helped to set a course for scholars and activists through the 1970s. To subvert sexism one need simply (in theory if not politics) vault the barricade between the public and the private. Such a feminist strategy was already in heavy use as Rosaldo wrote. In 1970 it provided the substance of perhaps the most memorable slogan of the new wave of feminism, The personal is the political. The strategy was activated by demands to place a whole spate of women's issues which originated in the private sphere—abortion, child care, housework, domestic violence, etc.—on the agenda for public discussion and legislative action. Scholars took up a similar strategy as they set to work rewriting a historical record that heretofore had been notably reticent about both women and private life. Entering into the families of the past, discovering a female world of love and ritual, compiling voluminous lists of women's voluntary associations, historians of American women publicized a past once veiled in privacy. In the process, the vocabulary of privacy as well as of gender was fundamentally altered: the private home became a site of domestic feminism; women's sphere was a domain of woman power; organizations with an exclusively female membership were invested with public significance.

This activism and scholarship had the unanticipated consequence of blurring the distinction between private and public as it had appeared in the theoretical blueprints of scholars like Rosaldo. Women's private relationships were recast as a domain of sexual *politics,* a term usually associated with the public sphere. Women's private spaces were found to be easily and repeatedly penetrated from the public domain by judicial constructions of child custody or the economic power that husbands brought home with their paychecks. Conversely, woman's work in her private place—be she socializing children, keeping boarders, silently inflating the GNP with her unremunerated housework, or providing for social welfare through a ladies' relief association—sent a steady, strong current of influence into the public domain. If, then, the boundary between the public and the private depended on the maintenance of exacting boundaries and refined gender distinctions between the two, then were not both spheres mere chimera?

Having done herculean service a few years earlier, the public/private distinction seemed about to dissolve. The spheres themselves were sometimes dismissed as fictions constructed by a patriarchal culture. Writing in 1980, Michelle Rosaldo herself confessed to some second thoughts on the subject. The mounting diversity of ethnographic evidence, as well as a revival of essentialist and oppositional thinking among feminists, propelled Rosaldo to place the public/private divide in the rapidly filling dustbin called the "dualisms of the past." "Home versus public life," she wrote, "appeared to have a transhistorical sense, at least in part, because it corresponds to our longstanding ideological terms, contrasting inner and outer, love and interest, natural and constructed bonds, men's and women's natural activities and styles." Such oppositional modes of categorizing human experience, she concluded, "will prove inherently problematic for those of us who hope to understand the lives that women lead in human societies."[3]

This distrust of dualistic categories is not a recent product of postmodern epistemology.[4] It is in the best spirit of the twentieth-century women's movement as depicted by Nancy Cott. The feminism born of this century, as described by Cott, operated on a paradoxical premise. While the new feminists of the second decade honored female solidarity based on sexual identity and acted in the interest of the second sex, they parted with the nineteenth-century woman movement by rejecting rigid definitions of woman, especially those that could be attributed to biology.[5] Many of Rosaldo's revisions of the position she took some six years earlier were undertaken in this spirit, by way of disputing essentialist categorizations of women and men and questioning the private/public distinctions drawn around them. She wrote in hopes of directing attention beyond those bounded spheres to the set of social relations whereby men and women actively constructed their own world of meaning. At the same time, Rosaldo was reluctant to jettison her original schema entirely. Rather, she rephrased the distinction between public and private, male and female, not as ontological categories or accurate depictions of behavior, but as cultural constructions imposed on a far more complex world of inchoate experience.

By virtue of their power in the creation of meaning, those categories are still deserving of feminists' attention. As long as these concepts retain such resiliency in modern Western culture, their theoretical obituaries are premature. Quite independent of their role in policing the genders, the terms *private* and *public* remain charged with value, albeit weighted with varying, contested, and shifting references. The term *privacy* is invested largely with positive value in the modern West. Since the Enlightenment, the private sphere has served to represent a domain of inviolate individualism, a barricade against the power of the monarch and the state, the place in which to cultivate a refined sense of the self, a refuge from the menacing world of strangers.[6] When paired with this liberal construction of privacy, the public becomes charged with negative value; it poses as the iron hand of the state or the anomie and danger that lurk in public places. Yet the term *public* also has its champions, from the admirers of the Greek polis, to the cosmopolitan spirits who savor the multifarious stimulations of the public thoroughfare, to social critics who lament the fall of public man.[7]

The power of the terms *public* and *private* in language and in our imagination is reflected in their continuing ability to shape and comprehend social behavior, albeit in very untidy, historically specific ways. It would be a foolish iconoclasm that destroyed a terminology capable of discerning societal variations between the sociability of a feudal manor and a suburban bungalow; between the fervor of a nineteenth-century political campaign and the poor turnout on recent election days; or between streets where women walk only under cover of the chador and roadsides lined with women wearing the skimpy garb of joggers.

This last homely example suggests the most compelling reason why the term *public,* in particular, has not lost all its analytic utility: the public still bears a very clear mark of gender. The distance between women and the public domain, marked in fundamentalist Moslem societies by the veil, purdah, and denial of the vote to women, can also be seen on the front page of the *New York Times,* where women rarely appear in the public gallery of the powerful. Cross-cultural surveys of gender roles find the greatest sexual asymmetry in the political arena, where men greatly outnumber women in positions of power. In 1980, Rosaldo summarized the still-pervasive gender asymmetry of the public as follows: "I know of no political system in which women individually or as a group are expected to hold more offices or have more political clout than their male counterparts." Rosaldo went on to note that the gender imbalance of the public adheres to cultural and spatial as well as to political relations: "women may have ritual power of considerable significance to themselves as well as men, but women never dominate in rites requiring the participation of the whole community."[8]

Gender asymmetry singles out the public side of this imbalance as especially deserving of attention. The relative absence of women in public life denotes not just segregation but stratification and hierarchy. In public, men speak for and act upon the community as a whole, including women. A reciprocal power does not accrue to women by virtue of their stature in the private realm. Similarly, the public can often incorporate or overrule private interests, but not vice versa. Nor should it be forgotten that the public arena is also the only legitimate agency for the use of force. It is only the sphere commonly labeled *public* that can issue pronouncements that pass as an overriding consensus, that presume to represent the common good or the general welfare. The public domain is also the crucible of a community's prestige system where, as Sherry Ortner has pointed out, men are situated to establish status for both sexes, and where women rarely reciprocate and never dominate. The term *public* continues to serve at least four critical purposes in feminist theory: as a reference for cultural values, as a crudely serviceable classification of social behavior, as a space denoting especially blatant gender asymmetry and inequality, and as a center of concentrated power.[9]

Up to this point in the historiography of American women, the public sphere has been studied either obliquely or through the narrow channels of the suffrage movement. One group of historians of women has approached the public domain by following the course of their female subjects as they moved slowly but persistently outward from their customary niches in the private sphere. Historians wisely began their search for women where they could most easily be found and were in the greatest numbers—in the household, the female sphere, and women's associations. Yet almost inevitably historians found even nineteenth-century middle-class women trespassing across the border of the private realm—entering reform movements or taking their domestic concerns to the halls of government. At the same time, even the most accomplished female trespassers into the public realm, the women reformers of the Progressive era, still left traces of their private origins in their metaphors of social housekeeping; their promises to purify and clean up politics; and their persistent refusal to challenge sexual differences, especially the reproductive and domestic roles assigned to women. By the turn of the century, definite limits to women's passage into the public domain were clearly visible. Theirs was still a women's politics, its agenda defined primarily around the needs and interests of women and children and its membership largely confined to one sex and most often a middle-class, Protestant sector of womanhood. Hence, Paula Baker argued, in her astute survey of politics and gender between 1780 and 1920, that women inhabited a separate political culture, which she termed "The Domestication of Politics." If the minimal dictionary definition of *public,* pertaining to the people as a whole, is applied to these nineteenth-century practices, then women's politics remained hamstrung by its roots in privacy.[10] Those historians who followed women along the second path into the public domain, through the suffrage movement, implicitly accepted a truncated definition of the public, focusing on but one manifestation of citizenship—that is, the exercise of the franchise. Moreover, the suffrage movement would reach its goal at a time when electoral politics was losing its grip on male citizens, as indicated by declining voter participation rates and the expansion of political bureaucracy.

Because these critical but relatively oblique and narrow points of entry into the public arena have led women's history into either domestic captivity or political irony, it is time to adopt a different strategy. While acknowledging that much of women's historical experience has been enclosed in a relatively private domain, these essays undertake the search for women from a direct, relatively unobstructed, squarely public vantage point. My starting point is neither the realm of domesticity nor women's associations but the public sphere itself. If, on the one hand, women are seldom found in this otherwise commodious but ill-defined space, we need to examine the mechanism whereby that sphere was created and maintained as a masculine province. How did public man characterize the women who were banned from his lofty domain? What were the public consequences of this exclusion for men as well as for women? On the other hand, if females are discovered acting effectively in the public arena, it raises a question of more than passing interest: how can women lay claim to and make use of the public citadels that continue to elude their sex?[11]

Before this investigation can proceed, an attempt to specify some of the characteristics of the public is in order. One wry commentator has aptly described this indefinable term as "a complex of processes seeking to encapsulate . . . an ambiguous and well-worn (not to say shop-soiled) distinction."[12] The term *public* is found neither in the *Dictionary of the Social Sciences* nor in lexicons of historical usages such as Raymond Williams's *Key Words.* This would seem a strange fate to befall a common noun that is so prominent in the language of politics and an adjective that designates the most familiar places of amusement, citizenship, and education. Those who would attempt to harness this ubiquitous word to a single precise definition, however, are soon lost in a maelstrom of conflicting meanings. Perhaps the most common way of anchoring the term *public* is to tie it to an institution such as the state and to set it in polar opposition to a private place, the family. Such concrete institutional parameters of public and private soon dissolve in a host of socio-spatial gradations, from the individual soul to a global community. Those who would consign the family to privacy meet up with anthropologists' arguments in behalf of the jural and political significance of kinship. The search for moorings along the spectrum between private and public has spawned intermediary concepts such as Hegel's civil society and Hannah Arendt's "the social." Feminist theorists like Anna Yeatman enter the fray by then refining the distinction between the social and the domestic. Any attempt to define the public will also collide with ideological presuppositions, the most prominent of which is the liberal's tendency to restrict the public to a mere aggregation of private interests and the communitarian's contrary attachment to the notion of an organic common good that stands above and apart from individual preoccupations. The prospects of finding a neat definition of the public seem bleak and are beyond my theoretical reach.[13]

But what eludes strict definition is hardly meaningless. For millennia, political theorists have invested the term *public* with special value. Philosophers from Aristotle to contemporary feminists confirm the importance of the concept and provide guidance in writing its history. In the writings of twentieth-century political theorists—of Hannah Arendt and Jürgen Habermas, in particular—the public becomes a richly evocative term, a linguistic marker of highly privileged meaning, both moral and political. Arendt constructed perhaps the most olympian notion of the public. Drawing on classic political theory, especially Aristotle, Arendt theorized a "public realm," which extended beyond governmental institutions to a world where citizens might share equally in self-government and deliberate as peers about their mutual concerns. Concurring with the ideal political formulations of ancient Greece, Arendt invested the polis with supreme value; it is in the public realm, not in privacy or isolation, "that humanity is most fully present and perfectly exercised, where some semblance of immortality is achievable." Arendt's public was clearly a social and historical as well as an idealized realm, a place like the Acropolis where citizens came together; for "only where things can be seen by many in a variety of aspects without changing their identity, so that those who are gathered around them know they see sameness in utter diversity, can worldly reality truly and reliably appear."[14]

Jürgen Habermas shares ardently in Arendt's veneration of the public but widens its domain beyond classic political ideals to the social, political, and discursive practices of the modern world. His description of the public sphere will serve as the initial blueprint for locating the public historically. "By the public sphere we mean first of all a realm of our social life in which something approaching public opinion can be formed. Access is guaranteed to all citizens. A portion of the public sphere comes into being in every conversation in which private individuals assemble to form a public body. They then behave neither like business or professional people conducting private affairs, nor like members of a constitutional order subject to the legal constraints of state bureaucracy. Citizens behave as a public body when they confer in an unrestricted fashion—that is with the guarantee of freedom of assembly and association and the freedom to express and publish their opinions—about matters of general interest." Habermas states emphatically that the public sphere is not coterminous with the state. Rather, his public sphere mediates between society and the state; it is that place where "the public organizes itself as the bearer of public opinion." Habermas, in sum, emphasizes a feature of the public implicit in Arendt, the ability of that concept to articulate and validate processes that promote open discussion among a wide spectrum of social actors on a wide range of concerns. Like Arendt, Habermas privileges the deliberative aspect of the public, its capacity to bring citizens together to rationally present, discuss, and reach a consensus about the general good. His early work on the public sphere set the stage for a "theory of communicative action," which elaborately specifies the conditions under which claims to a public good can be assessed.[15]

Other political theorists have called both Arendt and Habermas to task for placing implicit limitations on the openness and inclusiveness of their hallowed public sphere. Arendt, as Hanna Pitkin has demonstrated, seems relatively unconcerned that the polis excluded the majority of Greeks—slaves and women—and hardly disguises her distaste for the "household" concerns they might carry into the public realm. Similarly, Nancy Fraser has faulted Habermas for construing the citizen as a male. His larger theory of communicative action is riveted with polarizations that implicitly place women outside the public sphere, consigned to a realm more natural and private than the apollonian and rational world of public discourse. At the very least, any construction of the public sphere must acknowledge and account for the historical exclusion of women and gender issues. By restoring the quest for justice to the center of the Aristotelian public realm, Hanna Pitkin sets the stage for such a reassessment. With its "roots in human need and its consequence for power," justice pertains to all members of a community and admits all issues into the realm of public discourse. Among those whom Pitkin would enroll in the public quest for justice is the housewife who "learns for the first time that she is not alone in her misery and boredom, that what troubles her is part of social structure that can be altered." Such expansion of the public sphere is as necessary for men as for women, for "in so far as [he] did not really see the slaves and women around him," the Athenian citizen "did not know himself or his community."[16]

Feminist theorists from Mary Wollstonecraft to the political philosophers of the 1980s have challenged the public sphere to incorporate women and their uncommon concerns. Noting that theories of the public rarely take cognizance of gender differences and that classic republicanism was overtly disdainful of women, some contemporary feminist thinkers reject the concept itself as patriarchy parading as universalism. Iris Young points out that the Enlightenment notion of the public presumed some impartial, transcendent, aridly rational consensus, disconnected from the diverse interests and experience of real men and women. Influenced by postmodern philosophy, feminists such as Young and Fraser see the gender restrictions of political theory as a synecdoche for a general intolerance of social multiplicity. By feminist standards, male political institutions, no less than women's associations of the nineteenth century, are socially restrictive and hence imperfectly public. Feminists need not, however, turn their backs on the ideal of the public. Rather, like Iris Young, they might call for the creation of a "heterogeneous public life"—one fully accessible to women, attentive to the concerns that they embody in any given historical moment, and open to the full range of social differences that inhere in any complex society.[17]

The body of political and social theory to which I have elliptically alluded does not define the public; instead, it points to a set of ideals that is, I believe, well worth pursuing. The classic notion of the public, amended by Habermas's theory of communicative action, validates social spaces and political practices that foster exchange of opinion between citizens. Feminist political theorists push at the boundaries of the public by holding that sphere to the highest standards of openness, accessibility, tolerance of diversity, and capacity to acknowledge the needs of a heterogeneous membership. The term *public* evokes aspirations for an arena where women can strive, along with men, for empowerment and justice. It is a prize that feminists still covet for the female sex. In the end, it is this moral and political ideal that motivates my search for women in public.

This theory offers little guidance to historians, and especially students of nineteenth-century America, as to where they might actually locate the public. Arendt's Acropolis is far removed from Ben Butler's New Orleans. Habermas's conceptualization of the public sphere harks back to seventeenth- and eighteenth-century circles of the philosophes. "It is no coincidence," he writes, "that these concepts of public sphere and public opinion arose for the first time only in the eighteenth century." The demise of the Old Regime removed politics from the private chambers of monarchs and replaced the public display of their authority with multiple arenas for creating public opinion: republican clubs, insurgent movements, the café intelligentsia, and, above all, the public press. This public sphere, however, had decided social limits. It was the exclusive domain of the bourgeoisie. In Habermas's judgment, the very emergence of the public sphere was historically dependent on those bourgeois limits. Unrestrained public discussion with the intent of arriving at common goals could not be sustained once workers and the propertyless (not to speak of women) demanded entry into its august halls. Hence, Habermas's history of the public sphere is truncated: it emerged in the eighteenth century only to be fractured by English Chartism and the French Revolution of 1848. In a brief allusion to the United States, he suggests that the mainstay of public discourse, the press, had degenerated into a mere commercial enterprise as early as the 1830s. The public sphere was already deteriorating into a bastard form, which Habermas called "mass democracy." Under this political system, installed early in this century, consensus arrived at by individuals engaged in public discussion was replaced by competition between private—albeit large, well-organized, and well-publicized—interest groups, such as corporate capitalists and trade unions, each seeking exclusive benefits from the state.

If Habermas's chronology is accurate, it casts the public sphere as a very fragile entity, its history and prospects easily thwarted in heterogeneous societies. Born in narrow social circles during the Enlightenment, it could not withstand the challenges of social diversity, democratic insurgency, and women's public claims which buffeted Western republics early in the nineteenth century. The olympian notion of a sphere of rational deliberation may be incompatible with genuine publicness, with being open and accessible to all. These essays set this quandary in a social and historical context. They test the capacity of the public sphere to accommodate the female gender in a time and in places of social diversity and democratic challenge—three American cities, New York, New Orleans, and San Francisco, between 1825 and 1880.

The choice of these sites for my exploration is based on their claim to a vigorous public culture. In these places during this time, the value of publicness was undisputed and manifest in a variety of ways, the first of which is political in nature. The fledgling American republic was born of a revolution that wrested political authority from the private chambers of George III and the Board of Trade. By 1825, Americans had endorsed popular sovereignty, demanded public accountability, and adopted "universal" white manhood suffrage. Within the new nation, as in other times and places, the standard of publicness was raised with most exuberance and force in the open spaces of cities, London's cafés, the streets of Paris, and the Boston Common. In the last century as today, New York was renowned for its robust and contentious politics; New Orleans was loved for its public festivities; and San Francisco acclaimed for its cosmopolitan urban style. By 1825, the spirit of publicness was also installed in specific institutions and displayed in a vigorous popular culture. A public politics was exercised in mass-based parties, ubiquitous public meetings, and a fervor to construct city halls. Public opinion was churned up by a thriving popular press. (For example, newspapers reached an estimated one hundred thousand readers in New York City in 1850.) Urban culture found public expression in popular lectures, public amusements, and exuberant, elaborately orchestrated public ceremonies. The very word *public* seemed ever on the lips of urban residents, called nightly to "public meetings," bombarded with advertisements addressed "to the public," and praised for their "public spirit." Although these three American cities differed from one another in various and important ways, I have not conducted any explicit comparison of the three and have shied away, for the time being, from quagmires of significant contrasts such as the undeniably unique meaning of "the public" in Creole New Orleans.[18] Rather, by basing this study in three locations, north, south and west (each with its distinctive English, French, or Spanish heritage), I hope to give some breadth to generalizations about public life.

If, by the second quarter of the nineteenth century, American cities had wholeheartedly embraced the spirit and practice of publicness, the decades to follow would severely test the public's fortitude. The pressure of population was staggering. Each cityscape was bloated by a tenfold increase in the number of residents: between 1820 and 1880, New York's population grew from 123,000 to 1.2 million; New Orleans' grew from 27,000 to 216,000; and San Francisco, an "instant city" in 1849, harbored 234,000 souls three decades later. Each a port city, New York, San Francisco, and New Orleans had to absorb a constant stream of transients and newcomers. The public sphere was also hard-pressed to accommodate an increasingly diverse citizenry: at midcentury, nearly half the residents of each city were foreign-born or nonwhite. The city of New

Orleans was cleaved by race and caste. African-Americans, slave and free, dominated the city numerically in 1820, but by 1860 were less than 20 percent of the population. With the influx of emancipated slaves after the Civil War, blacks came to constitute more than one-third of the city residents. African-Americans were a small but very visible minority in New York and San Francisco, while the latter city was the begrudging host to thousands of Chinese, who were nearly 8 percent of its population in 1870. The final demographic factor that fractured the public sphere was the sex ratio. The proportion of women in the urban population did not conform to the parity of birth rates but varied from city to city and fluctuated over time. San Francisco had the most skewed ratio of men and women. Women were rare apparitions on the streets of the gold rush town, and as late as 1870 males still outnumbered females 3 to 2. Women held a significant edge over men in New York, while the ratio was reversed in New Orleans. To anyone attuned to gender differences, the proportion of women in the nineteenth century was sufficiently variable to tilt the equilibrium of the public sphere.

Finally, the nineteenth-century urban public was subject to the disruptive impact of a changing economic structure. At the beginning point of this study, the economies of New York and New Orleans were dominated by merchants, shopkeepers, and artisans joined together in relations of interdependence and hierarchy. The relatively calm surface of the preindustrial city was nonetheless buffeted by robust growth in the commercial sector. These three port cities were regional hubs of a volatile export and import trade and would maintain a strong commercial and financial segment throughout the century. In 1880, trade and transportation accounted for 25 percent of all jobs in New York, 30 percent in San Francisco, and over 33 percent in New Orleans, where commerce remained the dominant economic sector. With so much of their economies devoted to commercial exchange, these cities inevitably experienced a collision between material interests and financial power, which introduced further discord into the public domain. By 1870, all three cities boasted significant industrial sectors as well. Manufacturing accounted for 25 percent of all jobs in New Orleans, 33 percent in San Francisco, and 41 percent in New York, where industry dominated the local economy. All cities by this date harbored at least a few large-scale manufacturing enterprises employing wage laborers, who gave new definition to the cleavages of class. This conflict rocked the public arena of all three cities during the great labor struggles of the 1870s. These cities, in sum, set an increasingly diverse, volatile, and discordant stage on which nineteenth-century Americans would enact a public life.

And enact it they did. The public stage of these cities was in fact far more expansive than the staging ground of most political theory. I have traced the public life of the nineteenth century far afield of conventional locations for politics, into a cultural and social context of publicness that concentrated in four urban institutions, each the subject of one of the essays that follow. In Chapter 1, I turn my sight on the most ebulliently public and ornately staged dramas, those civic ceremonies that were repeatedly mounted during every calendar year in all three cities. On officially designated holidays—that is, in time consecrated to public festivity for the people as a whole—the city displayed itself at its highest level of generality. On these occasions, gender differences were publicly acknowledged, albeit in contorted ways and largely without the active participation of women. Public ceremonies provide the occasion to ferret out the cultural meaning attributed to sexual difference in the course of widely attended and festive conventions of the public. This is the site where public meaning is created and displayed.

In Chapter 2, the focus shifts from the temporal to the spatial manifestation of publicness. Admittedly, most urban turf was dedicated to private enterprise and domestic sociability; the cityscape of shops and houses was only rarely broken by open space and cut through with a narrow grid of public thoroughfares. Yet many social and political opportunities lurked in these streets, squares, and parks, spaces that by definition were open to women. This chapter traces the kaleidoscopic patterning of women's occupation and use of urban public space. Women were channeled into selective sectors of public space, where their movements were charted by both gender prescriptions and class distinctions. Public territory was divided into a patchwork of male and female, homosocial and heterosexual regions. This is the arena in which gender differences are acted out in the habits of everyday life and presented to the public as social action.

In Chapter 3, I turn to the commonest reference of the term *public*, to politics. It was in the nineteenth century that the American city became defined politically as a public sphere. At the turn of the century, states still followed the English practice of vesting the governmental powers of municipalities in a private charter of incorporation, thereby making urban self-government a privilege rather than a right. Only in the nineteenth century did cities like New York secure state charters that vested sovereignty in the local citizens. In the wake of such reforms in municipal government, the volume of public business, the range of public improvements, and the size of the political bureaucracy swelled geometrically.[19] This administrative and legislative sector of the public sphere would seem to be the least hospitable to women, who, after all, were denied the chief means of exercising popular sovereignty, the vote and elected office. Yet women did find themselves written into public law, subject to the coercive power of the state, armed with the right of petition, and capable of influencing public officials. Still, the imprint of women on urban politics was small and highly restricted. In fact, gender was most likely to enter the political arena amid public debates relating to sexuality, most especially prostitution. Hence, Chapter 3 dwells in particular on this realm of expressly sexual politics. In the formal political arena, "public" translates into decisive action and ultimate power, which impinges on male and female alike.

Public administration and city ordinances do not, however, exhaust the political manifestations of the public. To confine politics to these mechanical matters, as William Sullivan puts it, "reduces the public realm to formal institutions in which the conflicts among the 'interests' of society were umpired and negotiated, draining public life of intrinsic morality and significance."[20] Therefore, my fourth and final chapter searches for gender politics at the level of public discourse, the realm of public opinion that is so central to political theorists like Habermas. To access this realm of discourse, I have turned to the same arena that Habermas extols as the forum of public deliberation, the city newspaper. The nineteenth-century press spotlighted partisan political campaigns and the sectional rivalries of the Civil War as the themes of the most vocal public discourse. The search for women in this sector of the public yields the most meager and disturbing results, including the unseemly encounter between Benjamin Butler and the "ladies." Women appear irregularly and surrounded with the most distortion. Yet the female citizens of nineteenth-century cities battered at the walls of the public sphere, relentlessly and with a variety of ingenious tools, handkerchiefs and brickbats among them. Their efforts can tell us something of the process, pitfalls, and possibilities that women encounter in our continuing quest for a secure and equal place in the public sphere. In other words, Chapter 4 implicates female subjects and gender codes in the making of public life in its broadest meaning.

The motive for these exploratory incursions into a vast expanse of public space is not just to claim new turf for historians but to underscore the importance of opening new space for women—the exhilaration of the ceremonial, the freedom of the street, the empowerment of political engagement, and the human possibilities of the public sphere. Hanna Pitkin presents the promise of the public this way: "Only in public life can we jointly as a community exercise the human capacity to think what we are doing and to take charge of the history in which we are constantly engaged by drift and inadventure." Only the public is big enough to accommodate the goals to which this feminist historian stubbornly aspires, gender justice and the equality of the sexes. In the process of injecting women into the history of the public, these essays raise basic questions about the democratic project of reconciling social diversity and public responsibility.

1

Ceremonial Space

*Public Celebration
and Private Women*

O n November 26, 1855, after nearly a month of planning and prolonged public meetings, the citizens of San Francisco gathered to celebrate the Allies' victory at Sebastopol during the Crimean War. This relatively esoteric event provoked an exuberant public festival, complete with a parade, a Te Deum, a hundred-gun salute, and a public banquet attended by between four thousand and five thousand high-spirited citizens. The dinner guests were invited into a pavilion especially constructed for this "grand jubilee" and treated to hundreds of gallons of wine, a multi-course meal, and a dessert that re-created the battle of Sebastopol in confectionary. By the time of this last fantastic course, the revelers lost all pretense of public etiquette: they stormed the dessert table and reenacted the Crimean War by pelting one another with cake crumbs. Such civic exuberance was "purely Californian," according to the local press, and indeed was never demonstrated with quite such panache in either New York or New Orleans. Like public dinners elsewhere, however, the San Francisco frolic was a masculine festival. Women could be found only on its margins. The ladies of San Francisco were invited to circle the pavilion before dinner, observe the elaborate preparations (including the celebrated cake), and then demurely leave the site of public festivities to the menfolk.[1]

This colorful example of the many civic ceremonies mounted in nineteenth-century cities gave public expression to a blunt and familiar gender asymmetry: in public, it would seem, men were vigorous social actors, women a docile audience. This essay explores the voluminous record of such public ceremonies, searching for a larger presence and more active agency of women. The results of this investigation reveal how civic ceremonies displayed the urban public in deeply gendered imagery. The dualism, distortion, and silences within these ceremonial codes created a treacherous language in which to conduct the civic affairs which will be detailed in subsequent chapters.

This essay locates nineteenth-century public life in time as well as in space; it examines those special occasions when the residents of New York, New Orleans, and San Francisco declared a holiday and designed ceremonies calculated to capture the attention of a vast audience. The designation of a civic holiday is, in itself, a powerful demonstration of a public culture, enjoining the citizenry to put aside their private predilections and order their comings and goings according to a common schedule. The event that occasioned a holiday, be it a victory in the Crimea or a more commonplace anniversary like the Fourth of July, was a popular cause for celebration. Such ceremonies were usually called by public officials, extolled by the public press, planned at public meetings, and open to the public in general. Historians who are attentive to what transpired on these occasions are witnesses to a public creation of meaning, including the popular construction of masculinity and femininity.

Anthropologists have long been mining public ceremonies for evidence about local cultures. Clifford Geertz's interpretive method has enshrined community rituals as the "stories a culture tells about itself." Summarizing the anthropological literature, John Skorupski has designated ceremony as a cultural performance that says, "Look, this is how things should be, this is the ideal pattern of social life. It gives to the people concerned an image of a harmonious, well-ordered, undisturbed social universe." Although the ceremonies enacted on civic holidays often originated in, and functioned as, this kind of summarizing symbol, or "capsule of a culture," other investigators have read them in a more diversified, dynamic, and conflicting way. At the very least, any ceremony is open to multiple interpretations by diverse actors and observers. Public rituals can serve to identify and evaluate differences within a community, including the distinctive places of male and female. Holiday festivities can also expose strains in the official culture, even call forth opposition to a supposedly dominant ideology. Mikhail Bakhtin's interpretation of carnival in early modern Europe is the most exuberant rendering of this aspect of public holidays. "The carnivalesque crowd in the marketplace or in the streets is not merely a crowd. It is the people as a whole, but organized *in their own way*, the way of the people. It is outside of and contrary to all existing forms of the coercive socioeconomic and political organization, which is suspended for the time of the festivity." Victor Turner charts a middle course between the unifying and oppositional interpretations of ceremonies, plotting out a social drama complete with liminal episodes that open prospects for changing as well as solidifying the culture being celebrated.[2]

The popular celebrations enacted in American cities during the nineteenth century provide evidence for all these interpretations. Those rites that received public sanction, left an extensive public record, and are the chief evidence employed here tend, however, to conform most closely to the model of the summarizing symbol. This essay speaks only in the language of the highest public repute, that written boldly on the city streets in times of general celebration. The cacaphony of tongues spoken by marginal social groups is relocated to the background of these major civic productions. Still, a wide range of citizens in New York, San Francisco, and New Orleans witnessed these public celebrations a century ago, and the muffled voices of many anonymous men and women blended into the official sounds of ceremony.

The yearly calendar was littered with holidays of ancient and recent creation. The natural cycles that are commemorated in rural cultures left at least a residue in the modern city in the regular New Year's festivities, in occasional pageants marking May Day, in a harvest festival, metamorphosed and Americanized into Thanksgiving. The latter holiday was strongly associated with Puritan New England and provides one example of the continuing power of the Christian calendar to command public time in secular cities. While Thanksgiving and Christmas were the only religious holidays in New York and San Francisco, New Orleans' Catholic origins were honored on Shrove Tuesday and All Souls Day.

Nineteenth-century cities did not, however, depend on ancient excuses for celebration. Probably the greatest source of new holidays was the brief history of the Republic, giving cause for celebration on July Fourth and Washington's Birthday in all three cities, the anniversary of the Battle of New Orleans in the city of the same name (and Bastille Day in the French Quarter), Evacuation Day in New York, and Admission Day in San Francisco. The second major innovation in the annual public rites was, tellingly, a manifestation of the ethnic differentiation of the population, St. Patrick's Day being the most extensive such festival. African-Americans and immigrants from China also found a small slot on the municipal calendar, publicly celebrating the anniversary of Emancipation and the Chinese New Year. Finally, city residents celebrated unique events as well as recurrent anniversaries. The major justification for such ceremonies was a giant step in the march of technological progress. All business was suspended when thousands of citizens took gaily to the streets to celebrate the Erie Canal, the Transcontinental Railroad, the Brooklyn Bridge. All in all, the nineteenth-century city was the site of a major expansion in the number and variety of American ceremonies.

The most fertile period in the growth of public ceremony was between 1825 and 1850. It was then that individual civic improvements sparked ornate celebrations, when July Fourth became the major secular holiday on the urban calendar, when St. Patrick's Day established the legitimacy of celebrating national origins. At the midpoint of the nineteenth century and increasingly after the Civil War, however, public ceremony lost something of its exuberance, encountered increasing disfavor among select classes, and took more rigid and controlled forms. First, the middle classes withdrew into private and domestic celebration of public holidays while taxpayers complained about public expenditures for holiday entertainment. Only rare and extraordinary occasions, like the centennial of the Declaration of Independence, the completion of the Brooklyn Bridge, and the end of Reconstruction in the South, inspired widespread and enthusiastic public ceremony in the 1870s.

The characteristic form of civic celebration also changed over time. The beginning point of my analysis, 1825, was marked by especially ornate and festive celebrations. In that year, both the opening of the Erie Canal in New York and the welcome of Lafayette to New Orleans prompted elaborate festivities featuring civic pageants, multiple processions, and a communal feast—bringing as many as three thousand guests to a common table. San Francisco's celebration of the victory at Sebastopol, although three decades later in chronological time, conformed to this pattern and occupied a similar stage in the development of a newly founded city. By contrast, relatively routine annual anniversaries in the 1820s and 1830s were often more like festivals than ceremonies, with the population taking to the streets in a carnivalesque, Bakhtinian spirit. On New Year's and Christmas, city streets were filled with gangs of young pranksters emitting a din of cowbells, firecrackers, and festive gunfire. Mardi Gras in New Orleans brought masked revelers into the public spotlight, and July Fourth found New Yorkers gathered around City Hall to eat, drink, and be merry.

By 1850, when celebration had become both more frequent and more organized, Americans had found their ceremonial métier in the peculiar cultural performance of the parade. Filing through the streets with banners and a band was an everyday occurrence in the antebellum years, a mode of celebration enjoyed by hundreds of militia units, trade associations, fire companies, political parties, reform associations, ethnic brotherhoods, and simple revelers. On the major festive days on the public calendar, all these elements of the polity joined together in one long train, as many as fifty thousand strong. An elaborate parade was the central ceremonial act of July Fourth, the moment at the midpoint of the calendar year when the public displayed itself in its brightest and most variegated colors. This simple ceremonial form, a mobile line-up of the city's preconstituted social groups, was an ingenious method of displaying a diverse social structure and a heterogeneous culture. First, the parade encoded the social differences of the big city and then bound them together in the self-discipline of the march and the abundant organizing energy of volunteers and city officials. By 1850, the procedures of the parade had been finely tuned. Thousands congregated at the signal of the starting gun, assumed their prearranged places in line, and filed, in relatively good order, through streets lined with police officers. Such celebrations bespoke a diverse, exuberant, but well-ordered public.[3]

The parades of the second quarter of the nineteenth century were the high point in democratic and participatory celebration. In the contentious urban history that followed, the diverse ethnic and class groups splintered off into separate associations with their segregated holidays. When a fuller public reconvened for ceremonial purposes after the Civil War, the parade was a truncated version of those of the past, featuring largely the military, the Irish, and the working classes. The central focus of ceremony was more likely to be a spectacle than a communal rite, placing most of the urban population in the role of passively watching a military parade or the phantasmagoria of a fireworks display. Still, days were set aside for the purpose of public celebration, if not coordinated ceremonies. At least some vague images of a public spirit wavered in the becalmed holiday air.

From 1825 into the 1880s, public time and the rites that it occasioned were clearly marked by masculine signs, most often crafted by male hands. Prior to the 1840s, celebrations were either rowdy male encounters or the manufactured products of the city fathers. Men sat down to public dinners without their consorts, or reveled in rowdy masculine play in which harlots were the most prominent female participants. The heyday of democratic ritual, typified by a July Fourth parade in the 1840s, was masculine to the core: an all-male entourage marched with manly strides and acted out men's social roles—the citizen, the soldier, the tradesman. The central ritual in the spectacles of the late nineteenth century also evoked masculine power: a military procession orchestrated by city bureaucrats displayed the force of the state whose armed might had preserved the Union.

Amid these decades of public celebration, women more often marked time by a private calendar. Women's diaries only occasionally took notice of public holidays. A July Fourth entry in the journal of Nellie Wetherbee of San Francisco noted, "Staid in all day and saw the procession and all there was to be seen from my window. Pleasant day." Anne Fader took in the celebration in the same city in 1876, but only because "I feared that on the anniversary of the next I might not consider it convenient to attend." Miss Fader was expecting to be a more retiring married woman in another year. The diary of a married woman of New Orleans named Jane West Benedict provides a similarly sparse record of public ceremony. In 1872, when Mrs. Benedict was a new mother, she did take her infant son to view the King of Carnival. But thereafter her diary became reticent about public festivals. Benedict regularly noted Christmas and New Year's in her journal but only to record indoor intimacies, to note the gifts she showered on her children on Christmas and number the guests who paid a call on New Year's. To Mrs. Benedict, the most memorable days were private matters, sacred only to her family: the anniversary of her marriage; her children's births; their first teeth, words, and steps. By focusing on the minutiae of temporal advances in young life, and selecting a birthday or other moment in the private life of the individual as the most cherished anniversary, middle-class mothers like Mrs. Benedict were creating a rival to the public method of demarcating festive time.[4]

Were I simply to delineate the calendar dates honored by women and men, the result would undoubtedly calibrate the life span of women primarily in private time. But this is not my intent. Rather, by carefully scrutinizing public ceremonies I hope to demonstrate that women left a consequential, if sometimes muted, mark on those events that publicly displayed urban culture. From the first, and with increasing force and intricacy, women were symbolically incorporated into the image the city projected of itself. Furthermore, by the second half of the nineteenth century, women had created some public rituals all their own. Finally, the total fabric of public culture was woven from male and female strands and patterned with gender distinctions.

The Public Man and His Private Consort: Gender and Ceremony in 1825

My story begins in 1825, at perhaps the high-water mark of American civic pageantry. In that year, the citizens of New Orleans and New York conducted two extravagant ceremonies, the first to welcome Lafayette to the city and the second to celebrate the completion of the Erie Canal. In New Orleans, the whole population streamed into the streets and squares for a full four days of festivities, beginning with a procession composed of the civic and merchant elites who escorted Lafayette into the Place d'Armes, where they passed through an arch of triumph especially constructed for the occasion. There followed a sequence of speeches, receptions, and banquets in which everyone from the city's attorneys to a contingent of "colored citizens" paid their respects to the French visitor. The New York rites in celebration of the Erie Canal were concentrated on just one day, November 4, but were equally ornate. The focal point of the ritual was the intersection of two processions. The first was a parade of boats that passed through the canal, down the Hudson, and out Long Island Sound for an aquatic ceremony. Barges full of state and local dignitaries watched as a vial of water drawn from Lake Erie was solemnly poured into the Atlantic. Around midday this flotilla returned to the Battery, where its occupants joined a more mundane procession composed of some seven thousand citizens and especially large numbers of artisans and the humbler classes of New York.

The actual physical presence of women in these early ceremonies was small and largely passive but nonetheless highly visible. A welcome from the ladies of the city was publicly read during the ceremonies at the Place d'Armes, prompting Lafayette to turn directly to a contingent of women to convey his effusive thanks. In the days that followed, the Gallic hero of the American Revolution interrupted his visitations with his fellow men to call on distinguished ladies— the daughter of Henry Clay, the sister of a French general, the wife of a congressman, and a celebrated local author. One early plan for the civic festival called for another more public and prominent role for women. The mayor of New Orleans had put forth a fanciful proposal that Lafayette be entertained by a restaging of the Battle of New Orleans, to take place on the historical site up the Mississippi River. He proposed that the French general be escorted to this dramatization of local history in a fleet of steamboats carrying "the daughters, the mothers, the wives, the sisters of those who fought on January 8 [1815]."[5]

As it turns out, a procession of this sort did take place in 1825, not in New Orleans but in New York. Among the vessels traveling to the ceremonies on Long Island Sound was a barge bearing the name the *Lady Clinton*, a homage to the wife of the governor and canal promoter, De Witt Clinton. This ceremonial vessel carried Mrs. Clinton, along with the wives of other canal promoters such as Cadwallader Colden, the consorts of other state and local officials, and "ladies of distinction from our sister states." This fashionable entourage constituted a formidable female presence in the very center of public festivity. A "select committee of the corporation," appointed to arrange for the safety, comfort, and entertainment of these ladies, filed an official report noting that "every precaution was used to prevent any accident. The barge was safely secured to the Commerce, and being superbly decorated, and crowded with ladies, elegantly attired, presented a most beautiful spectacle. . . . such a sight was never before beheld." Even more auspicious than this solicitous placement of women on the public waters was the ritualized disembarcation of the passengers aboard the *Lady Clinton.* "Upon reaching the Battery, the ladies formed a procession, Mrs. Clinton and Mrs. Colden at their head; the band of music preceded them, and the Committee conducted the ladies from the Battery to the Bowling Green, where they were handed to their carriages, and proceeded to their respective homes." The ladies, in other words, had actually formed a parade.[6]

This public appearance of real women was dwarfed by quite another ceremonial expression of femininity, the display of female icons in order to impersonate civic virtues. On each side of the New Orleans Arch of Triumph stood colossal statues of Liberty and Justice. These female allegories, familiar sights in both France and the United States since the eighteenth century, also appeared on the engraved invitations to the Erie Canal celebration. As in France, the image of Liberty had been toned down by this point in time; rather than being poised for revolutionary battle she reclined politely upon her sword, where a Liberty cap perched coquettishly. These female symbols were not the exclusive property of the artists employed to design the ceremonial props. In the New York parade, a full retinue of feminine allegories appeared in the procession of tradesmen. The Fancy and Windsor Chairmakers' banner featured a female figure with cornucopia and fruit, emblematic of peace and plenty. The Shipwrights and Caulkers had in tow two female figures called the "Genius of America" and the "Genius of Liberty." One fire company represented industry by a woman with a spinning wheel. The printers used a woman to convey their reverence toward the Genius of Literature, while the students of Columbia University exhibited their more academic classical knowledge by using Minerva to personify Wisdom.[7]

Women, in the flesh and in fabrications of plaster and silk, were highly visible in these early processions. But they did not enter this public ritual of the young republic to represent either themselves or their sex. The female participants in these ceremonies, those on board the *Lady Clinton* in New York Harbor or attending the audiences for

Lafayette in New Orleans, were almost all consorts of elite males. They were not, like the contingents of males, enlisted into the public culture in the manner of popular sovereigns. "Tradesmen, merchants and citizens of all professions" were "respectfully invited to convene meetings of their representative bodies, and appoint on their behalf, a committee of two persons" to help plan the ceremonies. By contrast, women's place in the ceremonies was simply "arranged" by a committee of males. The "marked attention" accorded them did not honor female individuals or recognize women as one of the separate groups that composed the polity; rather, it was put forth as "a token of the profound respect which is due to the matrons and daughters of the Republic." Furthermore, only those women connected to elite males assumed even this ceremonial role, more a relic of aristocracy than an expression of the democratic insurgency of the 1820s.[8]

The appearance of women in these early ceremonies should not be interpreted as an invitation to equal participation in politics or culture. Nothing could have been farther from the minds of the City Fathers. Occasionally, as in this, the thirteenth and last official toast at the Freemasons' dinner for Lafayette, this presumption was made explicit. "The Fair Sex—Excluded by necessity from participation in our labours; we profess equality, the presence of woman would make us slaves, and convert the temple of wisdom into that of love." This was a homely rendering of the republican theory of gender, which Hanna Pitkin has uncovered in the writings of the classic republican, Machiavelli. As objects of male sexual desire, women appealed to the passions that would inevitably corrupt civic virtue.

These sexual allusions, intimations of a republican scheme of gender politics, often accompanied feminine symbols into early American political culture. A poem written during Jefferson's presidency, for example, praised "O Liberty thou Goddess! . . . Profuse of bliss and pregnant with delight . . . and smiling plenty leads thy wanton train." Such explicitly sexual symbols continued to grace civic and ceremonial culture in the 1820s. The female embodiment of Liberty affixed to the invitation for the Erie Canal celebration exposed a bare breast, while the ode composed for the occasion centered on the trope of sexual congress between a Virgin Erie and a brawny Neptune. Another toast to Lafayette, which won "tremendous cheers," read as follows: "The noble of nature versus the noble of title and privilege—the one a virgin pure; the other a painted harlot." The seal of the City of New Orleans featured an Indian maiden rendered in erotic detail, nude to the waist with sensuously heavy breasts. By equating women with sexuality, American republicans justified their exclusion from the political citadel of rationality and virtue. Once the civic tribunals had been purged of the female embodiment of sensuality and passion, however, their gender could assume a benign ceremonial representation; cast as the dutiful spouses of elites or as demure emblems of civic virtues, women could decorate public ceremonies. The matron of the early republic was untarnished by direct political experience and unthreatening to male civic virtue: she was a "virgin pure."

While female civic allegories occasionally invoked male sexual desire, they were largely mute on the questions of gender, that is, they rarely made reference to the actual social roles and cultural values assigned to females. The only symbol carried in the Erie Canal celebration that seemed to refer directly to the gender experience of females was the personification of industry by a woman at her spinning wheel. Liberty, Justice, Wisdom, and Prosperity held few substantive references to actual female experience. The cordwainers' banner even eschewed the spinning wheel as a feminine symbol of industry, choosing instead a "female figure in a white dress and purple robe, holding in her left hand a scroll with the words—'industry rewarded in America.' "[9] Woman, beautiful of form and splendidly attired, evoked a being different from, apart from, and attractive to the male creators of civic culture, and as such she served as a canvas on which to paint abstract values in appealing but transcendent fashion. The female body was a transitive semiotic device: it passed meaning beyond women themselves to civic values cherished by male citizens. Whether as the consort of the elite, the invocation of sensuality, or the pedestal for classic iconography, female symbols

Seal of the City of New Orleans. From the microfilm of a New Orleans city directory of the 1860s. The seal dates from before 1825, according to the best evidence in the Louisiana Division, New Orleans Public Library.

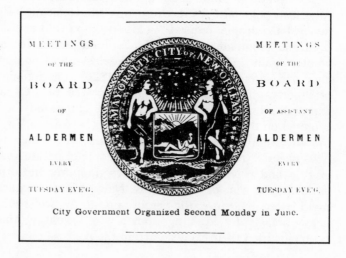

MEETINGS OF THE BOARD OF ALDERMEN EVERY TUESDAY EVE'G.

MEETINGS OF THE BOARD OF ASSISTANT ALDERMEN EVERY TUESDAY EVE'G.

City Government Organized Second Monday in June.

served as much to exclude as to incorporate women into the robust civic culture of 1825.

This gender pattern was regularly repeated on the ceremonial days of the 1820s and into the 1830s. Spontaneous, raucous, and noisy occupation of the streets by men remained the central mode of celebrating Christmas, New Year's, July Fourth, and Mardi Gras. In New York in 1825, New Year's was "celebrated in the streets with rather more noisy ceremonies than usual." A ramshackle parade, accompanied by the cacophony of "drums, tin kettles, rattles, horns, whistles," roved through much of the city. But before it disbanded around 2 A.M., this band of young men made a stop on the Bowery and issued their own manifesto about woman as sex: they pelted a brothel "with balls of lime and flour and other white substances, until they had changed its colour from red to white." According to the city press, the only women who joined in such "cowbellions" were themselves harlots.

The masked crowd of revelers that celebrated Mardi Gras in 1854, at a time when such shenanigans were frowned upon by a more decorous American press, was described as follows. "Boys with bags of flour paraded the streets, and painted Jezebels exhibited themselves in public carriages, and that is about all." Mardi Gras also gave male revelers the chance not only to exclude respectable women and cavort with harlots but also to take female roles themselves. The *Picayune* reported in 1838 that many of the maskers "were dressed in female attire, and acted the lady with no small degree of grace." A favorite antic was to create irreverent and incongruous couples, to pair the pope or Father Mathew with a painted lady, for example. Like the sexual reversals of European carnival as described by Natalie Davis, the cross-dressing of Mardi Gras did not challenge gender hierarchy.[10] The carnivalesque festivity of New Year's and Mardi Gras, like the organized civic pageantry of 1825, acted to exclude most women as it encoded their gender in sexual metaphors.

One holiday tradition dating from the early nineteenth century proved an exception to male domination of ceremonial life. In fact, it dramatized, in a semipublic manner, the gender relations of the more respectable classes. This was the custom of New Year's visits, most honored in New York but prevalent in New Orleans and soon in San Francisco as well. The higher social circles inaugurated the new year in a ritualized enactment of the interchange between the occupants of rigid gender spheres. Writing in 1833, one obedient practitioner of this rite described the male's role as follows. "Fortified with his list of parties, or where to call, we began at nine in the morning, and at five in the afternoon we ceased, having visited 67 homes." The female's role was to don her finest dress, provide a groaning board of delicacies and an ample supply of libations, receive her gentlemen friends, and then proudly count her callers. Lucy Jones of San Francisco reported her New Year's celebration in 1875, when the custom had become less popular: "We were all arrayed in our best. I received our gentlemen friends by eleven o'clock. We had quite a number of callers." A historian of this era neatly noted the gender choreography of celebration: "All maledom empties into the streets—all ladydom remains at home." This New Year's rite was a set piece, played out in public time, to celebrate women's private place.[11]

The Explosion of Ceremony and the Expression of Difference: 1830–1860

The urban elites who orchestrated the public ceremonies of 1825 and inaugurated the practice of New Year's visits lost some of their cultural authority soon thereafter. In the age of Jackson, the popular classes took a larger hand in the creation of public symbols, igniting an explosion of new holidays and refining that distinctively American method of celebration, the parade. The first new holidays and the accompanying parades were direct products of the rise of party politics. July Fourth was nurtured into a public holiday in New York by Tammany Hall Democrats and was initially regarded with suspicion by Federalists and Whigs. New Orleans' favorite patriotic occasion, the anniversary of Jackson's victory in the Battle of January 8, 1815, had similar origins. The opponents of the Jacksonians soon claimed another anniversary, the birth of George Washington, as their special holiday. From the 1830s through the 1850s, the rival parties in New Orleans and New York staged additional celebrations of partisanship by erecting and ceremonially unveiling monuments to their party heroes, Washington, Jackson, and Henry Clay. The second major incentive to creating new celebrations was ethnicity, laced with politics. It was amid the assaults of nativist parties that the Irish carved out a place for themselves on the public calendar and made St. Patrick's a major American holiday, the occasion for the most exuberant and tenacious parading.

The parade genre itself bears a striking resemblance to the democratic political culture, which emerged in the same period. Parades were a kind of cultural analog to popular sovereignty. The elected officials of the city appointed a committee, which then called a public meeting where almost any association of citizens might apply for and receive a place along the line of march. The groups that answered the call and whose names were proudly displayed in the program of the day included professional societies, bands of artisans, trade unions, ethnic benevolent societies, fraternal orders, militia companies, and reform associations, most notably bands of teetotalers. The central act in this public performance was a cultural equivalent of representative government. By marching in the streets, the citizens displayed themselves rather than abstract symbols of either authority or virtue. And thousands joined the march, from college students to humble cart men, from Anglo-Saxons to Celts, blacks as well as whites. The organizers of parades seemed determined to welcome the entire city into their celebrations, reserving the last marching unit for "citizens and strangers." Despite the masculine, martial posture required of paraders, it was theoretically possible that cultural democracy could be expanded to include both genders. After all, by 1848 some women had served notice that they wished to be included within the voting public. Could they not demand ceremonial representation as well?[12]

The evidence to support such a hypothesis is very scant. It is extremely rare to find contingents of women or even stray females adopting the parade as a ceremonial form of their own. From Pennsylvania comes evidence of an actual female marching unit called the Female Infantry and Lancers, known locally as the Fairy Guards. But no such apparition appeared in New York, San Francisco, or New Orleans. There are a few allusions to women walking as auxiliaries within parades of striking workers, but not as members of the proud battalions in a major public ceremony. Two temperance contingents in the parade that celebrated the completion of the Croton Aqueduct carrying water into New York City had feminine names, the Happy Wife and the Lady Franklin. Fire companies bore such names as the "Lady Washington." But those who marched behind these feminine banners appear to have been entirely male. In fact, that brief parade of elite ladies celebrating the Erie Canal in 1825 was the only major public procession of females before 1880. The chief ceremonial product of democratic civic culture, the parade, served once again to mark off public ceremonial space as masculine territory.[13]

Women were acknowledged in public ceremonies in the antebellum period in two less direct ways, however—not as participants but as audience and symbol. First of all, the presence of women on the sidelines of the parade was invested with new significance; secondly, their images were carried in the procession itself in new variety and profusion. Prior to the 1840s, the female audience at public ceremonies was only casually noted in accounts of public ceremonies; the newspapers perfunctorily commented that all ages and sexes mingled in the holiday crowd. After 1840, editors were increasingly attentive to women spectators and scanned the balconies and windows along the parade route for the pastel hues and white handkerchiefs that signaled a reassuring female presence. In addition, the organizers of public holidays often set aside special places from which women could view the ceremonies. The Fourth of July parades in New York in this period often concluded at the Tabernacle in lower Manhattan, where an audience composed chiefly of ladies waited to hear an oration. Newspapers in San Francisco and New Orleans advised the ladies on other occasions that they would find similar accommodations at such places as Platts Hall or Mr. Clapps Church. The City Fathers of San Francisco, eager to recruit ladies to this rough settlement of frontiersmen and fortune hunters, actually provided flower-strewn carriages in which women might travel at the end of parades. By midcentury, special stands for the ladies were regularly installed along the margins of parades or in the public squares or halls where the ceremonies concluded. The public audience had acquired an official and more defined gendered aspect.

The symbolism of the antebellum ceremonies also reveals the mark of gender and a subtle transformation in the cultural meaning attached to womanhood. This new femininity was installed in a social and cultural context that altered and magnified the cultural meaning of sexual difference. The list of classic goddesses had been radically truncated by midcentury, leaving only Liberty and her twin, Columbia, who were joined by a few allegories of ethnicity, chiefly the Maid of Erin. The installation of the Maid of Erin in the pantheon of female symbolism was in fact an omen of the ethnic turmoil in the ceremonial public. For example, those Fairy Guards of Pennsylvania, the rare case of women actually marching in the parades of this era, were auxiliaries to nativist societies desirous of ridding the polity as well as public ceremony of immigrants. New York City nativists, although reluctant to send women into the line of march, were also fond of female symbolism. The goddess of Liberty made one of her most noted appearances in 1850, embossed on a banner of a contingent of United Americans. Liberty was cast in a critical ceremonial role: she passed the scepter of Anglo-Saxon culture from George Washington to the leader of this nativist association. In short, gender, represented by a few female participants and by a more abundant profusion of female symbols, entered antebellum public culture at an ominous moment, at a time when the ethnic differences within the polity were becoming more apparent and more divisive.

Celebrating the completion of the Croton Aqueduct. J. Clarence Davies Collection, Museum of the City of New York.

The celebration conducted in 1856 to mark the completion of the Atlantic Cable was a visual feast of banners decorated with literary allusions, carried in procession, and draped over storefronts all along the parade route. Their creators, be they businessmen or marching artisans and benevolent societies, reveled in gender symbolism, especially metaphors of a marriage between England and the United States. The newlyweds were variously labeled "Albion to Columbia, Hudson to History," "Field to Fame," or "Niagara and Agamemnon, with their consorts Gorgon and Valorous." The couple might recite their vows in "the church of Progress" or before "the Altar of Commerce" and consummate their union in "the bed of the Ocean of Science and Enterprise." These metaphors were something more than irresistible sexual tropes for a deep-sea connection of cable between England and the United States. In fact, the Atlantic Cable ceremony, unlike earlier ceremonial representations of gender relations, did not resort to a purely sexualized rendering of the relationship between men and women. The "wanton train" of Liberty had been replaced by a proper wedding ceremony. The image of the harlot was upstaged by that of the bride. Where the sexualized symbolism of women in republican ideology and ceremony served politically and ceremonially to exclude women, this evocation of proper Victorian coupling embraced women as partners in a union between Victoria's realm and American culture. When nativists portrayed their kinswomen as virtuous brides, they also were setting up an implicit and invidious comparison with the sexual license of immigrants, thereby affixing the sexual mark of exclusion on the grounds of ethnicity rather than gender.

The trope of marriage articulated not just an international alliance but also, and preeminently, an ethnic bond, drawn between native-born, Protestant Americans and their British relatives. The banner over the Gallery of Decorative Arts dubbed the progeny of this union, crudely but pregnantly, "the Anglo-Saxon Twins." The transparency over Laura Keene's theater put the ethnic subtext of this celebration bluntly: "There is no such word as fail for Saxon Blood." The whole celebration was a poorly disguised celebration of nativism. The parade that day was especially well populated with Protestant Anglo-Saxon benevolent societies and skilled tradesmen of the same national origin and religious affiliation. Irish Catholics, conversely, were scarce in the line of march, and their New York spokesman, the editor of *The Irish American Weekly*, disparaged the whole event as a nativist festival.[14]

Although the Anglo-Saxons took the cultural offensive for one day in 1858, they did not succeed in driving the great waves of Irish immigration back across the Atlantic, out of the voting booth, or into a subordinate position in public ceremony. Indeed, the Irish stubbornly continued to parade through city streets during the most virulent episodes of nativism in the 1850s, and they forced city business to a virtual standstill for one day annually. On March 17, the Irish not only honored St. Patrick but also took up the legacy of female symbolism. The Irish-American ceremonies outdid those of the native-born in the homage paid to the ladies in the audience, recounting, for example, how "the fair sex showed itself in a profane display of green ribbons, shawls, and dresses, as well as the enthusiastic manner in which they greeted the celebrants with waving handkerchiefs from every point which offered an elevation above the moving crowd." Just as quickly and with special panache, Irish-Americans adapted the Goddess of Liberty as their own female allegory. The *Irish American Weekly* opined that the best banner in one parade was that of the Ancient Order of Hibernians from Brooklyn, on one side of which was embossed "a beautiful figure of Hibernia crowned with a wreath of shamrocks with a splendid Cap of Liberty worked in green velvet embroidered richly with gold."[15]

Once the nativists and the Irish-Americans had commandeered female allegory for their own purposes, the Goddess of Liberty lost some of its transcendent symbolic uses. Metamorphosed into the Maid of Erin, for example, the female allegory evoked ethnic diversity, not an abstract and unifying political ideology. The use of female allegories to represent an ethnic partition in public culture had a particular symbolic utility and logic. Ethnicity, after all, was a matter of birth, marriage, and kinship, not citizenship or political ideology; it practically and necessarily extended to women as well as men. The bonds between Anglo-Saxons, like the symbols of the Atlantic Cable ceremony, were perpetuated by endogamous marriages. The identification of second-generation immigrants with the native land of their parents required that maids as well as sons of Erin maintain loyalties to Ireland. While this subtle recasting of gender symbolism still used female images as conduits for largely male concerns, especially the evolving ethnic references of partisan politics, it also made wives and daughters direct parties to the new social identities they articulated. If not tradesmen, voters, or militia men, women could identify as Irish or Anglo-Saxon, Catholic or Protestant.

By the mid-nineteenth century, these female emblems of ethnic identity also began to take on a more pointedly feminine meaning. Images of women found on the banners and in the speeches of Irish associations, for example, evoked a series of associations with feminine characteristics and female roles. When Ireland was represented by a young maiden, this figure assumed a feminine posture, head bowed, eyes tearing, docilely lamenting the subordination of her countrymen to Great Britain. Alternatively, Ireland was represented as a mother, lovingly and unconditionally embracing her scattered children. A banner carried in a St. Patrick's Day parade by the Longshoremen of New York pictured a touching domestic tableau: two children were placed on either side of a "beautiful female figure" and were accompanied by the inscriptions "Whatever you do for the little ones" and "Faith Hope and Charity." The Longshoremen, like many another antebellum fraternity, found the female association with charity a handy symbol for their mutual benefit programs.[16]

Irish-American women as well as male associationists and newspaper editors were party to this feminine reading of ceremonial iconography. By 1860, the wives and daughters of members of Irish militia companies and benevolent associations had found a small but active role at the margins of public ceremonies. On St. Patrick's Day morn, they frequently presented homemade banners to their kinsmen who had assembled for the parade. These artifacts often laced Irish identity with feminine values. The ladies of St. Mary's Church in San Francisco presented a banner with the words "Benevolence, Temperance and Libraries" on one side and the slogan "Be Sober and Watch" on the other. The banners of Irish temperance associations, if not actually wrought by female hands, also projected values associated with femininity and privacy. Mothers seemed behind the scenes when some one hundred young boys marched in the St. Patrick's Day parade under banners identifying them as the "Temperance Cadets of the Blessed Virgin Mary" and boasting, "All's Right: Dad's Sober." With or without the complicity of women, Irish-American public ceremonies came to embrace some of the doctrines most germane to women's sphere. In 1865, for example, the Father Mathew Total Abstinence Benevolent Society translated this increasingly popular ideology into the slogan "Sobriety the true source of domestic happiness."[17]

By 1865, the coupling of femininity and domesticity had achieved something of a cachet in public ceremony, especially among the advocates of temperance. Beginning in the 1840s, contingents of teetotalers were the major feature of both July Fourth and St. Patrick's Day processions in all three cities. In some years, temperance companies were the only processions to be mounted on July Fourth. The native-born had taken the lead in embracing feminine iconography, typified by those New York temperance companies with names like the Happy Wife and the Lady Franklin. Women were more prominent in the backstage ceremonies of the antebellum temperance movement. Temperance festivals conducted in public halls and churches gave women a central role singing songs, reciting odes, leading prayers and occupying special seats. In sum, women were associated prominently with another new entry in the vocabulary of urban ritual. They were both allies and symbolic props in a campaign to attach public value to personal habits of sobriety.

By the 1860s, a certain circularity is evident in the history of women and public ceremonies. On the one hand, both women and feminine symbols were more prominent in and around public ceremonies. Yet the meanings they conveyed to the assembled public evoked incipient doctrines of privacy. Temperance was a private habit of individuals and not, like the earlier female personifications of Liberty and Justice, a civic virtue that could only be realized in public. Both temperance and ethnicity, furthermore, gave public definition to familial loyalties and associations, rather than to a politically and publicly expressed municipal consensus. The women who entered the public ceremonies as symbols of ethnicity or backstage allies of the temperance movement did so against the backdrop of an increasingly vocal and elaborate doctrine of domesticity. By 1860, it was clear to any literate middle-class observer that a "Happy Wife" did not parade through the public streets but, rather, remained at home, ministering to her family.

In other words, this particular apparition of women glided through the civic ceremonies of the 1840s and 1850s, leaving behind a paradox: the public celebration of the virtues of private life. Although the female had secured cultural representation in public ceremonies, she conveyed prescriptions for domesticity. For some, especially middle-class Protestants, the feminine image of the tranquil home signaled a retreat from the public and participatory expression of civic culture. After their attempt to regain the offensive in ceremonies like temperance parades and the Atlantic Cable celebration in the 1850s, native-born Protestants of the middling social ranks began to withdraw from public places and to eschew public rites on civic holidays. The Fourth of July found these groups journeying to private retreats—picnicking with their families on Lake Ponchartrain near New Orleans, leaving San Francisco for the sunshine across the bay in Oakland, or listening to polite concerts in Central Park. The closest thing to an old-fashioned Fourth, according to the New York papers, came on St. Patrick's Day. Even then, the principal marchers in this vestigal parade were working-class associations like the Ancient Order of Hibernians.

Feminine Ceremonies: 1850–1860

The middle classes and the native-born retreated from public space on most holidays after midcentury, but they did not forfeit their claim on public time. The holidays that closed the calendar year, Thanksgiving and Christmas, increasingly bore the dual imprint of the middle class and of domesticity. The rising star of these holidays on the public calendar was enthusiastically charted in the newspapers, and with special fervor and verve in Horace Greeley's *New York Tribune*. In 1844, the *Tribune* was still somewhat partisan toward public holidays: "Our festivals come rather too near together since we have so few of them. We value a means of marking time by appointed days because man, on one side of his nature so ardent and aspiring, is on the other so slippery and indolent a being that he needs the incessant admonitions to redeem the time." Concurrently,

Greeley was irritated by the saturnalian and masculine celebrations of holidays characteristic of the early nineteenth century. In the Christmas edition of 1841 he equivocated: "We would not check the innocent hilarity of the occasion, though we may not improperly suggest that the festivity of Christmas should be chastened and hallowed by the consideration of its Divine Origins. . . . May its mirth be entwined with innocence, and its pleasures those which detract nothing from the health of the body and the purity of the soul."[18]

By 1844, the *Tribune*'s annual Christmas homily clearly enunciated the proper holiday strategy, that of marking public time with private ceremony. In addition to discouraging rowdy public antics on July Fourth, Greeley enjoined Christians to revise their ritual calendar by celebrating December 25 as a day of fireside amusements and special deference to children. His logic went as follows: "Were all this right in the private sphere, the public would soon right itself also, and the nations of Christendom might join in a celebration, such as 'Kings and Prophets waited for' and so many martyrs died to achieve Christ-Mass."[19] Greeley continued his campaign to privatize and Christianize the holidays through the next decade. In 1849, he devoted his Christmas editorial to a homage to Santa Claus. A few years later, a voice from the far West chimed in with this celebration of domesticity, calling Christmas "the day so sacred to memory, so cherished by association and so hallowed by ties of home." The San Francisco editor spoke forlornly from a settlement of bachelors: "Heaven speed the day when we have many real homes in California. Women alone can create homes."[20]

After 1850, the holiday editorials were more complacent. The *Alta* exclaimed of Christmas in 1854 (when the San Francisco sex ratio was not quite as egregiously out of balance), "Its pleasures here are chiefly associative and its associations are all of the fireside kind." Back in New York, where women were abundant, Greeley confidently assumed that the celebration of Christmas had been given over to children and to childish innocence. "It is a good thing to feel oneself a child again, to grow young as the year grows old, and indeed to be a nation of children at Christmas time would be a 'consummation most devoutly to be wished.' " This transmutation of Christmas into a domestic celebration focused on childhood was welcome news to the cities' shopkeepers and to the advertising departments of the newspapers. Tuttle's Emporium on Broadway began running its Christmas ad campaign on December 4, 1855, and encouraged mothers to patronize both a "Doll Department" and a "Toy Department." Department stores elsewhere joined in the celebration of Christmas as a time for the private purchase of the accouterments of domesticity. The newspapers throughout December were splashed with the hallmarks of the new holiday tradition: "TOYS, TOYS, TOYS," "DOLLS, DOLLS, DOLLS."[21]

By midcentury, Thanksgiving had been added to the official list of public holidays, and cities north, south, and west could boast two domesticated dates on the public calendar. Once merely a New England tradition, commemorated by a day of rest, prayer, and public worship, Thanksgiving became an occasion for family dinners and the gluttonous consumption of turkey. It was largely through the efforts of Sarah Josepha Hale, editor of *Godey's Ladies' Book* and a leading spokeswoman for domesticity, that President Lincoln proclaimed Thanksgiving a national holiday in 1863.[22] Yet as early as 1850 the proponents of the domestication of Thanksgiving and, to a lesser extent, Christmas had begun to widen their social horizons. The memory of the Pilgrims' first harvest inspired attention to the plight of the poor and generated appeals to leave home to assist less privileged citizens. In the 1850s, this impulse became the rationale for a new holiday ritual, a ceremony designed primarily by women.

This invention consisted of a ritualized feeding of poor children conducted by charitable societies. One of the earliest rituals of this kind was enacted on Thanksgiving Day in 1850 by the benevolent ladies of New York, who had converted the Five Points Brewery into a city mission. In this ceremonial act, the ladies clearly set the calendar according to the clock of female reform. "Thanksgiving was approaching, and we resolved for a little time to lay aside our ordinary duties, and by change of occupation, to find relief, and bestow gladness." The ladies proceeded to translate the labor and skill peculiar to their sex into the elements of a ceremony. They set about the task in a whirlwind of housewifery—"turkey, chickens, and meats of every kind mingled in sweet confusion with cakes, pies, fruits, etc—evergreens on the floors, crockery on the window-sills and benches, huge piles of clothing waiting for distribution, visitors pouring in, childish faces peeping though every window and open door—commands, opinions, directions issuing from every quarter."[23]

There was something more in this scene than the domestic disarray prelude to a Thanksgiving meal. Relocated to a charitable institution, the women of the Old Brewery soon constrained this chaos into a stylized dramatization of their gender role. The ceremony was first of all an enactment of feminine principles of magnanimity and piety. "Three hundred and seventy poor, neglected, hapless children, placed for an hour in an atmosphere of love and gladness, practically taught the meaning of Christian kindness, wooed and won to cling to those whose inmost hearts were struggling in earnest prayer for grace and wisdom to lead them unto God." These motherly gestures, observed through the sentimental lens of a "tearful eye," were made public on Thanksgiving Day, and in the same gesture transmitted beyond middle-class families, to "children who seldom know a parent's care."[24]

By commandeering public time to enact this symbolism of evangelical femininity, these women also inscribed their own reading of class relations on public culture. First, they presumed that they were entitled to assume a parental relationship to the children of their social inferiors. They affixed their own domestic ideology on the objects of their beneficence. Not just any needy child could participate in this ceremony. "The ladies were trying to select, first our Sunday School Children, and next any who seemed hopeful. These were washed and dressed, and then each received a ticket which admitted them to the mission-room." In subsequent years, the ladies were even more selective. The children "now were simply informed that they must come clean and well dressed from their homes" or "they would not be fed." In other words, these churchwomen had translated economic differences into the classifications of housewives, the clean and the dirty.

With their cast chosen, cleaned, and coached, the cultural performance could begin. "The lamps were lighted, and the signal was given. Hundreds of visitors stood in silent expectation and in a moment the sound of childish voices was heard, and they entered in regular procession singing—

> The morn of hope is breaking
> All doubt now disappears,
> For Five Points are waking
> To penitential tears."[25]

The ladies of the Five Points Mission had clearly designed this ceremony with an audience in mind. Their clean and pious charges were paraded before a congregation of benefactors to provide evidence of the efficacy of their program of domestic rehabilitation. These women aimed not just to feed the hungry and break bread with one another but also to demonstrate publicly their power to save the poor, both spiritually and materially. Not incidentally, they hoped to persuade the audience of wealthy men to contribute to their coffers. By drawing the benefactors into their holiday rites and publicizing their performance in the press, the women of the Five Points Mission demonstrated perspicacious acumen at public relations.

The public display did not end here, at a carefully controlled meeting of rich men and poor children. Another audience was assembled along the sidelines of this female ceremony. After the children had been fed, "notice was given to the visitors that the company now about to assemble were the 'outsiders,' about whom we knew nothing save that they were poor and wretched, and all were warned to take care of their watches and pocket-books." These guests, residents of Five Points unaffiliated with the mission, were greeted as both unworthy and irredeemable: "ragged, dirty, forlorn. . . . we could scarcely hope to snatch these from the vortex." By inviting the unwashed to their Thanksgiving table, the organizers of the ceremony provided a public display of the dichotomy between the worthy and the unworthy poor. We can only guess the impression such rituals might have had on the "outsiders," who were scorned even as they were fed, and who watched their children being inducted into middle-class, Protestant, domestic culture. Certainly such rites do not echo the relatively egalitarian and pluralistic message of the American parade.[26]

With this virtuoso dramatization of class and gender relations, a select group of women laid claim to at least a portion of the ceremonial stage on this one public holiday. In fact, before the Civil War the public calendar had begun to acquire a certain gender segmentation. While men claimed the political anniversaries—July Fourth, Washington's Birthday, and January Eighth—as times for masculine marching, women staked their semipublic claim to the winter holidays—Christmas as a paean to domesticity, Thanksgiving as a pageant of female altruism. The pattern was not perfect: in small ways, images of femininity fluttered over and around all the holidays, and throughout the calendar year. Female charitable institutions held ladies' fairs throughout the seasons to demonstrate the magnanimity of their sex as they solicited funds from wealthy men. Sunday School processions were a summer ritual in San Francisco, sometimes joined in by both female students and female teachers. By 1860, women had even poached upon the masculine territory of the public calendar. The *New York Tribune* reported that a "Novel Exhibition" occurred on July 3, 1848: "The ladies have gotten up a floral exhibition and Pic Nic on Randall's Island for the benefit of children cared for by public charge." Displays of flowers and provision of strawberries to poor children clearly put a feminine garnish on the national birthday. In such ceremonies, women eschewed political oratory and shied away from the public spotlight of the parade route. Nonetheless, they embellished public time with their self-wrought feminine symbols and moved beyond the confinement of privacy. By associating their ceremonies with publicly funded institutions like the asylums on Randall's Island, moreover, some benevolent women encroached symbolically upon the state itself. The *Tribune* said of the beneficiaries of this female ceremony: "Though not their natural parents the city extends over them such protection as effectually guards them against evil and prepares them for future usefulness." It was women who evoked the domestic metaphor for this welfare function of the state. Even before the Civil War, women, as actors and organizers as well as symbols, had opened their own small beachhead on the public calendar and in public consciousness.[27]

Spectacle and Difference: The Ceremonial Signs of Gender in the 1860s and 1870s

During and after the Civil War, women became even more prominent in public ceremonies, and feminine iconography loomed ever larger and bolder over the holiday streets. The star of womanhood rose over a new cultural landscape, however, on a less crowded but more spectacular public stage. To put it baldly and in the terms of anthropologist John MacAloon, public ceremonies became less like rituals and more like spectacles. While the former term connotes the participation of a significant portion of a community in some public drama or stylized public action like the parade, the spectacle displays powerful and evocative sights and sounds before a vast and relatively passive audience. This swing in the pendulum of American cultural history, from participation toward passivity, has also been observed by Lawrence Levine, especially in the theater audience.[28]

The transmutation of ritual into spectacle could be seen even along the parade routes of the 1870s. The decades following the Civil War were not as prolific of parades and public ceremonies as the antebellum years had been. Still, certain events demanded that the public be convened for celebratory purposes. If nothing else, the hundredth anniversary of the Declaration of Independence warranted ceremonial recognition. The city of New York, like San Francisco and New Orleans, managed to get up quite a procession for July 4, 1876; a large number of associations, predominantly ethnic brotherhoods, marched on this occasion. Yet they did so at night, when the flickering lights of torches could not clearly illuminate the identity of the participants nor the mottoes inscribed upon their banners. The torchlight procession gave ceremonial preeminence to visual and aural sensation, the pattern of light and the crescendo of music. It was also in this same period that another light show—fireworks, always a small part of the day's festivities—became a central event on the Fourth of July. New Yorkers gathered in one of more than a dozen public places or perched with their families on the roofs of tenements to enjoy the fireworks, a less active and public manner of observing the Fourth than marching in a common procession or gathering for an oration. The columns of newsprint once devoted to listing the different social groups that constituted the parade now carried detailed descriptions of pyrotechnic exhibitions. The quality of the spectacle can be gleaned from this example of but one of the eighteen displays mounted in one of fourteen different parks in New York in 1875. "Open with rainbow wheel, which changes instantly to temple, the base adorned with diamond lights and lancework, on which are placed four pillars supporting a cornice on which is inscribed in letters of gold, 'the Union Now and Forever;' the whole surrounded by an eagle; on each side will be placed trees of colored wheels and Roman candles, discharging stars of crimson, white, amethyst, purple, orange, jacinth, lilac, violet, emerald and gold; concluding with a discharge of rockets, mines, bombshells, etc. etc."[29]

If one were to detect a representative symbol in such a phantasmagoria, it most likely invoked associations with gender: masculine signs like the eagle or the profile of George Washington were coupled with the silhouette of the Goddess of Liberty or Columbia. By the late nineteenth century, these female allegories had been purged of direct political or ideological meaning. One newspaper reporter perfunctorily described the gender display as "George Washington and the usual litany of goddesses." Similarly, two invocations of gender stood out in the July Fourth parade still mounted in San Francisco in the 1870s: the uniformed ranks of the National Guard were directly followed by a wagon carrying the Goddess of Liberty and her court representing the states in the Union.

While sons and daughters of the Confederacy were somewhat cool about celebrating the national birthday, even in 1876, they mobilized in the wake of defeat to celebrate their local traditions. The annual parade of the New Orleans Fire Company, the major municipal institution to maintain autonomy during Yankee occupation, became the focus of celebration for unregenerate Confederates. The festivities conducted on March 4 in the 1870s were a symphony on the theme of gender difference, with stereotyped parts designed for each sex. The men's role was to march through the streets towing steam engines; the ladies decked the machines in flowers and looked on in admiration. As the *Picayune* put it in 1872, "It is a manly—it is a splendid service. These drilled and resolute men—these powerful engines, covered with the emblems and expression of affiliation and gratitude—the throngs of applauding women and children, proud of their defenders, in these constitute the 'pomp and circumstances' of a war which leaves no widows to mourn, and no victims to execrate its bloody progress.''[30]

When New Orleans rebels wrested political control from Radical Republican government, they invented a new tradition to celebrate their local loyalties. The day they commemorated was September 14, 1874, when vanquished sons of the Confederacy organized into White Leagues, took up arms, and temporarily ousted the Radical Republicans from the seat of power. Again, gender difference was the primary social distinction honored in the ceremony that marked redemption. The White Leagues marched proudly through the streets in civilian garb. The only ornamentation of this stark presentation of the political power of white males was enacted on the sidelines, and by women. As the champions of their race and sex passed by, the ladies of New Orleans donned white dresses and waved handkerchiefs of the same color.[31]

A similar apparition of femininity appeared on the streets of New York a few years later when it came time to celebrate the opening of the Brooklyn Bridge. Newspaper reporters who covered that event were hard-pressed to find much interest in the major ceremonial act, the short procession across the bridge consisting of President Arthur, scores of city commissioners, and the Seventh Regiment of the New York National Guard. When observers looked for more engaging images in a sea of passive spectators, two things caught their eye: first, the lines of military authority cut through the crowds by cordons of soldiers and policemen; second, the sartorial splendor of the ladies, their pale, frothy garments and their fluttering handkerchiefs presenting a veritable phalanx of white. The same pattern recurs in the major spectacles of the late nineteenth century. The imagery is polarized around the masculine and the feminine: the soldier and Miss Liberty, White Leagues and ladies in white, presidential power and feminine decoration. Gender dimorphism in and of itself was perhaps the dominant motif of these modern American spectacles. If female symbols had approached parity with ceremonial evocations of masculinity, both sexes had been denuded of more specific social or ideological references, be they ethnic banners, tradesmen's tools, reformers' causes, or the slogans of civic virtues.[32]

There was, however, one apparent exception to this pattern. Even as parading and participatory civic rituals were dwarfed by the spectacles of the 1870s, real women were installed at the dramatic center of the public display. Beginning in the 1860s, feminine allegories were cast not in marble, ink, or silk but in the flesh, enacted by real women. Usually personifying the Goddess of Liberty and the states in the Union, these young women were transported through the parade itself in carriages or on decorated wagons. Previous processions had assigned the role of living allegory to men or young boys. Early in the Republic, elite adult men would don costumes to represent some civic symbol, to impersonate yeoman farmers, noble savages, or George Washington. In the age of representative democracy, when men displayed themselves and not abstract symbols, juveniles were chosen for this role. In the Erie Canal celebrations, for example, twenty-four apprentices represented the states of the Union. A few parades of the 1840s placed young girls in this role, and by the 1860s it was the standard place of ingenues, usually relatives of the parade organizers and reputedly the prettiest girls in the city.

Once civic symbolism was conveyed by living women, whose names were boldly printed in the program of the day and in the newspapers, gender acquired new meaning and enhanced evocative power. The garrulous accounts of ceremonies found in the Irish press suggest some of the associations these living allegories might stir in a spectator's imagination. Of two "beautiful young ladies," representing Liberty and the Maid of Erin in the St. Patrick's Day parade of 1866, the *Irish American Weekly* wrote:

> The latter is the full flush of youth and beauty, eyes sparkle brilliantly and a complexion which might shame the rose, and with long flowering curls hanging over her shoulders—she rode a spirited horse which pranced as if proud of his fair burden. She dressed in white and wore a red, white and blue scarf, with a Phrygian cap and seemed the very personification of youth, health and beauty. The other was dressed in a rich green riding suit with hat and veil to match. She was also very beautiful but her face bore a down and out look which occasionally lit up with a smile. Her sister [the personification of Liberty] cast a triumphantly patronizing glance upon her. The appearance of these two young ladies was the signal for enthusiastic cheering which continued until the procession was over.[33]

If one can believe rare accounts like this, the women who personified the Goddess of Liberty and the Maid of Erin made a powerful impression on the audience. But what precisely did the young women who assumed this novel ceremonial position say, convey, or evoke? The historical and ideological content of their message is slight. The Phrygian cap, for example, seems a picturesque costume, an accessory worn by a pretty girl rather than an invocation of the ideology of the French Revolution. This observer was more intent on reading the facial expressions of Miss America and Miss Ireland. What he

The Maids of Erin: "St. Patrick's Day in America," 1874. Published and printed by Th. Kelly; designed by Hogan; drawn by Lucian Gray, J. Clarence Davies Collection, Museum of the City of New York.

spied there was a contrast between the vitality of America and the depressed condition of Ireland under English rule. The actual human face, and that of a woman, was a transparency off which the receptive audience could read not civic virtue but patriotic and ethnic sentiment, not ideas but feeling. But even these social and civic references paled beside the sheer physical attraction of nubile womanhood. The St. Patrick's Day parades dating from after the Civil War were the first ceremonies to exhibit what would become a fixture of the American parade. The female body itself, with a minimum of iconographic trappings (and soon a dwindling of drapery as well), became a focus of public ceremonial attention. Women were no longer allegorical, hardly even symbolic; their bodies in themselves were ceremoniously presented for public view. The raw physicality of the female form was the cause of admiration, narcissistic or sexual, from male or female. Woman had become spectacle.

An occasional ceremony contained a more elaborate and detailed script for the display of gender difference. After the Civil War, New Orleans celebrated Mardi Gras in a dense pageantry, rich in literary and political allusions. The spontaneous masking and revelry of the antebellum period had been challenged, if not supplanted, by a costly pageant organized by carnival clubs of Anglo-Saxon businessmen. The spectacular tableaux they mounted on wagons often carried explicit political messages, such as those of the 1873 procession, which burlesqued Radical Reconstruction as the sport of apes. More often, the parade seemed a hedonistic fantasy. In 1871, the different units of the procession each enacted an episode from Spenser's *Faerie Queene*. The oldest, most exclusive carnival club, the Mystique Crewe of Comus, presented a simulated orgy, enacted by men and men dressed as women. Cross-dressing had been commonplace in the earliest carnivals, when Mardi Gras gave males license to play with gender roles, both impersonating women and parading sexuality. The text that accompanied this carnival of a later day interpreted the gender drama in quite another way. The *Picayune*'s commentary read the orgy scene as an illustration of "the fearful power of dissipation in unsexing its victim, desecrating the exquisite purity of womanhood, rendering effeminate the man made in the image of god." By the 1870s, the press tried, probably unsuccessfully, given the resilence of Mardi Gras festivity in New Orleans, to convert even the bacchanalia of carnival into a parable about the importance of maintaining sexual difference.[34]

When some enterprising businessmen tried to organize a carnival in New York City in 1877, they mounted a parade that featured real women rather than men masquerading as such. The female actors in this drama included "a lovely young maiden, wrapped in an American flag, at her feet an Eagle and a shield" and "a pretty Venus in a shell drawn by stuffed swans and attended by immense bull frogs." In this instance, the intended use of living female symbolism was quite explicit: the flag-draped damsel sat atop a brewery wagon, and Venus ornamented a huge bottle of patent medicine. Already in the 1870s it seems that some ingenious salesmen had divined a novel use of female symbolism, as a mode of advertising their products. This particular ceremonial usage of gender came stillborn into urban public culture at that time. The New York carnival was denounced as "merely an advertising panorama" and was promptly discontinued. Other, noncommercial uses of the female body in civic ceremony were not questioned. In the 1870s, living female symbols appeared in a variety of public ceremonies, on St. Patrick's Day, July Fourth, and, in San Francisco, on May Day when "a beautiful little blonde girl" was crowned the queen of the spring festival.[35]

While living female symbols such as the Maid of Erin or the Venus of patent medicine were archetypes of female objectification, women entered the ceremonies of the 1870s in more self-directed

The German Regiment, Steuben Volunteers, receiving the American and Steuben flags in Front of New York's City Hall, May 24, 1861. *Frank Leslie's Illustrated Newsletter.*

ways as well. In fact, they created little ceremonies of their own on the margins of the public spectacle. By then, it was commonplace to find women ritualistically presenting banners of their own design to bands of marching men. In all three cities, the more intrepid allies of militia companies and other male associations actually wrote, and sometimes delivered, their own speeches before these promiscuous and public audiences. Even the more retiring ladies of New Orleans utilized this opportunity to make a personal contribution to public culture. A Miss Sancier "delivered a pretty little address" as she presented a banner to the Benevolent Sons of Louisiana in 1871. On that banner the seamstresses had placed the mascot of the Crescent City, a pelican, which they rendered not as a proud figure but as a wounded bird with a bleeding breast. The ladies posed behind a feminized façade and voiced their discontent under the rule of Radical Reconstruction. Woman's voice became audible in the Crescent City in 1877 when a Miss Jane Donnelly delivered a brief address as she presented an Irish flag to the Mitchel Rifle Company. Her words were actually printed in the public press. Miss Donnelly presumed to interpret the symbol she presented: "In the Irish tri-color the warring colors of the clans of Ireland are united; the green and yellow are joined together by the white bond of peace and love over which rises the sun of Irish Unity, an omen of the success which has ever flowed from the effort of a united people." In small rituals like this, enacted on the border of the major public ceremonies, women like Miss Donnelly could at least put ethnicity into their own words, and might even counter the martial bravado of the Mitchels' rifles with symbols of "peace and love."[36]

After the Civil War, women's ceremonies absorbed more time and space on the public calendar in both the North and the South. The origins of the major ceremonial product of the Civil War, Memorial Day, can be directly traced to females. As Gaines Foster has described in detail, Ladies Memorial Associations were organized throughout the South soon after the war. From their beginnings in simple gestures of bereavement at the gravesides of fallen rebels, Memorial Day ceremonies mushroomed into a full-scale civic ritual. In the spring of each year, women orchestrated a Confederate holiday complete with processions, speeches, suspension of business, and specially constructed civic space—monuments and cemeteries commemorating the war dead. This annual event was inaugurated in New Orleans in 1874 by the Ladies Benevolent Association and bore its feminine signature. The women eschewed "noisy demonstration, no parade, no gathering," choosing instead simply to carry flowers to the graves of their fallen heroes and kinsmen. The ladies had turned the tables on male ritual forms: before an audience of five thousand they walked beside their children in a melancholy procession to the gravesites.

The inventors of this ceremonial tradition, however feminine their public gestures, were not shy about claiming cultural power. The records of the Ladies Benevolent Association contain a piece of self-promotional prose that praised this civic rite not only as a "tribute to the dead" but also as "the consummation of Southern women's indomitable energy." To gauge the success of their publicity campaign one need only look to the pages of the city press, which printed the association's text without alteration or abridgement. Throughout the South during the 1860s and 1870s, such ceremonies were organized by Ladies Memorial Associations and constituted "virtually the only cultural expression concerned with the meaning of the war." Southern women had exploited the vacuum of cultural power that followed defeat and had placed their own mark on the public calendar. Transported to the North as Decoration Day, these rites of spring demonstrated that women and feminine sensibilities laid a large claim on public culture in the last quarter of the nineteenth century.[37]

In the North, this encroachment on public time was evidenced by an acceleration in the feminization of the winter holidays, Thanksgiving and Christmas. When Samuel MacKeever offered the reading public his *Glimpses of Gotham* in 1880, he spotlighted the holiday of Christmas and thereby captured a moment in women's time—domestic, privatized, under the jurisdiction of housewives. According to MacKeever, the clergy's claim on the holiday had been reduced to a few ill-attended church services, and only a few men of a certain age still honored the old revelry of Christmas mummery and merriment in the streets. The "average young man—say the hard-working clerk, for instance" celebrated a subdued "bachelor holiday . . . during which he is expected to eat a great deal of turkey, play considerable billiards and punish untold hot drinks." For the majority of most ages and both sexes, however, Christmas was a family celebration, commemorated around the hearth and at the dinner table. Yet, in order to mount this domestic celebration, women took to the public streets. The holiday season was the time when city thoroughfares were most congested, as women flocked to city shops in search of holiday gifts and victuals. "These are pre-eminently the shopping days," wrote MacKeever, "and no study of New York would be complete that did not embrace a consideration of Gotham's comely matrons and lovely daughters when they are on what might be called the extravagant rampage." Both fashionable Broadway and the less expensive shops of Sixth Avenue were awhirl with women in the month of December. This public display smacked of a feminine conspiracy to MacKeever, who pictured Christmas shoppers as wives and daughters "conspiring against . . . [the] financial well-being and peace of mind" of breadwinners.[38]

The Christmas season in the 1870s was not entirely given over to an alliance between women consumers and male shopkeepers. As MacKeever put it, "All the missions, schools and the charitable associations which begin at the Five Points and seem to crop up everywhere between that section and High Bridge will be scrubbed until little ears and noses are awfully sore, and then, after singing a lot of chilling hymns, they will be set loose upon the provender." With the proliferation of charitable dinners in the seventies came a few innovations and variations in this feminized ceremony. Some matrons, embracing a more relaxed and humane celebration and a more progressive view of childhood socialization, dispensed with didactic exercises and allowed their charges to eat and play freely for a day. Others refined the requirement to sing for one's supper into an even more elaborate public dramatization of domestic values.

The latter development is illustrated by an account of the ceremonies conducted at the Olivet Mutual Sewing Relief Annual Festival in New York in 1877. The little girls who benefited from this charity conducted a demonstration of something called "the kitchen garden method of instruction," designed by a Miss Huntington. The choreography of domestic propriety was described in the press as follows: "Keeping time with the music the little girls took their places at the tables, each with a complete set of small dishes, knives, and forks before her. Then they sang in concert verses descriptive of the rules of setting the table properly and elegantly." The hand of women's history upon this ceremony could not be heavier. It was conducted by women for female children, and it elevated the most prosaic activity of the middle-class housewife, setting the table, into a public ritual. The ceremonies of the 1850s that had dramatized salvation through maternal evangelism had, by the 1870s, metamorphosed into a reenactment of woman's mundane domestic roles for secular and public purposes.

By 1880, this fully feminized rite had commandeered the public side of the privatized holiday calendar. The Thanksgiving edition of the *New York Herald* in 1874 devoted a full page to brief descriptions of charitable dinners in a score of public institutions. Their headlines interpreted the public meaning of Thanksgiving as a parable of "The Rich and the Poor" or "How the Sick and the Needy Were Cared For by the Well-To-Do." In 1879, one charity fed eight thousand children and issued credit marks to the girls who were well-mannered at table. On the same holiday a year later, Mrs. Huntington was at work once again; this time, her sponsor was none other than Mrs. John Astor, who provided gifts and refreshments for the residents of a girls' lodging house. Theodore Roosevelt also recalled the powerful impression left by witnessing such rites as a child. The participation of both the doyenne of the higher New York circles and a future president in these ceremonies would suggest that women had created a public ritual of considerable consequence. While ostensibly honoring privacy, women left home, crossed a class divide, and leapt into public consciousness and onto the public calendar. By 1880, these rituals of class and gender were highly publicized, and they monopolized their own special quarter of the city press's holiday report. Under the heading of "At the Public Institutions" came abundant testimony that women had installed themselves and their gendered values at a critical nexus of urban culture, where rich met poor and private charity converged with public welfare.

Summary and Conclusion

By 1880, women had broken out of the chrysalis of female allegory to become a visible and active presence in public ceremony. A
brief review of their advance into public culture will suggest some of
the multiple and malleable meanings of the ceremonial construction
and elaboration of sexual difference.

The earliest ceremonies appearing in my account presented the
female side of gender difference primarily as feminine allegories of
abstract civic virtues and political ideals. This system was set in
place long before 1825, in America and in England and France. The
eighteenth-century origins and functions of such allegories as the
Goddess of Liberty have been examined by a number of historians,
chiefly Europeanists such as Lynn Hunt, Joan Landes, and Maurice
Agulhon. To simplify and summarize their argument, female allegories solved a problem of representing political authority after the
monarch, be he George III or Louis XVI, had been deposed. A feminine representation of the civic whole replaced the courtly rituals that
formerly dramatized the frankly patriarchal authority of the king.
Liberty was so remote from venal political power that she could unite
the public mind around those abstract principles that challenged
monarchical authority without evoking private male interests. This
recourse to female personification of public ideals was premised,
however, on a republican suspicion of the female sex, the embodiment of those passions that corrupted the citizen's virtue and reason.
This construction of sexual difference warranted the exclusion of
women from participation in the actual deliberations of the public
sphere. The political exclusion of women created an opening in civic
culture for the Goddess of Liberty and her retinue, who could become benign but decorative vehicles for conveying abstract
principles.[39]

The female allegory entered American public ceremony early in
the history of the Republic, before the Jacksonian revolution of popular parties and universal white manhood suffrage. Allegories of
Liberty and Justice reigned in New York and New Orleans as late as
1825, along with civic elites who dominated early processions and
pageants and who, in a survival of aristocracy, still extended the
symbolism of their high social and political status to their kinswomen, like "Lady Clinton." To the popular architects of the pre-
mier ceremony of the Jacksonian era, the parade, feminine allegories
and the public appearance of ladies seemed less attractive, less necessary. Democratic celebrants did not pay homage to some abstract
image of civic virtue or political ideology but honored themselves,

claiming the authority—whatever their class, ethnicity, or favorite voluntary association—to participate fully and in their own right in public life. Women, however, failed to appear in the mainstream of these more democratic ceremonies; they were still barred by some covert yet powerful gender taboo.

Yet a closer look along the sidelines, at minor ceremonies, and in the iconography of parades reveals a pivotal reconfiguration of gender during the 1840s and 1850s. Female symbols, and perhaps a few women themselves, joined the contingents of nativists, Irish, and temperance reformers who made the city their parade ground during those years. In the process, the content of female symbols changed in two important respects. First, women became references for the kinship ties that marked ethnic differences within the polity. Second, women were vehicles for representing incipient feminine values, especially the tenets of an emerging cult of domesticity.

Women advanced toward the stage of civic ceremony at a time when the public sphere was becoming riddled with social distinctions, as the virtuous public citizen was splintered into multiple private identities. The precise role of women in this recasting of public culture is difficult to chronicle. Yet we know that women did in fact work along the sidelines of the public sphere, in voluntary associations and as writers, to develop ethnic identity, instill temperate habits, expound the doctrines of domesticity, define middle-class culture, and expand the private sphere.[40] This eventful women's history, conducted just off the public stage, helped to navigate a circular turn in the history of gender and ceremony. Women entered upon the public ceremonial stage primarily to represent private values and to reinforce the division of the Republic into separate ethnic constituencies. Women's history and women's culture also contributed to the decreasing popularity of marking public time with public festivities, especially among the middle classes. The second sex was clearly implicated in the ineluctable process that fractured public culture and spurred a retreat from public spaces on celebratory occasions.

After the Civil War, and especially during the 1870s and 1880s, women took up a new place in the rarer but more spectacular public ceremonies. Now they seemed to represent, if not themselves, gender itself. Appearing as living symbols in the St. Patrick's Day parade, or as a flurry of white handkerchiefs at a patriotic observance, images of womanhood rarely denoted specific values, be they home rule for Ireland, Anglo-Saxon lineage, or temperate habits. Instead, there seemed to be something visually and culturally satisfying in the female presence itself. First, feminine decorations softened the looming power of the state and modern technology; they were paired with both President Arthur and the Brooklyn Bridge. This relationship was presented forthrightly in a July Fourth parade in San Francisco in 1872 when Liberty and her court rode in a wagon called the "ship of state." Second, the female image seemed to disarm and dissolve the contentious differences in industrial America. She was without a class, without a party, and bespoke differences that could be ascribed to nature rather than politics or economics. In the major public spectacles of the late nineteenth century, gender seemed to function as circus; in the play of masculinity and femininity, the audience could forget political differences and social divisions. Gender was the difference that unified, a key symbol in a ceremony that entertained a mass public.

Yet even as a tattered public culture was being stitched together in increasingly spectacular, massive, and abstract ceremonies after the Civil War, women themselves were designing an array of celebrations of their own. They put a mark of privacy on public time, by converting Thanksgiving and Christmas into domestic reveries, and simultaneously extended their ceremonial reach out into public space, especially by designing holiday rites for public and charitable institutions. In these dramatizations at public institutions, women spoke (more candidly than any politician would dare) in a condescending language of class. Under the benign veils of domesticity, women articulated a hierarchical ordering of the social divisions of industrial society. The convoluted process that brought women into public ceremony culminated in these public acts, ritualized translations of difference into hierarchy and inequity.

Having located gender in this compromised position in public life, what can we conclude about those ceremonies that anthropologists suggest can reveal "the essential life . . . the distillation and typification of the corporate experience"?[41] Do these ceremonies constitute a capsule summary of nineteenth-century American urban society? They certainly testify to a widespread compulsion and an assiduous effort to create such summarizing and unifying symbols. The organization of public time in the nineteenth-century city served more to impose cultural order on a heterogeneous population than to release, in Bakhtinian fashion, the suppressed animosity of the popular classes. Certainly these ceremonies failed to invite the entire populace to freely express themselves publicly or turn social hierarchy topsy-turvy. The official civic culture of the nineteenth century, even in its most democratic moments, recognized only the most well-behaved among the poor, the foreign-born, and racial minorities.

Yet even the staid and official public ceremonies that have been the subject of this essay were far more than simple enactments of cultural hegemony by a narrow class of cultural impresarios. Many marginal social groups, including women, found their way onto the stage of public ceremony. Conversely, no single group, including those armed with the greatest social and economic power, had free rein to stage public ceremony exactly as they wished. Even the elite City Fathers of the 1820s had to share the stage with humble artisans. As a consequence, most public ceremonies provide an incomplete but hardly monolithic portrait of the composition and interrelations of the population at any given moment in time. Yet, in order to imprint their values or self-wrought identity on a public ceremony, individuals and groups had to pass through many obstacles, screenings, and compromises. By the time they appeared on the public stage, they projected highly selective images of themselves. This is especially true for women, who broke through the gender exclusions of republican civic culture only to assume publicly the constraining ceremonial costume of domesticity and femininity. The ceremonies of these three cities chart a painstaking transition in the public meaning attached to the female sex, from the excluded "other" evoked by the classic female allegories of 1825 to the honorable stereotypes of the beneficent ladies at the public charities and Memorial Day processions of the 1870s. Women's image in the public mind had become more vivid, more embellished with concrete gender references, but was still a pallid representation of the diverse experience, multifarious roles, divergent values, and distinct interests of their sex.

But women were more than one of the myriad compromised and calculated social categories within the symbol system of urban culture. The elaboration of gender symbolism served not only to define women but also as a kind of master metaphor of social difference itself. Early in the nineteenth century, sexual difference served primarily to differentiate men from women and to mark off the public sphere as masculine territory. In the 1830s and 1840s, more refined gender distinctions buttressed the social boundaries within the public, helping to recast social identity in terms of ethnicity. During the 1870s, those ceremonies enacted in the name of charity gilded class divisions with gender symbols. Simultaneously, an increasing array of feminine symbols articulated a differentiation of social space, giving new cultural power to the private sphere and undermining the publicness of ceremony.

The genius of sexual difference was that it served symbolically not only to divide but also to reunify the public. Early in the century, female icons symbolized civic virtues, to be revered by all men. When female allegory reappeared as a spectacle of gender dimorphism a half century later, it served to dissolve other social differences in the supposedly natural dualism that diffused through every class and every ethnic group. Concurrently, the ceremonies enacted largely by women at the public charitable institutions had in a single stroke divided the public between the rich and the poor and then bound them together again on hierarchical but benevolent terms, dramatizing "how the sick and the needy are cared for by the well-to-do."

In sum, the incorporation of sexual difference into public celebrations did both less and more than represent women. The increasing attention to and participation of women hardly displayed a realistic portrait of the female population before the ceremonial public. At the same time, female symbolism and women's rituals spoke in terms that had broader references than the experience of the female sex. Less than a reflection of sex roles, more than the representation of male and female, gender inscribed on the holiday calendar a comprehensive language of social difference. The language of gender had its own shifting vocabulary; sexual classifications such as harlot and virgin gave way to the gender classification of femininity. Gender difference also supplied a sequence of terms to connect other nouns in the sociolinguistics of the city: classic female allegories represented civic virtues to be honored by all men; references to wives and mothers evoked ethnic solidarity; ingenues impersonating Liberty awed and galvanized a mass audience. As this vocabulary evolved, furthermore, the language of public ceremony became increasingly transfused with gender terms until by the last quarter of the nineteenth century male and female difference loomed spectacularly over the social landscape as the difference that unified. The men and women of the city had worked out in public time and public space a whole set of terms, references, and repeated usages through which the bewildering stimuli of the city became intelligible. All these linguistic elaborations on sexual difference provided ways of seeing and knowing the city.

Nevertheless, a workable and coherent sign system like the public language of gender should not be confused with the actual operations of a society. Social and political differences could not all be resolved by evoking attractive symbols or eliciting cheers from a holiday crowd. In fact, on a number of occasions violence erupted in the very midst of these public ceremonies. In addition, those motley participants in holiday festivals were required to make decisions about public policy that would affect them in different and mutually disagreeable ways. These public ceremonies did, however, help provide a language, an imperfect, but inveterately human, means of communicating between individuals and across social divisions. The residents of New York, New Orleans, and San Francisco carried the language they had learned in public celebrations into their everyday encounters on the city streets and into their formal deliberations at City Hall. The centrality of gender in that language strongly suggests that women would somehow make a mark on the other locations of the public to which I now turn, the spatial and the political.

2
Everyday Space
Gender and the
Geography of the Public

O n a return visit to the United States in 1904 and 1905, Henry
      James was chagrined to find the women of his native land
      conducting themselves in a manner that he called "as public
as possible." James was not speaking of the assault of suffragists and
progressive reformers on the formal public podium, nor was he commenting on recent changes in the comportment of American women.
His cranky essay on the "speech and manners of American women"
was provoked by a "haunting reminiscence" of schoolgirls who "took
possession of the public scene" a quarter-century earlier. These students at a young ladies' seminary on Mount Vernon Street in Boston
"had been turned out . . . to the pavements of the town, and with
this large scale of space about them for intercourse they could scarce
do other than hoot and howl. They romped, they conversed, at the
top of their lungs from one side of the ample avenue to the other;
they sat on doorsteps and partook of scraps of luncheon, they hunted
each other to and fro and indulged in innocent mirth quite as if they
had been in private gardens or a play-room."[1]

This depiction of the ease and confidence with which American
women occupied urban public spaces was not the isolated impression
of Henry James. A Mexican visitor to San Francisco in the 1870s
proclaimed that "the typical American woman lives in the street. She
goes everywhere and everywhere she is received with preferential
civility." An Italian tourist to these shores went so far as to pronounce
that "the public here is a common noun of the feminine gender."[2]

Yet such scenes of women in public, witnessed by a number of
observers in a variety of times and places, have largely escaped the
attention of historians. The bulk of the scholarship created by historians of women over the last fifteen years has located female subjects

in more private and retiring places. Sequestered in their homes, gathered together in churches, charities, and women's associations, observing the businesslike decorum of suffrage conventions, the female characters in this historical record rarely exhibit the *joie de vivre* of those young women on the streets of Boston. But if that image is more than a figment of Henry James's prodigious imagination, it can tell us much about the meaning of gender a century ago.

Social space, especially the everyday uses of city streets, serves as a scaffolding upon which both gender distinctions and female identity are constructed. Woman's status is often, perhaps inappropriately, defined in spatial metaphors of woman's place and the female sphere. An individual's sense of self, and the degree to which that self is at core male or female, evolves through associations with place, memories of familiar and centering spaces, where men or women feel they properly belong and most comfortably reside. By its very definition, however, public space defies exact boundaries between male and female spheres. In spaces theoretically open and accessible to all, women can mix with a multiplicity of others, both male and female, rather than ensconce themselves among their own sex or with like-minded kin and close associates. Therefore, male-female distinctions are put to a severe test in public space. On the one hand, the behavior of men and women in public can be orchestrated so as to lend a special legitimacy and sharper definition to gender differences. The dualistic gender symbols displayed in public space on holidays and described in Chapter 1 would seem to support this interpretation. On the other hand, gender distinctions might be corroded by the informal, everyday uses of public space by real men and women. The spontaneity, diversity, and volatility of life on the streets of the big city might not be so easily corralled into neat distinctions between the dualistic classifications of male and female.

This essay will explore these alternative and fundamental implications of the relationship between gender and public space. The chief location of this public and diurnal enactment of gender difference was the city streets, slim paths marked out in monotonous grid patterns, cutting their way through a densely built environment of dwelling houses and places of business. The private jurisdiction over city space was also interrupted by a few public squares in New Orleans, and somewhat fewer in New York and San Francisco. After midcentury, large urban parks were situated at the outskirts of this densely built-up urban space. Over the course of the nineteenth century, the cityscape also became littered with spaces that were semipublic in character, places such as theaters, department stores, and places of commercial amusement, which provided ready access from the streets for those who could pay the price of admission.

To chart the borders of public and private in urban space is an exercise in social geography, "the understanding of the patterns which arise from the use social groups make of space as they see it, and of the processes involved in making and changing such patterns."[3] The patterns of social geography were especially irregular and confusing in the three sites of these essays, New York, San Francisco, and New Orleans between 1825 and 1880. First of all, as the political and physical boundaries of these cities strained to contain a mushrooming population, their residents forfeited the traditional means of ordering people in space, through detailed personal knowledge of most of those they encountered on a daily basis. As one contemporary put it, the city was the habitat of "strangers in a strange land."

A second means of imposing orderly patterns on the burgeoning urban population was also unavailable to the residents of nineteenth-century cities: the assignment of specialized urban functions and different social groups to separate spatial zones. Neither the multiple functions of a mixed urban economy nor the diverse ethnic, racial, and class groupings of the metropolis were neatly sorted out in urban space before 1880. Only a few omnibuses and rail lines carried select portions of the population to segregated residential districts. As New York's population topped one million in the 1870s, only the privileged could find refuge in a few middle- and upper-class areas like Fifth Avenue and Greenwich Village. Even these segregated spaces were measured by blocks, not wards, and bordered immediately on the residences of the foreign-born and lower class. The latter groups rarely took up residence in compact ethnic villages in New York. In San Francisco, only the Chinese, blacks, and Italians had any measurable residential concentration. New Orleans was unique in sorting its population into three politically separate municipalities between 1837 and 1850, one notably French, another Yankee, and the third foreign in origin. But even this ethnic compartmentalization was imperfect, brief, and undercut by the mixing of classes and races in each of the three districts. Neither was the map of the big city zoned according to specialized land usage. Although each city could boast at least the rudiments of a central business district by midcentury, its diverse population had to share common neighborhood services on an everyday basis. Shops, factories, and dwelling units still abutted one another on the city streets. Only in the age of automobiles, suburbs, and electronic communication would distinct social groups and different economic functions be assigned to distinctly separate territories.[4]

Above all, the streets themselves defied attempts at segregation.

The big city of the industrial age was first and foremost a market-place, circulating goods, services, and people in a dense physical environment cut through with narrow public arteries. Along the way to producing, buying, and selling, strangers routinely crossed each others' paths, often making brusque physical contact. On the streets of "the great metropolis" of New York in 1867, Junius Browne observed that "beggars and millionaires, shoulder-hitters and thinkers, burghers and scholars, fine women and fortune tellers, journalists and pawn brokers, gamblers and mechanics, here as everywhere else crowd and jostle each other, and all had and fill their places in some mysterious way."[5]

The social geography of the big city might indeed seem mysterious to its residents. Denied both personal knowledge of their fellow citizens and the refuge of precise social segregation, they were destined to "crowd and jostle each other" every day on the public streets.

Stranded in this limbo between the face-to-face communities of the past and the more segregated social geography of more recent times, the city dwellers of the last century devised intermediary methods of imposing order on the urban maelstrom. Junius Browne exhibited the first such method. He had made a literary career out of penetrating the mysteries of the city streets and imposing what Lyn Lofland has called categorical knowledge, a refined set of human types from "shoulder-hitters" to "fortunetellers," on what the less sophisticated saw as "a huge conglomerate mass of people." By 1880, an army of flaneurs cum journalists shared Browne's acumen for imposing cognitive patterns on the heterogeneous spaces of the city. They traveled the city streets, block by block, mapping the haunts of the rich and the poor, the Irish, the German, and the native-born, the black, the white, and the Asian, the virtuous and the vile.[6]

Everywhere they went, these journalists categorized places as well as people, superimposing cultural districts on a socially mixed city. Their "mental maps" and skill at "reading" the city, to use Kenneth Lynch's astute formulations, entered the vernacular as well. In New Yorker parlance, the city was divided between the affluent West Side and the modest East Side, between the dollar and the shilling side of Broadway, and between Fifth Avenue opulence and Five Points misery. The smaller, more manageable population of San Francisco was symbolically polarized between Nob Hill and South of Market. Similarly, residents of New Orleans had recourse to the symbols of the French Quarter and the Garden District to mentally anchor their city in the turbulent seas of urban heterogeneity. By the third quarter of the nineteenth century, urbanites in general had

defied an untidy social-spatial reality and had sketched the rudiments of a mental map that sorted the city's motley population into
a few reassuring categories.

This cognitive method of ordering public space was supplemented
by a second geographical innovation, one that entailed more concrete
spatial and institutional changes. By the 1870s, urban residents could
look to a new order of semipublic places whose specialized functions
and regulated activities facilitated a more decorous and controlled
manner of interaction between strangers. Public parks, shopping
districts, and sanitized public amusements were the spatial land-
marks of this strategy of social geography. Those who gathered in
these discrete points on the mottled map of the city could enjoy the
art of public mingling in a relatively controlled and unthreatening
environment.

When either the cognitive or the institutional method of ordering
public space failed, cities resorted to a third technique, the enactment
of laws. City statute books were stocked with coercive and quaint
rules about behavior in the streets—prohibitions of everything from
obscene language to spitting in the streets to presenting a maimed or
hideous body to public view. By midcentury, all three cities had
instituted police forces whose major function was to monitor public
behavior. The majority of arrests in nineteenth-century cities were
prompted by infractions of public order—failure to conform to proper
street etiquette by displaying drunkenness, boisterousness, or "indecent" behavior. These legal controls combined with urbanites' mental
maps and the proliferation of semipublic institutions to create some
semblance of order amid the confusion of urban public spaces.

Women were key figures in this tapestry of public space. In a few
notable cases, they were actually the architects of urban space. A
lady was instrumental in creating perhaps the most enchanted public
space in the nation, New Orleans' Jackson Square. The revitalization
of that space in the 1840s was largely the work of Baroness de
Pontalba, who erected and gave her name to the gracious block of
apartments that enclosed one side of the square, and who then pres-
sured the City Fathers to improve the whole magic piazza. Another
class of women remodeled the built environment of the North, but
for more than aesthetic reasons. Reform-minded women in New York
were among the first practitioners of urban renewal, converting the
civic eyesore of the Old Brewery at Five Points into an evangelical
mission (see Chapter 1). The benevolent women who constructed
orphan asylums, industrial schools, and homes for the friendless also
left a feminine mark on the city skyline.

With these notable exceptions, however, the cityscape of the

Jackson Square, 1850. Historic New Orleans Collection, Museum/Research Center, acc. no. 1940.3.

nineteenth century was largely the handiwork of men. Most mental maps were drafted by masculine hands; businessmen shaped and drew profit from the gender patterns of commercial space; and male officials and landscape architects broke the ground for urban parks. Nonetheless, the female occupants of public space were very much on the minds of nineteenth-century urban planners and cartographers. Because their traditional behavior and status were turned topsy-turvy in the big city, women's conduct on the streets was monitored with special care. Heretofore, women's social status had largely been circumscribed by the spaces and relations of the household. In farmhouses, artisans' shops, and small, face-to-face communities, most women were under the close surveillance of fathers, husbands, and civic patriarchs. Now, the city streets offered them new attractions, new freedoms, and a veil of anonymity under which to pursue them.

The evolving urban marketplace could not, of course, afford to place the female population under house arrest. Women were a substantial portion of the city's labor force; in 1870, they constituted one-third of the work force in New York and New Orleans, and one-sixth in San Francisco. A significant minority of women lived on the streets, where they accounted for about half of the cities' vagrant population. Women of all classes took to public spaces for routine shopping and occasional recreation. As workers or as consumers, they circulated through streets crowded with strangers. As a consequence, gender became a key element in the three major strategies of nineteenth-century urban geography: woman's movements along the mental map of the city were carefully charted; places for her amusement were the centerpiece of the new network of semipublic institutions; and her regulation and protection were preoccupations of ordinances pertaining to public order. The placement of women on the public map would have important consequences. Would the big city beckon women into promiscuous enjoyment of urban freedom? Or would access to public space be severely restricted for the second sex?

The Public Domain and the Public Man: 1825–1840

The amorphous social geography of the early nineteenth century was not particularly precise about the spatial boundaries between either male and female or public and private. Before 1840, the configuration of people in urban space conformed roughly to the concept of the public domain as formulated by Philippe Ariès: for most residents of New York, San Francisco, and New Orleans, the household was still a center of production, retail business, and professional practice. It was also the site of relatively open socializing rather than a cloister for immediate kin. The household's border with the streets and squares was permeable and heavily trafficked. New Yorkers fondly recalled a domain early in the nineteenth century where they regularly enjoyed "social meeting of friends and neighbors, indulged in good dinners, long chats, pleasant walks, and rides in lumbering coaches." A lady of New Orleans recollected that "in the gay season then the whole city was one neighborhood, courtyard doors all open, balcony touching balcony, terrace looking on to the terrace. Society was close, contiguous, continuous."[7]

Although the nostalgia that enveloped such recollections casts some suspicion on their reliability, they were grounded in references to actual physical space. Memories of old New Orleans were anchored not only in the balconies of the Vieux Carre but also in the cherished wooden sidewalks of the city, the banquettes. "Families seated on their front banquettes until quite late at night, as though it were their common saloon, and the kindly feeling that each had for

"Sunday in New Orleans—The French Market," 1866, drawn by A. R. Waud. Historic New Orleans Collection, Museum/Research Center, acc. no. 1951.68.

their neighbors; it was like a country village." A short walk to the Place d'Armes, later Jackson Square, extended this casual sociability and diversified the social circle. Sunday afternoon around the square found Greek ice cream vendors, Choctaw Indians, "mulattresses," children, gentlemen, soldiers, and opera stars, all "commingled together in incessant motions, offering the ever vying and dissolving views of the kaleidoscope." In New Orleans, the public domain was especially elaborate, extending from sidewalks to public squares (in the American section as well as the French Quarter) to the lively promenades along the Levee and Canal, Chartres, and Royal streets. While the public domain was not as racially integrated as these romantic recollections implied, the art of public mingling was enjoyed by everyone. African-Americans gathered each Sunday in Congo Square for their own exuberant socializing, music, and dance.[8]

Portsmouth Plaza served the same catholic purposes during gold-rush days in San Francisco. It served as the city's rustic and ill-kept living room, a place for miners and fortune seekers to pitch their tents, a warehouse and retail stall for newly arrived merchants, and a place of sociability for everyone. In the instant city of the 1850s, when the plaza's bustling public grounds were surrounded by only a few domestic dwellings, the spatial distinction between private and public was grossly inappropriate. In the habitat of snugly settled Knickerbockers, the public domain had its own spatial centers. City Hall Park was a gathering point for the whole populace—the front lawn of the public's house, whose doors were opened to all for a public reception on New Year's Day. The Battery, the promenade along the docks of lower Manhattan, provided another place of public resort and personalized sociability: "It was the afternoon resort of children, and in summer the evening resort and promenade of citizens. Ladies could visit it with impunity even unaccompanied by a gentleman."[9]

To the extent that the informal socializing in American cities early in the nineteenth century approximated a public domain, it was relatively careless of male/female distinctions. If the streets, banquettes, and squares were an extension of the household, they were an appropriate habitat for both sexes. The editors of New Orleans newspapers looked forward to the appearance of upper-class women on the streets. The coming of springtime, the subsiding of a storm, the conclusion of a summer of epidemics was routinely greeted with the comforting notice, "The ladies are out on the street again." In San Francisco, where women were outnumbered at least four to one, both ladies and harlots were greeted gallantly in public places. Nor was doing business in public seen as especially untoward or unfamiliar behavior on the part of women. The woman huckster was a familiar and colorful presence in the public markets, which were centers of indiscriminate socializing in New York until the 1840s and long thereafter in New Orleans. Women like Aunt Katy Barr, at her stall in New York's Union Market for half a century, maintained their stations at the center of commerce and sociability and became cherished figures of urban folklore. As Christine Stansell has shown, the comings and goings of women in the walking city were marked by class and sexual distinctions more than by those of gender. While the wives and daughters of the elite were singled out for patriarchal protection, escorted through the streets by their kinsmen, poor and unprotected women were likely to be the sexual prey of upper-class dandies.[10] But as long as the everyday sociability of the city moved effortlessly outside households and through the streets, women's movements across the city map might be relatively untrammeled and poorly charted.

Yet, not all of urban social space was a seamless interweaving of the public and the private early in the nineteenth century. In fact, the public side of the spatial domain took on an increasingly visible, formal, and discrete quality between 1825 and 1840. The earliest examples of this distinctly public space were male preserves. This was the era, after all, when the public role of citizen was especially hallowed and was extended with the suffrage to all adult white men. The public status of the male citizen was registered in social space. Politics was given spatial and architectural definition by public halls, like that of Tammany, the prototype for many other partisan head-quarters that transplanted political discussion to specialized places, set apart from the heterosocial space of the home and the public domain. Women rarely passed through the classical portals of these public halls to enter a major center of public discourse. If a woman dared to tread within, she was likely to be branded a deviant or a pariah. When, for example, the radical Fanny Wright spoke at Tam-many Hall in the 1820s, she was dismissed as a "lady man."[11]

The places of commercial amusement that proliferated between 1825 and 1840 also marked off public space as the realm of public man. The first theaters were largely male sanctums. When Tyrone Power performed upon the New York stage in the 1830s, he counted only twenty females in the audience at the Park Theater. The city's first restaurants, along with a growing number of cafés and coffee houses, were occupied almost exclusively by men, who for the first time lunched outside the home. The exceptions to this male monop-oly actually reinforced gender segregation. The females who fre-quented these places of refreshment and amusement were regarded as harlots, as "public women." The same adjective that denoted civic honor when applied to men labeled females as sexual pariahs.[12]

The commercial amusements were but one sector of an increas-ingly formal and spatially contained public sphere. Men of a variety of classes began to mark off public turf as an extension of their jobs. Merchants' exchanges were accounted among the most impressive public buildings erected in each city during the antebellum period. More humble, but nonetheless architecturally notable, mechanics' institutes soon followed. The civic culture of New York in the early national period, as described by Thomas Bender, brought citizens of a variety of social ranks together in publicly funded literary institu-tions. But women never entered this male domain.[13] In the decades before the Civil War, in sum, an increasing number of formalized public places dotted the cityscape. These urban sites were often architecturally bounded or set off from the street by the cost of entry, and most of them were off-limits to most women.

Concurrently, as a wealth of literature in women's history has demonstrated, the domestic space was acquiring a distinctly feminine definition and was being set off from the street by an increasingly dense screen of privacy. A fissure in the public domain was now clearly visible: the result was two spatially separate sectors, one public, one private. The first clientele of the formally defined public space, as we have seen, was markedly masculine. Those firemen, tradesmen, militiamen, and politicians who paraded through Chapter 1 gave ceremonial definition to public space and laid claim to the streets themselves as masculine turf. The approximate date of the 1840s can serve, then, as a rough benchmark in the gender geography of public urban space. It was then that the trajectory of historical geography left women mingling in the old public realm of informal sociability or newly ensconced in their Victorian domiciles, but barred from the formal public spaces newly opened to men.

The Cartography of Gender: The Endangered and the Dangerous

The first evidence of the change in this *modus vivendi* is visible in literary accounts of everyday life on city streets. Around the midpoint of the nineteenth century, the ever-loquacious newspaper editors, a new breed of reporters who prowled the streets in search of human interest stories, and a few urban reformers set about drafting ever more elaborate maps of the city streets. They coded public urban space in terms that are now quite familiar: the streets became a place of danger. They also charted the boundaries of gender on the map of the city, but in ways that diverge from the mental maps that are commonplace today. The cartographers of gender at work during the latter half of the nineteenth century did not picture the streets as places where women were especially vulnerable and men the most likely predators. Neither the endangered nor the dangerous had such simple, dichotomized gender designations a century ago.

First of all, warnings of urban danger were issued to men and women alike. Naïfs and visitors of both sexes were warned against walking the streets after nightfall. Even as fearless an urbanite as Walt Whitman warned against such foolhardy escapades, journalistic men-about-town sought police escorts when they ventured into the most notorious slum districts, and Charles Dickens took two body-guards with him on a tour of Five Points. From the newspaper columns came daily headings, "Stabbing Affray," "Shooting Affray," "Another Horrible Murder." These commonplace warnings about the physical dangers lurking on the streets were seldom coded by gender in the nineteenth century. In fact, men seemed more often the victims of street crimes than women. Sensational murder cases in New York sometimes claimed men as victims and women, either prostitutes or paramours, as executioners. (No analog to Jack the Ripper stalked the American press filling women's imaginations with images of the sexual dangers lurking in the streets.) When women were the victims of violence, it most often occurred in the private spaces of the tenements. The crime report in the *New York Tribune* on February 23, 1867, was as good a measure as any of the sex ratio for street crime. On that day, when "more than the average amount of crime" was reported to the *Tribune* office, one women was shot indoors in a "vile den," while three men met violence on the street—one shot and killed on the Bowery and two others "stabbed by rowdies."

Although both men and women were alerted to the dangers of the city streets, they were warned of different species of threats. By most accounts, women were exposed less to bodily harm and more to a violation of their delicate sensibilities. Perhaps the most extreme expression of this sensitivity was recorded in San Francisco in 1855 when an organ grinder was arrested and fined the hefty sum of $50 "for affrighting the women and children of Henry Street into 'conniption fits' by exhibiting a monster in the shape of a deformed indian. The sight was truly disgusting." The regulation of begging on the streets was also construed as a mode of protecting sensitive females. When a beggar displayed a decrepit arm, by way of demonstrating to passers-by that he was incapable of manual labor, the *Alta California* commented that "it may be imagined how shocked ladies have been encountering these wretches in their promenades for healthy exercise."[14] In New Orleans, the gallant editor tried to shield the truly ugly sight of a slave auction from woman's gaze, but for aesthetic and sexual rather than political or moral reasons. For ladies to promenade near slave sales would expose them to scantily clad chattels, and the leers of black men.[15]

According to newspaper accounts, the lecherous gaze of men was not confined to a single race and could be found in every quarter of each city. The city streets were littered with voyeurs, the ubiquitous corner loungers and hoodlums whose major avocation was girl watching. Like the "hordes of ruffians who loitered around the firehouse on Worth and Broadway in 1857," their "only occupation seems to be to hang around the enginehouse and the nearest rumshops, insulting and abusing women and strangers and making themselves as offensive and dangerous as possible." All three cities passed ordinances against insulting women in the streets, an offense that provoked more than twice the number of arrests as rape. The sensitive ears of ladies were reputedly offended by playfulness as well as insult. Firecrackers were tolerable to men, according to the *New*

Orleans Picayune, "but when females are selected as the object it becomes extremely reprehensible."[16]

Although male writers posed primarily as protectors of women's acute sensibilities to public insult, they clearly felt personally threatened as well. Not just their refined tastes and morals, but their pocketbooks, their bodies, and their egos were placed in jeopardy on the public streets. Professional cartographers of street life warned men as well as women of an array of threatening personages on the public streets: there were beggars, vagrants, a panoply of specialists in thievery, and of course streetwalkers. The beggar personified all the dangers that awaited men in the street. Characterized as a devious person of business, the beggar posed a challenge to the marketplace intelligence of the males he or she accosted on the streets. The "smarter sort" calculated to increase their earnings by assuming pathetic costumes and recounting bathetic sob stories. They "hired" accomplices and operated by sophisticated business techniques; some reputedly were organized into joint stock companies. A New York cartman who prided himself on his knowledge of the street confided that "I have often heard it said that these professionals owned a fine large hall somewhere down on the 'points' where they assembled and enjoyed themselves in high carnival when the business of the day was over." According to journalists, public space was densely populated with wily street people who made their livelihood off gullible men. The *New York Tribune* advised male readers: "Don't hang around corners where vagabonds of either sex resort. You will be spotted and apt to get a bruised face and lose your watch and money."[17]

Fears of beggars encoded another critical element in the gendered

"Beauties of Street-Car Travel in New York," drawn by C. S. Reinhart, from a sketch by M. Woolf. *Harper's Weekly,* May 20, 1871.

cartography of the nineteenth-century city. The population that posed these multiple threats to public man contained large numbers of women. In other words, the dangerous as well as the endangered urbanite was often portrayed as a woman, who in turn preyed on both sexes. Dangerous women assumed their most threatening guise as prostitutes. The greatest moral risk that women encountered on the public streets was presented by these members of their own sex who converted public space into an erotic marketplace. Images of chance meetings and near collisions between virtuous and sinful women were a mainstay of urban gender cartography. Antebellum moral reformers posed "Purity, enshrined in the loveliest form of womanhood" strolling alongside "womanhood discrowned, clothed with painted shame." Two decades later, journalists pictured harlots and ladies rubbing shoulders with one another on the haughty thoroughfare of Broadway. They told of the dangerous and the endangered inhabiting the same ice cream parlors and brushing their embroidered and flounced sleeves at the counters of dry goods stores. The propinquity of vice and virtue in urban space held endless possibilities of contamination. George Ellington's imagination concocted one of the more exotic scenarios: a lady traveling on one of the Broadway cars streets unknowingly passes a brothel where her son or husband is "enjoying the society of Africans."[18]

For men, the prostitute posed a threat that was more palpable, physical, and lethal than such contrived images. Male readers of the daily press heard dire warnings such as this: "Investigations made in a very large number of cases where bodies have been found floating in the water showed that the victims were last seen alive in the the company of the female frequenters of these hells of the metropolis or in the dance-halls."[19] The fearful possibility of meeting death by female hands was conjured up around dance halls and low-class dives, public spaces where men and women often came together to transact sexual commerce. The men who frequented such places courted the greatest danger of urban life. When the battle of the sexes was staged on the streets, men could be cast in the role of victim.

The imagery of male victimization was already apparent in 1850, when George Foster portrayed the prostitute "snaring her victim and trapping him to her den." In the 1860s, Junius Browne characterized prostitutes as "those who pace the street day and night in search of victims, whom they debauch and rob if they can." George Ellington, writing in the 1870s, warned men that even in the fashionable quarter on Twelfth Street near Fifth Avenue, "they pass the doors of this house every day in crowds, little knowing how near there is a trap set for them and all their sex." Girls as young as ten preyed on men from their stations at the intersections of busy streets. Street sweepers and flower girls were under suspicion of prostitution or worse. Some of them were alleged to have blackmailed gentlemen with charges of seduction. The readers of this lurid literature were instructed to see the streets as a sexual battlefield, even more dangerous for men than for women. Dangerous women had set deadly traps at the most vulnerable site in a man's psyche: his sexuality.[20]

At such a volatile point in the urban imagination, the rhetoric of sexual danger grew more extravagant. As late as 1850, urban literature still harbored some sentimental images of the prostitute, evoking fallen angels, both "frail and vile." In the decades to follow, the dangerous female was banished from the pantheon of true womanhood. "There are spots in the great city," said one writer, where "women lost to modesty and neglectful of person and attire, seem even more degraded than the beastly men around them. . . . Decency shudders that such a creature bears the name of woman." Junius Browne impugned the femininity of the dangerous woman by questioning her maternal instincts. "Even maternity is not sacred" in the vice districts, where woman "gives nourishment from the gross, all exposed bosom to the already infected face." George Foster expelled another female from the circle of true womanhood with an equally graphic image of "flabby-breasts, as lascivious as . . . a new milch cow."[21]

Once deprived of the maternal crown of her femininity, the dangerous female lost her humanity as well; her most frequent label became "the savage female." The verbs that described the interaction between the savage woman and the city male evoked images of physical contamination. She infested, polluted, defiled, repelled, and sickened. Richard Buel, writing early in the 1880s, was a virtuoso of this visceral rhetoric. Of the women of New York's Water Street, he said: "So repulsive is their exceeding degradation as would almost make a gentleman heave his heels to look on them." Buel characterized a congregation of women on Bleecker Street as "of a type which is so repellent that we cannot suffer the defilement of their touch. . . . shoved down on the scale of life till they are a part of the city's sewage."

Buel and his cohort of urban writers had decisively and categorically cordoned off the dangerous woman, had banished her to the lowest regions of the urban imagination. He could not, however, remove her from the city streets. She was there to infest, defile, and threaten the body and soul, the very being of men. She was, in his language, a "bloodsucker."[22]

Accounts of everyday life in the city streets fractured the false universalism of polite gender symbolism. The chaste, domesticated, altruistic feminine image displayed in public ceremonies could not accommodate the diverse manifestations of womanhood on the public streets, especially not those females who took their very identity from those social spaces—the streetwalkers, the public women. The cartographers of gender devised a dualistic classification of womanhood in order to account for the discrepancies between the feminine ideal and the untidy realities of gender on the streets in everyday life. In so doing, the chroniclers of urban life implicitly acknowledged that gender was deeply divided by class. The endangered lady was clearly of the middle and upper classes; the dangerous woman came from the ranks of the poor and laboring classes. Accounts of the demimonde served in fact as the literary context in which intricate schemes of social stratification were played out. The popular literature of prostitution was structured around a crude class analysis, as the authors took their readers on a tour that began among affluent madams, proceeded to the modest rooms of harlots of the middling rank, and terminated in the degraded haunts of the streetwalker.

The category of the dangerous woman encapsulated racial as well as class distinctions. The most dangerous female inhabitant of the public streets was singled out by her skin color. Journalists often became apoplectic when they wrote of white men mingling with black prostitutes in the dives of lower Manhattan. In New Orleans, despite the fabled beauty of octoroons and the good repute of gentlemen who took them as their mistresses, white men carefully shielded their wives from social contact with dark-skinned paramours. In San Francisco, the Chinese prostitute assumed the role of "most thoroughly degraded specimen" of the dangerous sex. First, Asian-American women were defined as sexual slaves; then, their urban habitat became labeled as dangerous territory for the more chaste, vulnerable, and white of their sex. Editors warned that it was "absolutely impossible for a lady to pass anywhere near the precinct of these dens" in Chinatown. The urban imagination encoded class and racial differences in the categories of the dangerous and the endangered and played out these social distinctions within the female sex.

In the process, urban cartographers inadvertently exposed the ambiguities of gender identity and the arbitrariness of gender dualism. The discrepancy between biological differences and gender classifications became most highly visible in the haunts of the lower classes. On their excursions into the poor districts of the city, journalists were particularly disturbed by the difficulty of discerning gender boundaries. In slum districts, the sexes appeared to mingle freely and were poorly differentiated from each other in their behavior, their character, even in their appearance. The lodgers in a lower Manhattan police station were characterized as follows: "Men and women are alike in their filthiness, laziness, drunkenness. Both go out at daylight to wander the streets, begging food at basement windows, draining the dregs from the beer set outside the saloons, earning a dollar occasionally by some short job of light work and invariably spending it on liquor."

One of the greatest problems for Junius Browne in his forays into the dark side of the city was this gender ambiguity: "Old and young of both sexes are mingled everywhere. You hardly know the men from the women but for their beards and dress." One of the few female commentators on street life was similarly perplexed. Marie Louise Hankins observed of the poor that "in the women the distinction of sex is merely physiological. They swear and drink and fight like the most brutal men, often exceed them in coarseness and cruelty." Gender confusion was also a mark of racial difference. Observers of San Francisco's Chinatown were troubled by their inability to discern sexual dimorphism in the physiognomy and costumes of Asian-Americans. The festivities conducted by blacks in New Orleans' Congo Square were equally vexing; "men and women threw themselves recklessly into the arms of each other, without regard for age and sex."[23]

Those who observed the everyday behavior of men and women on the streets of the big city found repeated evidence of the inadequacy and ambiguity of gender classifications. Yet an army of writers and journalists remained defiantly at work plotting out intricate patterns of gender differences and gender relations in public space. When a simple, symmetrical opposition between male and female usages of public space proved inadequate, they acknowledged a division among women between the dangerous and the endangered. Their rigidly defined mental maps of city streets were riddled with the signs of gender difference and pockmarked with warnings of sexual threat.

The cartography of public spaces in nineteenth-century American cities invites some reference to anthropological interpretations of symbols of sexual danger, particularly the theories of Mary Douglas. This obsession with sexual differences conforms to Douglas's belief that "ideas about separating, purifying, demarcating and punishing transgressions have as their main function to impose system on an inherently untidy experience. It is only by exaggerating the differences between within and without, above and below, male and female, with and against that a semblance of order is created." Drawing exact and dualistic gender boundaries, in other words, is a frequent recourse of human cultures seeking to create symbolic order out of social multiplicity. The frequent association between treacherous sexual encounters and race and class relations is also in keeping with Douglas's typology of the symbolic function of sexual danger. Sexual dangers, according to Douglas, "are interpreted as symbols of other relations between parts of society, as mirroring designs of hierarchy or symmetry which apply to the larger social system. . . . The two sexes can serve as a model for the collaboration and distinctiveness of social units."[24] Female behavior, so obsessively charted on the streets, might stand in for other social differences that were imperfectly ranked and ordered in everyday life and poorly sorted in urban space.

The public spaces of nineteenth-century cities present an extreme case of what Douglas calls "untidy experience." The residents of nineteenth-century cities were destined to encounter an unseemly array of strangers every day on the city streets. Warnings of sexual danger and admonitions to maintain scrupulous gender differences might express and assuage the anxiety portended by such diversity. Moreover, sexual relations were particularly fitting representations of the potential disorder that lurked in the compact diversity of New York, New Orleans, and San Francisco. Males and females represented both opposites and intimates; despite their dichotomized social roles and cultural images, they shared the same households, bedrooms, and brothels. Theirs was a difference, in other words, that abided in immediate propinquity, as did the diverse occupants of the city streets. Relations with women, clearly the "other" in this largely male construction of urban geography, provided male writers with metaphors that neatly encapsulated the central problem of urban social space: how to create order and hierarchy in an environment where social differences coexisted in close physical proximity. Sexuality was perhaps the most powerful metaphor for the interplay of diversity and proximity in the big city. All the mental effort exhausted in trying to constrain the sexes and sexuality within cognitive and spatial boundaries expressed this compulsion to impose symbolic order on the tumult of nineteenth-century American cities.

But gender differences and the relations of the sexes were more than metaphors. The social relations of males and females were themselves being redrawn on the streets of the nineteenth-century city. The public man, as the urban cartographers repeatedly revealed, was not altogether confident of his position in the changing social spaces. To help him navigate the hazardous streets of the big city, journalists provided a map that pinpointed sexual dangers. Those dangers, furthermore, were often personified by women. The contradictory images of dangerous and endangered women testified that the members of the second sex were on the streets to stay and that their deportment in public space was still disquietingly unpredictable.

Constructing a Public Space for the Endangered

These mental maps of public space, however intricate and symbolically useful, provide a highly distorted and incomplete picture of the everyday uses of the city streets. Gender differences were imprinted on the city sidewalks as well as in newspaper type, and the correspondence between the two was hardly exact. Even as literary cartographers were drafting these mental maps, city dwellers were constructing and observing new gender boundaries. In small, jagged, but nonetheless material ways, men and women took new and separate routes through the city streets. The most visible gender boundary marked off territory that accommodated, protected, and loosely segregated endangered women.

The creation of the urban habitat designed especially for the ladies was not the work of journalists, writers, or reformers but of businessmen. Commercial entrepreneurs, ever eager to reap wealth in the urban marketplace, were the most energetic providers of urban public space especially for women. The pioneer in the business of gender differentiation was A. T. Stewart, who, in 1846, opened the first American department store on the corner of Broadway and Chambers in New York. Stewart's daring business venture both exploited a female market and experimented with the design of space. His marble palace, which operated on Chambers Street from 1846 to 1862, invited women into a commodious space just off the street where they could enjoy some of the amenities of urban sociability. They passed through huge doors into a large hall and then strolled aisles that bordered his merchandise much as the city streets lined private residences. They could promenade through a wide rotunda streaming with natural light from a dome above. They could linger in a public ladies' parlor on the second floor, whose giant mirrors, imported from France, refracted back their own images in this secure, sex-segregated crowd of strangers. Within the department store, women found an urban enclave in which to mimic the arts of urban mingling without incurring the risks of the world outside. When Stewart's moved uptown to Astor Place in 1862, this ladies' turf measured two and one-quarter acres of floor space. Here was ample territory in which to refine shopping into an urban occupation. As the *New York Herald* put it on the opening of the store, "Mr. Stewart has paid the ladies of this city a high compliment in giving them such a beautiful spot in which to while away their leisure hours of a morning."[25]

The feminine population of the department store soon spilled out into the street. Stewart had also imported plate glass windows, and he mounted displays within that transformed the street itself into terrain for a public female avocation, window shopping. The success of Stewart's experiment provoked the proliferation of department stores in New York and augmented the stream of shoppers, until twenty blocks of Broadway became a "ladies' mile." The tide of femininity shifted over to Sixth Avenue and was fed by a tributary of less affluent customers when Macy's emporium opened in the next decade. Soon women occupied a second major pocket of urban space on Fourteenth Street. In addition to enticing his clientele with the promise of bargains, Macy offered women such special services as a ladies' lunch room and ladies' parlor, thereby embroidering shopping with more opportunities to mingle with strangers. Once catering to city women had proved so lucrative, department stores spread rapidly to other urban sites. The editor of the *New Orleans Picayune* announced "Good news for the ladies" in 1868—"who cannot be expected to keep indoors, now that the weather is cleared up, should not fail upon their shopping excursion on Canal Street to drop in at the elegant store of Messrs. Guelbe and Nippert." Similar invitations were sent by the merchants of Market Street in San Francisco where Mary Magnin opened the department store named for her husband in 1876.[26]

In the third quarter of the nineteenth century, the department store became the centerpiece of an extended network of commercial enterprises that capitalized on a female market. Big-city hotels also cordoned off special places for women. The St. Nicholas in New York, the St. Charles in New Orleans, and the Cosmopolitan in San Francisco all boasted ladies' parlors and drawing rooms. Feeding a lady became another lucrative business as the central business districts of each city featured signs for ladies' dining rooms and ladies' restaurants. Ice cream parlors also became identified as women's spaces. Those public houses that did not offer segregated spaces for women smoothed the way for their sex by providing separate ladies' entrances. Theaters in central business districts courted the female audience as well, providing matinees and wholesome play bills catering to the amusement of a lady. A careful scrutiny of the commercial district could find less savory entertainments for women as well, among them female cabarets, oyster houses, and gambling houses.[27]

The retailer in a frenetic search for customers was the most energetic but hardly the solitary architect of gender-defined public space. By midcentury, voluntary societies had joined in the provision of quarters for women. San Francisco's Mercantile Library invited women into a ladies' reading room in 1870. Transportation facilities such as New York's ferry boats set aside special compartments for women. The public sector followed suit, providing ladies' parlors at City Hall, and even a ladies' place at the post office. In the New Orleans post office, the ladies enjoyed "a complete department" solely for their use, along with a separate entrance. The more parsimonious postal officials of San Francisco offered only a ladies' window.[28]

The provision of public space for women was a major civic project during the latter half of the nineteenth century. The accommodation of ladies and the ordering of gender relations was a major incentive behind the boldest public intervention in the private use and allocation of city space: the development of the great parks of New York, San Francisco, and, later, New Orleans. Frederick Law Olmsted, a publicist and planner of both Central Park and San Francisco's Golden Gate Park, proffered his designs as especially responsive to female needs, both of country girls, who came to the city in a "frantic desire to escape from dull lives," and of urban housewives, reputedly idled by their diminished household responsibilities. San Francisco's park promoters championed the ladies, whose sallow countenances bespoke their need for the healthy exercise prohibited by "the winds, the dusty dunes or mudholes" of the city.[29]

Few would dispute the merits of such a beneficent and chivalrous civic project, especially if it could be accomplished by locating parks on less valuable real estate along the cities' borders. When large urban parks were reclaimed from the rocky turf of Manhattan's Upper West Side in the 1850s and from the sand dunes of San Francisco two decades later, the urban landscape was revamped to accommodate the ladies. The San Francisco Park Commissioners classified their users by class and gender: first, "the respectable and well-behaved adult community"; second, the ladies and children, "who wish to enjoy themselves in a home-like manner"; third, the poorer classes who inhabited neighborhoods adjacent to the park; and fourth, "gentlemen who wish to speed their horses." Most accessible to the owners of horses and private carriages, the large urban parks provided their genteel users de facto segregation from the lower classes, male and female. Central Park was extolled as the piece of Manhattan real estate least frequented by prostitutes. The sanitizing of urban space was reinforced by a series of park regulations that prohibited "riots, boisterous or indecent conduct or language" and "publicly using provoking or indecent language." The urban park system, by design or de facto segregation, had a sanitary set of users and was thus a fit habitat for ladies.[30]

Still, park planners were even more fastidious in marking off the boundaries between the genders. Special sections of the park were set off as "retiring rooms for ladies," "ladies' refreshment houses," and "children's quarters." Section 9 of the Golden Gate Park regulations read, "No male person over the age of ten years shall enter any ladies toilet or playground for children, parents and guardians." When a father took exception to a sign in the park that read, "This lawn reserved for ladies and children," his plea for gender desegregation went unheard.[31]

The sexes were rarely sorted into such perfectly segregated places. After all, endangered men were also entitled to refuge in urban space. To that end, men were ushered into public spaces that had been sanitized by the presence of women. Horace Greeley of the *New York Tribune* put it bluntly when he observed that with a wife and child at his side, a man was unlikely to resort to riot and revolution. Places like large parks, set apart from the diversity of the city proper, were ideal spaces in which to reintegrate the sexes. Parks invited men out of raucous male assemblages into a space designed for family picnics, quiet walks, and high-toned concerts. The rhetoric of Junius Browne was calmed by the atmosphere of Central Park: "No sight is more pleasant than the laborer or mechanic on Saturday afternoon or Sunday with his wife and children luxuriating in the mere absence of toil and drinking in the breezes from the sea which cannot find their way into the close tenement quarter he calls a home." Many other organizers of urban entertainment resorted to the same strategy. One newspaper endorsed the recruitment of women into the audience for the national pastime, saying, "The presence of an assemblage of ladies purifies the moral atmosphere of a baseball gathering, repressing as it does, all the outbursts of intemperate language which the excitement of a combat so frequently induces." This prescription for treating urban ills became the rationale for a multi-phalanxed campaign to construct heterosocial spaces as barricades against urban dangers.[32]

The first public den of male sociability to be sexually integrated was the theater. Before ladies could gather there, however, the prostitutes had to be banished. The architectural and spatial devices that accommodated eros to thespians did not meet the scrupulous standards of Victorian heterosociality. George Foster reported that although "thick walls and wide stair-cases" barred "abandoned women" from the public entrance to the Broadway Theater, "it is

nevertheless true that one-quarter of the house is set apart exclusively for the use of [prostitutes] in which they nightly and publicly
drive their sickening trade."[33] A more effective system of segregation
was in operation at the French Theater of New Orleans. A passage-
way connected the Theater d'Orleans with the adjacent Orleans Hall,
a habitat of quadroons. It permitted gentlemen to pass unobserved
between the separate quarters of wives and mistresses.

At midcentury, such spatial hypocrisy was permissible neither in
the American Quarter of New Orleans nor in Northern cities. Led by
the construction of New York's elite Astor Place Theater in 1848,
each city could soon boast at least a few theaters that had been
thoroughly sanitized, their hefty price of admission chasing out the
rabble and their orderly tiers accommodating the respectable classes
of both sexes. New York's Academy of Music was a showcase of
respectable public amusement. Subdued programs of classical music
made it a gathering place for bourgeois couples and a model for a
new order of heterosocial public life. The Grand Opera of New Orleans was advertised as "The Ladies Theater" of the city.

A variety of other public places of entertainment opened their
doors to both men and women at midcentury. A small fee admitted
both sexes to the popular pleasure gardens of New York and San
Francisco, where they purchased a rustic ambience for casual socializing along with refreshments and musical entertainment. Niblós
Gardens in New York became a model of propriety and a thriving
business by 1850. "The secret," wrote George Foster, "was simple—
no woman is admitted at this house under any pretext, unless accompanied by a gentleman. The consequence is that rowdies avoid the
house, or if they visit it, have no inducement for misbehaving—and
respectable and quiet people freely come, with their wives and children, sure of being neither shocked by obscenity nor frightened by
violence." Pleasure spots such as Woodward's and Russ Garden in
San Francisco and Vauxhall Gardens in New York offered polite
public relaxation for the middle and working classes. The master
impresario of popular heterosocial entertainment was P. T. Barnum.
Barnum's sensational but wholesome shows brought women and
families flocking to the American Museum and turned the corner of
Fourteenth Street and Sixth Avenue into a place of public frolic,
congestion, and orderly mingling of the sexes.[34]

Another formalized social space, the public ball, brought the sexes
together in a regular and stylized manner. Always a mainstay of the
gay heterosociality of French New Orleans, balls became a staple of
urban public life in all three cities by midcentury; announcements of
public balls invited men and women en masse to take in this mode

of entertainment. Some balls were promoted by tycoons of the amusement industry to fill their halls, hotels, and pleasure gardens for a lucrative admission price or by subscription. Others were hosted as benefits for public charities; still others lent a heterosocial dimension to male voluntary associations. The sponsors of one ball at New Orleans' St. Charles Theater in 1858, for example, issued fifteen hundred invitations. The balls sponsored by Irish benefit societies brought as many as four thousand reveling men and women together.[35]

The reputation of the public ball was never entirely savory. Masked balls, in particular, were notorious for veiling sexual indiscretions and were regulated or banned in all three cities. The organizers of the more reputable public balls attempted to prevent the dance floor from becoming the haunt of prostitutes by denying admission to women who lacked male escorts. These public balls linked the sexes in carefully formalized and ritualized ways. A single ticket admitted one gentlemen, along with one to three ladies. Entering under male escort, then paired with men on the dance floor, women mingled with the opposite sex in a stylized and dispassionate public dramatization of heterosexual relations. Guests were issued the house rules along with the evening's program and were expected to conform to a rigid pattern for heterosocial mingling. The fashionable balls that eclipsed the promiscuous outdoor celebration of Mardi Gras after the Civil War exemplify this formalized choreography of heterosocial relations. A long set of instructions to the dancers began: "Gentlemen escorting ladies will leave them at the head of the main staircase, in the hands of the reception committee, and will then themselves pass by the left hand staircase to the third tier. No gentlemen will be allowed to occupy a seat even in the third tier whilst there is a lady without a seat . . . ."[36] The dance was an object lesson in heterosocial decorum, even as it offered women the pleasures of inhabiting a semipublic space.

The late nineteenth-century city offered women space in which to exert themselves in more vigorous ways than by waltzing. When the skating rinks of Central Park opened in 1858, literally thousands of women ventured out of doors in the winter cold for exercise and sociability. Many of them soon grew restless on the "ladies' pond," where the timid of their sex could tumble on the ice without a blush and glide along without fear of colliding with the rougher sex. By the 1860s, the gender segregation of the skating rink had broken down as bolder women jostled with the boys and men on the public rinks. Another sporting fad of the era, croquet, provided an additional opportunity for genteel mingling and polite competition between the sexes. Athletic contests between women were also permissible in some segments of the public. Numerous picnics of the Yankee benevolent associations, and the more frequent and lusty games of German gymnastic societies, featured women's athletic contests. Women raced one another in age categories and in special divisions of the married and the single. Female pedestrian and equestrian competitions also presented the familiar apparitions of women in public.[37]

Gender differences and gender relations were prominent in all these new public sites—the central business district, the array of public amusements, and the spacious public parks. Women had found their own privileged spaces, and both sexes could enjoy polite and stylized ways of coupling, courting, and fraternizing in public. Urbanites in general could see a reassuring pattern of heterosocial propriety on, and just off, the city streets. These areas, centers of both gender segregation and the decorous mingling of males and females, were most clearly defined for the upper classes, by means of "ladies' miles" and elite entertainments. But men and women of the lower classes could not be altogether excluded from such public amenities. Newspaper editors admiringly recorded the movements of working girls along the city streets, where they mingled among the pedestrians of Broadway, Canal, and Market streets, gathered before shop windows, and prudently apportioned some of their small wages for the finery and entertainment on sale there.[38]

The Costly Freedom of Endangered Women

Large numbers of women, from ladies to working girls, had by 1880 found a relatively commodious and sometimes exclusive place for their sex on the city streets. Women clearly used and enjoyed the new public freedoms afforded by changes in gender geography. First of all, those women who participated in the intellectual mapping of urban space—largely travelers from abroad, such as Fredrika Bremer and Frances Trollope—demonstrated that the city could be conquered, made familiar, and enjoyed by literate females. One American sojourner in the nation's most bustling city displayed how quickly and effectively some women could adapt themselves to the urban regimen. Lydia Maria Child's *Letters from New York,* dating from the 1840s, are a distillation of urban cosmopolitanism. When asked how she, a New Englander and devotee of nature, could live so contentedly in New York City, Child retorted, "Why need I sigh for green fields? Does not Broadway superabound with beauty?" Child ambled freely along this street, pausing on a summer's evening to hear a concert at the Alhambra fountain, feast on ice cream, rub shoulders with working men, and sigh, "What more could one wish for amid so many agreeable sights and sounds?" After orienting herself along the spatial axis of Broadway, Child journeyed confidently onto the less genteel Bowery. "They who think exclusive gentility worth the fetters it imposes are welcome to wear them. I find quite enough of conventional shackles that cannot be slipped off, without assuming any unnecessary ones." Even the rough-and-tumble amusements of the working-class districts and haunts like the Bowery Theater and Vauxhall Gardens were accessible, comfortable, and pleasurable to Lydia Maria Child.[39]

A generation later and across the continent in San Francisco, a less renowned woman named Lucy Jones took an even wider course along city streets, now lined with destinations expressly for her sex. In the course of a year, Lucy Jones made use of the following urban amenities: ice cream parlors, boat races, galleries, banks, charitable fairs, the Mechanics' Institute, the Art Association, public halls, the Mercantile Library, public gardens, parks, the opera, and an array of concerts and plays, all these in addition to church and Sunday School. Lucy Jones reached these multiple urban sites in carriages, by street-car, and on foot. She orbited between them according to a social schedule or by personal caprice—returning home "after much wandering." She was escorted by her "young friends," her aunt Mary, or her brothers, and occasionally sauntered off alone, often linking up with friends of both sexes along the way. Some sunny weekends Lucy Jones took in two or three events a day. Routinely she recorded venturing out of doors three times a week, if not daily, and any day she could amuse herself by simply "going down town." Lucy Jones was certainly neither constrained in her middle-class household, nor intimidated by the tumultuous social life outside.[40]

Working girls could hardly devote their young lives to urban amusement. They rarely had the time or the literary inclination to record their movements through the city in private journals like that of Lucy Jones. Their course through the city streets was charted, however, by observers from the middle class who were uniformly impressed by the joie de vivre and animation with which they journeyed to and from work, lingered around the shops, and frequented their own places of amusement—gardens, picnics, theaters, and dance halls. In fact, one species of working girl actually took her name from a public street. The Bowery Gh'al was named for a street that epitomized urban intensity, that was congested with every species of city dweller and lined with every variety of public entertainment: "Theater, Museum, Christy's, garden, concert and ball-room. . . . Chatham street theater and Bowery shops"; it embraced "the whole world of middle and lower life." The young women who took their name from that street and who are so vividly portrayed by Christine Stansell were fluent in the language of street sociability. They had their own way of perambulating through the crowd, a distinctively brisk and bouncing gait. They created a sign system with their attire. In 1850, their identifying garment was something called the polka or monkey-jacket, tightly fitted and so striking that it was mimicked by the ladies on Broadway. Liz, the Bowery Girl and pal of the archetypal Bowery Boy, Mose, practiced her favorite urban pastimes in commercial public spaces. "If Mose is most perfectly himself at the target-excursion, Liz never feels herself at home but at the theater or the dance."[41]

Another group of women found a more sedate way to occupy the streets and to navigate between the respectable and the dangerous classes. One member of this class of female reformers, the Quaker philanthropist Abby Harper Gibbon, guided Fredrika Bremer though the most unseemly neighborhoods of New York: "Whoever walks at her side through the abandoned haunts of New York may feel himself in safety. Her bright and mild countenance is known even in the darkest places as a messenger of light." The women of New York's Five Points Mission epitomized the stalwart public posture of female reformers. Despite initial trepidation about visiting this notorious neighborhood, they soon felt "no grounds for apprehension" and determined that it was "better and safer to go about here alone than in company with a gentleman." Roman Catholic nuns reportedly walked the streets just as confidently. "Few that see the sisters gliding like shadows through the crowded streets of the city on their errands of mercy ever realize the harrowing scenes at which they are present." For such women, who lacked the secular and epicurean esprit of world travelers, middle-class ingenues, and spirited working girls, charitable visiting excused many an adventure in public space.[42]

For all these women, city streets provided a more lively sociability than the monotonous routines of the household or the relative isolation of rural and small-town America. Annie Fader's girlhood residence of Petaluma, California, was a social wasteland compared to San Francisco. A walk downtown and a visit to church set the narrow parameters of her everyday life in Petaluma. No wonder that the word "dull" was the commonest adjective in her diary. "This dullness is enough to drive one wild. I really think I will expire."[43] The social whirlwind of the city was in marked contrast not just to the rural past but to the suburban future of many American women. Not yet sequestered in socially and ethnically homogeneous spaces devoted to private residential uses of space, nineteenth-century urban women were still a doorstep or a short walk away from the excitement of heterogeneous public space and diverse urban amusements.

This is not to say that all or even most women enjoyed untrammeled access to public spaces. Some trembled at the borders of their domiciles. This was particularly true of the Southern lady represented by Julia Le Grand of New Orleans. Miss Le Grand's journal, while teeming with keen social observations and astute political judgments, was also limited by its author's narrow and private social circle. When the exigencies of the military occupation of New Orleans during the Civil War compelled her to escort a woman friend to the city's center, Miss Le Grand's timidity in public bordered on agoraphobia.

> We paced up and down before that desolate-looking Custom House, listening to the drumbeats of the soldiers drilling upon the river bank; also to some few cannon. Dirty-looking soldiers guarded the different entrances, and vile-appearing negroes, in filthy clothes, looked from the windows. It felt quite as desolate as everything looked. How my heart ached for a brothers's strong arm on which to lean, or for that dear one, now lost to me forever. Well, we did not go up into the court-room. I escaped that shadow of infamy. After traipsing up and down for a full hour, and submitting to the gaze for that length of time of any infamous creature that chose to look at us, we walked to the City Hall.

Within the sanctum of the major's private chamber, Julia Le Grand found asylum from this painful exposure to public space.[44]

The degree to which women made use of public space was conditioned not only by differences in temperament, class, and region, but by stages in the family cycle. Most women found their social orbit narrow upon marriage and after childbirth. At the same time that Lucy Jones enjoyed such freedom and diversity on the streets of San Francisco, a young matron named Nellie Wetherbee inscribed a very different map of the same city in her diary. Her married life was a season of "home knitting"; "staid in all day"; "Nothing new today. I live over the same thing everyday." Mrs. Wetherbee had her urban amenities—journeys to Russ Garden with her husband, an occasional outing for ice cream or to attend a lecture—but this was frugal public fare compared to that of single women. The spatial threshold marked by marriage did not escape Mrs. Wetherbee's consciousness: "No festival-going now. I'm an old married woman. I cannot help feeling how different married life is from single!!!"[45]

"The Morning Walk—Young Ladies' School Promenading the Avenue." *Harper's Weekly*, March 28, 1868.

Mrs. Wetherbee recognized that women's social roles as wife and mother still bound them to the household and severely restricted their use of even the most inviting public spaces.

Whenever women did make forays into public space during the nineteenth century, furthermore, they paid a certain cost. In the very act of opening up urban territory for females, the architects of urban geography branded the women who walked the streets of the nineteenth-century city as either endangered or dangerous women, emblems of propriety and vulnerability or object lessons in social differences and sexual danger. When ladies and respectable working-class girls stepped out on city streets, they carried the cumbersome baggage of gender stereotypes. They were subject to intense male scrutiny. In 1880, Samuel MacKeever indulged the peculiar urban taste for girl watching with avidity, and reported it in revealing metaphors. "I saw New York female loveliness in all its Fall glory, and an expensive glory it is too. . . . I saw pretty women, pretty enough to eat, pretty enough to make a man think that perhaps there is some-

thing in cannibalism after all."[46] Women who took to the streets of
the city may not have been ingested by male predators, but they had
entered a field of sexual objectification.

Women's entry into the newly feminized spaces of the city also
lured them into commodity culture. Both ladies and working girls
were induced to purchase appropriate costumes for the occasion.
Sarah Dawson of New Orleans had internalized this prerequisite of
female public life in the capitalist city: "I must have some clothes
too! How can I go among strangers with a single dress?" Women's
movements through the streets were often hampered by the invisible
tentacles of the urban market. Her places of resort were commonly
commercial places of entertainment extracting a price of admission:
her major excuse for meandering in urban space was shopping. In
the 1840s, Lydia Maria Child, author of *The Frugal Housewife*, was
already warding off the seductions of consumerism that beckoned
from the sidelines of women's space on the street. Passing the shop
windows of Broadway, she took pains to describe the commodities
within in natural and immaterial terms, regarding them like "the
stars and the forests, without the slightest wish to appropriate them,
and with the feeling that every human being ought to enjoy the
fairest creations of art, as freely as the sunlight and the star glory,
which our Father gives to all."[47]

The daughters of the late nineteenth century, born not in the
moral and religious economy of preindustrial America but in an urban marketplace superabundant with commodities, bought the con-
sumer ethic wholesale. Their commonest everyday public diversion
became an exercise in commercial capitalism called "shopping" or
"going downtown." Nellie Wetherbee paced her movements through
public space according to her shopping list: "I bought black silk dress
and silk morning dress. Then around to Mrs. Burdett's and ordered
my underclothes . . . out shopping all day." Another San Francisco
woman seemed to recognize the false promises of consumption. Annie Fader, perhaps anticipating her conversion to socialism later in
life, tired of excursions to the commercial district. "Another dull day
its course has run and here we are yet. We went down town, but
what's going down town, it's like the rest of any amusements, perfectly unbearable." The glimpses of urban excitement caught between aisles of goods, the purchase of tickets, and encounters with
cashiers were to some women small and hollow rewards of a public
life circumscribed by consumption. Women's access to new kinds of
public space was welcome and enjoyable, but it had its limits and
exacted its price.[48]

The Space of the Dangerous

The new social spaces described above were set aside for endangered and decorous women and were only one sector in the gendered
geography of the nineteenth-century city. All along the urban map,
but concentrated in a few localities, were the haunts of menacing
women and the sites of sexual danger. The dangerous woman left
her mark on the physical space as well as the mental map of the city.
The signpost of her public place was sexual commerce. Manhattan,
San Francisco, and New Orleans were cities of relatively unbridled
eros throughout the nineteenth century. By the mid-nineteenth century, the sexual services sold by women had become a highly visible,
profitable, and public urban occupation, with its own peculiar historical geography.

The sexual geography of New York City has been meticulously
mapped by Timothy Gilfoyle, who charts the course of a great wave
of prostitution onto the public space of the metropolis. Prior to 1820,
prostitution was confined to a few concentrated blocks mostly near
the waterfront and conducted in the relative privacy of disorderly
houses. Thereafter, houses of prostitution proliferated throughout the
city; there were sexual service stations even in elite and middle-class
neighborhoods. Although by the late nineteenth century New York,
like San Francisco and New Orleans, had its red light districts, where
sexual commerce was more densely and flamboyantly displayed,
most urban residents were within walking distance of brothels.[49]

As sexual commerce spun its tentacles throughout the city it also
assumed a variety of new institutional forms. Concentrated in brothels and clustered around the docks and the theaters early in the
century, prostitution expanded into a new array of public amusements by the 1870s: concert saloons, dance halls, oyster houses, and
masked balls. The entrepreneurs who reaped profits from this vast
spawning ground for sexual vice could be outrageously public and
graphic in their mode of operation. The Belle Union of San Francisco
advertised that a female employee could be seen performing sex acts
with a boar. Visitors to New York could explore the bawdy palaces
of commerce in the fashionable districts with a printed guidebook in
hand, *The Fast Man's Directory and Lover's Guide,* or *The Directory to
Seraglios.* Sexuality in Five Points was hardly this discreet; prostitutes
displayed their wares from open windows and even copulated in the
street. Anyone who walked out upon the major arteries of the city
shared the streets with prostitutes; both Broadway and the Bowery
were flooded with prostitutes in the evening. "Here are two ladies
approaching us," wrote one Broadway voyeur, "magnificently attired

"John Allen's Dance House," 304 Water St., New York City, 1868. *Frank Leslie's Illustrated Newsletter*, August 8, 1868.

with their large arms and voluptuous bosoms half naked, and their bright eyes looking invitation at every passer-by hailing 'How do you do, my dear? Come won't you come home with me.'"[50]

It was this audacious publicness of urban sexual commerce that was most likely to inspire public outrage and provoke civic action. Houses of prostitution were divided into public and private categories: "in some localities they are conducted so secretly that the police scarcely dare assert their existence, while in others the painted occupants of them may be seen sitting by the open door, or coquettishly arranged show-window like spiders anxiously awaiting for flies." High-class and discreet parlor houses were largely immune to prosecution. The flamboyant lower-class brothels, with their open doors and windows, were prime targets for police raids.[51]

The public amusements that gave a bold and defiant definition to the sexuality of the city were also grist for the mill of moralistic voyeurs. Journalistic cartographers and reforming politicians made frequent excursions to the most highly visible dens of sexuality in lower Manhattan, south of Market Street in San Francisco, and on the waterfront in the Third District of New Orleans, reporting back on the antics of prostitutes in cheap theaters, oyster saloons, and grog shops. One urban institution had an especially unsavory and well-documented reputation for reaping profit from sexual vice. Often called a concert saloon or simply a dance hall, it was just a "dive" to New York police chief George Walling, who described these habitats of vice as places located "in various parts of town, where abandoned women congregate to try their charms on easily tempted men."[52]

In the urban imagination, the concert saloon was a place whose specialized function was to permit dangerous women to entrap vulnerable men. Ellington counted three thousand such establishments in New York in 1870, scattered from upper Broadway to the tip of the island. They employed seventeen thousand women, according to Ellington, all of whom practiced prostitution. Urban cartographers described these dance halls in intimate detail, down to the architectural fine points of the interior. The range of New York establishments offered to the consuming public extended from the more high-toned and renowned halls like that of Harry Hill's to the infamous "Black and Tan," whose mixture of races made the scene "all the more revolting . . . as bad as the imagination can picture." Walling described the life within the dance hall in more detail. "Devils in female form" performed a "dance of death" before the male victim, who "drinks and jokes with his female companions until reason and wit begin to dull. He enjoys in a low, sensual way their pawing over his face and whiskers and notices naught amiss when their light feminine fingers slip into his pockets and abstract his valuables."[53]

The dance hall—this highly public, sexually charged nexus between male and female, the dangerous and the endangered—provoked nineteenth-century officials to write the etiquette of gender in public places into law. By the 1870s, all three cities had enacted municipal ordinances to regulate the dance halls. The San Francisco statute imposed a midnight curfew on all places of amusement that employed women as entertainers or waitresses. New Orleans expelled prostitutes from the city's cafés. The New York statute regulating places of amusement contained this stipulation: "nor shall it be lawful to employ nor furnish or assent to the employment or attendance of, any female to wait on, or attend in any manner, or furnish refreshments to the audience or spectators." This law barred women from employment in a wide range of public places: "theaters, circuses, public gardens, public houses, public halls or premises or other place of public meeting, resort or amusement whatsoever." Sexual danger had become a rationale for legally restricting women's use of public space.[54]

By the 1870s, all three cities were also moving hesitantly toward legal restriction of prostitution itself. They acted, however, to control only the public aspects of sexual commerce. The chief codicil of the laws in all three cities did not outlaw prostitution itself but prohibited solicitation "on the public streets." In the 1870s, New Orleans barristers strained to establish precise borders between legitimate private vice and the unlawful public display of sexuality. That statute read:

> That it shall be unlawful for any woman or girl notoriously abandoned to lewdness to stand on the sidewalks in front of the premises occupied by her, or at the alley-way, door or gate of such premises or sit upon the steps thereof in an indecent posture, nor accost, call nor stop any person passing by, nor walk up and down the sidewalk or banquette, nor stroll about the streets of the city indecently attired.

Another ordinance prohibited prostitutes from occupying the first floor of those edifices that fronted public streets.[55]

The San Francisco ordinance dating from the same period legislated the means whereby prostitutes were permitted to communicate with the occupants of the streets, forbidding them to "solicit by words, gestures, or knocks any person passing or being on a public street." The language that restricted women's access to public space read more simply in New York, penalizing "common prostitutes or night-walkers" for "loitering or being in any thoroughfare or public place for the purpose of prostitution."[56]

The lawmakers of New Orleans and San Francisco drew the boundaries of prostitution not just at the intersection between street and brothel but also in specialized zones of the city. The New Orleans statute of 1866 read that "it shall be unlawful for any woman or girl, notoriously abandoned to lewdness, to occupy, inhabit, live or sleep in the lower floor of any houses or buildings within the following districts." The city legislators made the boundaries of permissible sexual commerce very narrow, limiting prostitution chiefly to a few slum districts near the river. The law in San Francisco dating from 1863 confined prostitution largely within the infamous red light district of the Barbary Coast. The freedom of the city, for this one conspicuous class of a single gender, was severely constricted. Those women who sought to make their living selling sexual services on the streets were forbidden to "occupy, inhabit, live or sleep" in private dwellings of their own choosing.[57] Prostitutes were a special class of citizens singled out to experience de jure residential segregation.

This early example of urban zoning, a striking exception to the laissez-faire principles of the nineteenth-century political economy, demonstrates the centrality of gender in the maintenance of order in a dense congregation of strangers. Still, the primacy of circulating goods and services through the market economy would not permit fastidious maintenance of these sexual boundaries. The statutes designed to contain prostitution carried small penalties, were rarely enforced, and at times were overruled by courts in the name of free enterprise. City people—men, women, and even prostitutes—still enjoyed relatively free use of public space. That space, however, was now criss-crossed with real and imaginary gender boundaries: the categories of proper and improper womanhood, the segregated territories of ladies, the places for polite heterosociality, and the spatial restrictions on prostitution. To create the last-mentioned rule of gender, moreover, citizens had taken the extreme step of coercive government action: they had emphatically politicized space. The next essay will follow the course of sex and gender directly into the political arena. But first, a few words about the broader implications of space for the generation of a collective female identity and politics are in order.

Appropriating Space for Women

Geographical theorists such as Henri Lefebvre and M. Gottdiener have argued convincingly that the appropriation of the social spaces of everyday life is an essential precondition for the political empowerment of subordinated social groups. As Lefebvre puts it, "Groups, classes and fragments of classes are only constituted and recognized as 'subjects' through generating (producing) a space." American historians have implicitly accepted this theory. Numerous scholars have rooted the development of working-class culture, black community, and feminist consciousness in shared spaces on the shop floor, in the ethnic neighborhood, within a female sphere. Women's historians have argued that the separate women's sphere that grew up around the household and the voluntary association during the nineteenth century nurtured, first, gender consciousness, then feminist politics.[58]

Yet the notion of women's sphere provides a particularly fragile and fractured spatial base, particularly when it is located in the domestic realm. The private home not only isolated women from one another but tied them intimately to members of the opposite sex. The emergence of a public space for women, as documented in this essay, was also fraught with contradictions and cleaved by the division between dangerous and endangered women. (Women's voluntary associations usually enrolled only the latter.) Women's public spaces in the nineteenth-century city were created by commercial and municipal decisions in which their sex rarely participated. Hence, they conformed to Lefebvre's notion of "abstract," rather than social, space and shared its limitations: "As long as everydayness exists in abstract space . . . as long as spaces (of work, leisure and residence) remain disjointed and re-joined only through political control, the prospect of 'changing life' will remain a slogan, at times abandoned, at times taken up again."[59] That plaintive phrase, "at times abandoned, at times taken up again" aptly describes the long, uneven, interrupted course of American feminism. The absence of a spatial center and anchor may help to explain the erratic and circular history of social movements for sexual equality.

Nonetheless, by virtue of their foothold in public space during the nineteenth century, women did appropriate some scattered turf on which to act politically and collectively. One example of how women politicized public space will illustrate this process. In the nineteenth century as in ours, women actively participated in the most heated political battles over public space, the struggles over racial segregation. When streetcar segregation was outlawed in New York in 1864, an unnamed precursor of Rosa Parks was at the center of the incident that provoked reform. The courts upheld the right of the widow of a black sergeant who met his death in the Union army to share vehicles of public transport with whites. In 1867, women were similarly instrumental in the demise of the New Orleanian method of segregating public transportation. The city had provided special cars, marked with a star, for African-Americans. While bands of black and white men battled over these spaces, women held the public turf with special tenacity. "Two colored women boarded a white street car and adamantly refused to leave, causing the white passengers to disembark in disgust." The African-American women held their ground, and the starred cars were abolished. This racial conflict over space was riddled with gender consciousness. The Radical Republican press took a special satisfaction in seeing white ladies forced to share the streetcars with men and women of color.[60]

Contests over public space did not, however, simply pit males against females, and women hardly presented a united front on the question of racial segregation. In New Orleans, white women joined the side of male segregationists. On September 13, 1874, the newspapers printed an "Appeal of the Women to the Men of New Orleans." The ladies assumed the role of the endangered to plead for a return to the regulation of race relations in public space: "our cheeks tingle with shame, that, in broad daylight, upon our most frequented thoroughfares, almost within your sight and hearing we are subjected to assault and insult!" These entreaties to make the streets safe for white womanhood were tendered from a feminine position that eschewed the ballot box or rostrum favored by "our Northern sisters" and asked only that men protect the "honor of your wives and daughters." A day later, five thousand armed men organized into White Leagues temporarily wrested power from the Radical Republicans. When women's place in public space thus became embroiled in New Orleans city politics, gender became Janus-faced, divided by racial difference.[61]

This particular dramatization of gender and race in the streets of New Orleans (to which I return later) demonstrates how difficult it is to sort the sexes into precisely bounded and separate spaces. Although sex denoted dualistic biological classifications around which symbolic differences were readily and routinely constructed, it did not ordain neatly segregated social spaces or automatic political alliances. The politics of the public streets divided women by race and class, and between the dangerous and the endangered. Gender was not a social category that automatically or immediately translated into a common identity or united politics for women.

Nonetheless, a variety of women made their way outside their homes and into public spaces between 1825 and 1880. In so doing they had found a place, however small, scattered, complicated, divided, and compromised, in which to begin to act collectively and politically. The stage of public space has been set for my next essays, which examine in more detail how women took their diverse interests and ambiguous identity into the sphere of politics.

3
Political Space

*Of Prostitutes and
Politicians*

During the summer of 1831, the leaders of New York City acted swiftly and effectively to curb public discussion of sexuality. A band of evangelical reformers calling themselves the Magdalen Society had published a report indicting Gotham as a breeding ground of sexual immorality. Their efforts to "expose public immorality, to elicit public sentiment, and to devise and carry into effect the means of preventing licentiousness" provoked angry public meetings, a grand jury investigation, and concerted opposition in the press. As the *Evening Post* put it, "The report should never have been printed, and being printed should be as speedily as possible suppressed." Opposition to the Magdalen Report was inspired not just by its lurid subject matter and its slandering of the city's reputation but by the flamboyant and unrestricted publicness of its methods, especially its flagrant disregard of the sensibilities of the female public. The *Post* went on: "These minute statistics of whoredom are pretty things truly, to have been read at a public meeting composed three-fourths of respectable females—pretty things, to be afterwards published and sent into private and virtuous families—pretty things for a husband to put before his wife, a father before his daughter."[1]

In the short term, the proponents of public reticence about sexuality would triumph: the subject of whoredom quickly disappeared from the press, and the Magdalen Society soon disbanded. Yet the question of sexuality had been placed on the public agenda, never again to be entirely erased. Once injected into the political sphere, sexuality would recurrently provoke vitriolic contests among an increasingly complex array of urban constituencies. Moreover, from the 1830s onward into our own time, women were open and increasingly vociferous participants in political debates about sexuality. The sexual politics of New York, San Francisco, and New Orleans all give credence to Barbara Hobson's assertion that women and feminists have been "the most constant and vocal actors in the struggles over prostitution policy."[2]

A survey of sexual politics in New York, San Francisco, and New Orleans also suggests some complications and qualifications of Hobson's argument, which is based on a careful and insightful study of the city of Boston. First, female parties to sexual debates in New York, New Orleans, and San Francisco were hemmed in and often bested by a larger and changing cast of political actors, especially male politicians of many persuasions and differing relationships to the polity. Second, women's role in political debate and public policy regarding prostitution takes on a different meaning when placed in the larger context of gender politics. Women's voice in these specialized debates about prostitution, however strong, also bespoke the limited range of action open to women in the urban public sphere. Of all the fundamental issues of gender justice and sexual equality that merited public discussion, it was sexuality, and most often the even narrower issue of prostitution, that most readily received public attention and provoked decisive governmental action. While many items on the political agenda, such as legislation relating to temperance, overlapped with women's interests, and although legislatures and courts were actively engaged in changing statutes related to women's property rights, sexuality was the issue that provoked the most direct discussions of gender in and around City Hall.

Because the issues relating to sexuality were especially likely to capture the attention of mayors, judges, city councils, and government bureaus, they provide a particularly revealing case study of the process whereby gender became public in the narrow political sense— that is, by provoking governmental action. Because the measure of political effectiveness within the framework of formal politics is the enactment of laws, I have traced the record of gender politics back from a sequence of municipal and state statutes. No equal rights statutes, no acts to enfranchise women, no legislative remedies for sex discrimination, no public provision of services expressly for women, were placed before municipal governments between 1825 and 1880. Rather, gender rarely appeared on the statute books; when it did, it was largely within those articles of the municipal code that defined punishable sexual acts. The major markers of gender politics between 1825 and 1880 consisted of, first, a spate of ordinances relating to sexual commerce and prostitution; second, the New York State law that made seduction a misdemeanor in 1848; and, third, the negative evidence of repeated failures in the 1860s and 1870s to

license and regulate prostitution. An examination of the public debates that surrounded these acts of government will flesh out one of
the most direct, formal, and explicit expressions of gender politics.

The Politicization of Sexuality: 1825–1850

Before the mid-nineteenth century, sexuality appeared on the public agenda largely in veiled and convoluted ways. A reading of the
ordinances of New York and New Orleans indicates that sexuality
became a public concern when it involved violence, threatened to
deplete public resources, or disturbed the public peace. The first
category of public concern about sexuality, its manifestation as personal violence, was registered in statutes that made rape a capital
crime. The second category of the public interest was represented in
laws regarding bastardy, an offense that spawned children who,
without the economic support of their fathers, were likely to become
dependent on public relief. The inclusion of prostitutes under the
vagrancy statues had the same rationale: like other public offenders
identified in that statute as lacking a home or a legitimate occupation,
streetwalkers threatened to become public charges.

It was the third classification of statutory sex offenses that generated the most action in the police courts of nineteenth-century cities.
Sexual immorality became the occasion of vigorous prosecution
largely when it disturbed the public peace. Controls on prostitution
in New York were buried in the city's disorderly conduct ordinance.
Women engaged in sexual commerce found themselves in exotic and
motley company, among "all persons pretending to tell fortunes . . .
jugglers, common showmen and mountebanks, who exhibit or per-
form for profit any puppet show, wire or rope act or other idle shows
. . . all persons who play in public streets or highways, with cards,
dice or any other instrument or device for gaming." Before midcentury, furthermore, sexual offenses clearly caused less public concern
than other species of disorderly conduct such as gambling and drunkenness. These omnibus statutes that were created to promote public
order also singled out the economic sponsors rather than the perpetrators of such nefarious activities for punishment: it was the "keepers
of bawdy houses," not those who committed sexual sin, who were
most liable to face prosecution under New York laws. In 1826, for
example, only 38 of 1,344 persons committed to the city prison were
labeled prostitutes.[3]

The statutes of the city of New Orleans were especially explicit
about drawing the border between sexual immorality and the criminal disruption of public order. The crime of prostitution was hidden

in the New Orleans ordinance that imposed a fine of $25 on "any woman or girl, notoriously abandoned to lewdness, who shall occasion scandal or disturb the tranquility of the neighborhood." The authors of such statutes seemed reluctant to outlaw prostitution; indeed, the very word, or any single noun denoting a female occupation, seemed unavailable as a stand-in for the cumbersome phrasing of the lewd woman statute. It would seem, furthermore, that women were even free to be "notoriously abandoned to lewdness," as long as they did not otherwise scandalize or disturb their neighbors. In the absence of an organized police force, and long before the appearance of vice squads, these ordinances were put into operation largely through specific complaints addressed to the mayor by the immediate neighbors of the accused. In order to justify a complaint about a bawdy house, the offended citizens argued before public officials that their sleep had been repeatedly disturbed, their businesses disrupted, or the funeral services of their loved ones blasphemed. In all three cities, such vague statutes were very rarely enforced early in the nineteenth century.[4]

The difficulty of obtaining redress of grievances against offensive sexual practices occasionally led citizens to make and enforce their own codes of sexual conduct. It had long been customary to apply the moral economy of the crowd to sexual offenses. Brothel riots, which commenced in the eighteenth century, continued well into the nineteenth, when the perpetrators, "gentlemen of property and standing" among them, still acted in community-sanctioned and controlled ways to enforce public order. Hundreds of citizens convened as a crowd and, with a calculated destruction of brothel property, ensured that houses whose disorderliness had become intolerable went out of business. Until at least the 1830s, these crowds rarely attacked sexual culprits personally, physically abusing neither lewd women nor their customers.[5]

The first attempts to target sexual vice in itself for public action came neither from city councils nor disgruntled neighbors, but emanated from the expanding spaces of civil society where public-spirited individuals combined to foster social and moral reform. The second decade of the century brought elite and pious New Yorkers into voluntary associations such as the Magdalen Society, which was founded in 1812 with the express intention of attacking sexual immorality. The handful of merchants who united for this purpose focused their reforming zeal on what they regarded as the most redeemable sex offenders, innocent women who had been recruited into prostitution. Their major accomplishment was to open an asylum for the rehabilitation of fallen women. They soon discovered, however, that their charges resisted reformation, even with the able and gentle efforts of the committee of ladies who managed the asylum. In 1818, six years after its founding, the first Magdalen Society disbanded.[6]

It took the perfectionist fervor that ensued from the Second Great Awakening to rekindle the fires of sexual reform. A young convert, John MacDowall, placed sexual morality at the center of the public sphere by writing the Magdalen Report, which so outraged public opinion in 1831. A missionary to New York's slums, MacDowall set his sights on saving women given over to sexual vice, enlisted the financial support of wealthy evangelicals like the Tappan brothers, and formed the New York Magdalen Society. MacDowall and his coterie both exhibited and exploited the spirited public discourse of the Jacksonian era. In his journal, which soon reached fourteen thousand subscribers, at public meetings, and with the famed report, MacDowall quickly accomplished the first goal of the Magdalen Society, to "create a public sentiment" on the issue of sexual sin. He also provoked a concerted and decidedly public response. On Saturday, August 21, "a large assemblage of citizens" came together at Tammany Hall for the purpose of taking into consideration the infamous report of the Magdalen Society. Arguing that it was "the duty of freemen of this city to have these matters investigated and not tamely submit to be thus publicly insulted," this ad hoc congress succeeded in convening the grand jury, who reported back with the assertion that the number of prostitutes in New York was lower than MacDowall's estimate by a factor of ten. Still, the Magdalen Society might, and did, congratulate itself for provoking a public discussion about sexual morality. Even the opposition conceded that, while his means were questionable, MacDowall's cause was in the public interest.[7]

Among those who took this new political issue most to heart were the evangelical women who had listened quietly and worked behind the scenes from the very inception of sexual reform. MacDowall's report had openly recruited "virtuous females of this city" for his crusade. It concluded with this salvo: "We behold you in short, employing all the peculiar influences of your sex—and in all your relations as wives, mothers, daughters, sisters, in promoting the interest and success of an Institution which, we wish you never to forget, is founded for the relief of the miserable of your own sex exclusively."[8] This explicit and public appeal to women did not go unanswered. Soon, evangelical women came center stage in the politics of sexuality, founding by the mid–1830s both a Female Benevolent Society with its own home for the rehabilitation of prostitutes and the

New York Female Moral Reform Society, the direct heir to John MacDowall's scepter of moral reform. The membership of the Female Moral Reform Society soon dwarfed the ranks of male sexual reformers. And then, when MacDowall's aggressive methods and questionable financial practices led to his expulsion from the presbytery, his organ of publicity was handed over to the Female Moral Reform Society and retitled the *Advocate of Female Moral Reform*.

The story of this reform association is a familiar one, its militant expression of the female interests at stake in sexual politics well documented by Carroll Smith-Rosenberg. The *Advocate* translated sex reform into a challenge to the double standard, an outlet for visceral antagonism to salacious males, an agency for helping women to secure employment, and, at least occasionally, a forum for women's rights advocates like Sarah Moore Grimké. Female moral reform also offered women an exhilarating opportunity to gather in public, an activity that the *Advocate* called "thrilling," and that, if we can believe the *Evening Post*, led women to outnumber men at public meetings called to discuss sexual immorality. The missionary activities of the society also provided women access to public space; teams of two to five men and women made excursions into the slums, where they conducted prayer meetings in brothels and taverns.[9]

The Female Moral Reform Society also charted a widening course through antebellum politics. As was typical of reformers and politicians in the 1830s, they set out to "use the press to enlist the public mind." Until late into the 1830s, the society was wedded to moral suasion as the best political method. By capturing the attention of the public, argued the *Advocate*, moral reformers would purify the hearts of individuals and avoid the unsavory world of "politics and politicians." At the same time, however, moral reformers were not averse to seeking either police power or state funds to support their cause. As early as 1831, MacDowall had proposed petitioning the legislature to undertake draconian measures to combat sexual immorality: "arrest every vagrant male or female and imprison them until reformed." By 1834, the Female Benevolent Society had gone to both City Hall and the State House to petition for financial support for their house of refuge. In 1838, the Female Moral Reform Society abruptly relinquished its aversion to "politics" and embarked on a campaign to convince the state legislature to outlaw seduction. After securing over four hundred thousand signatures on petitions in behalf of such legislation and after tenaciously lobbying public officials to support the bill they had drafted, Female Moral Reformers saw their sexual ideology become state law in 1848. The course of sexual politics seemed straightforward, from religious fervor to moral suasion to the halls of the government. The interests of the female sex were written into the final product of this first foray of women into the sphere of sexual politics: a statute that cast men as offenders and women as victims and that inflicted state sanctions on "any man who shall, under promises of marriage, seduce and have illicit connection with any unmarried female of previous chaste character."[10]

The political course of female sex reformers did not proceed without detours and contradictions. By the 1840s, the Female Moral Reform Society had veered off decisively in the direction of the private sphere, arguing that the surest remedy for immorality was to be found in the home, through the moral agency of mothers. From the first, moral reformers implicitly sorted out the sexes along a private/ public divide. The relatively small male wing of the movement, organized as the Seventh Commandment Society, assumed a more explicitly public role. Its magazine was called *The Journal of Public Morals,* and it was directed to "the public, the press, and the male part of the community." By midcentury, when the women reformers had renamed their association the Female Guardian Society, they effusively extolled domesticity: "of all the relations on earth none are more sacred than that of the mother." At the same time, the *Advocate* eschewed efforts to expand the formal public role of women. After Sarah Grimké's controversial appearance in the *Advocate* in 1837, its pages were closed to those women's rights advocates who took aim at all gender restrictions on political rights.

Concurrently, the wide-open public discourse embraced by sex reformers in the 1830s had been hemmed in by midcentury. The reformers increasingly directed their energies toward more staid and narrower institutional forms. Like the first Magdalen Society and the Female Benevolent Society, the Female Moral Reform Society invested much of its resources in an asylum for the rehabilitation of prostitutes. With this gesture, female moral reformers corralled their politics within the borders of a private institution that resembled a family dwelling. When their efforts at redemption were rebuffed by most prostitutes and proved incapable of reclaiming even a majority of the dwindling number of inmates, the female reformers drew in their net further, embracing only those women whose native-born, Protestant backgrounds and pious demeanors identified them as salvageable. In the end, the Female Guardian Society eschewed the whole enterprise of reclaiming prostitutes and took in only "reputable young women."[11]

Whatever their goals, whatever population they served, female reformers came to sort the public into unequal ranks and authoritarian relationships. The inmates of the Home for the Friendless, operated by the Female Guardian Society, were subjected to stringent controls, including regimented schedules. They had to rise at 5 A.M. and to bed down at 8:30 in the evening and were prohibited from leaving the asylum until that unspecified date when their reform was judged complete. When the female reformers enlisted the collaboration of the state in their projects, they also initiated coercive action against a subordinate population. In 1849, the Female Guardian Society, in league with other municipal benevolent societies, secured state power to take in children of "dissipated and vicious parents." The language of the statute bristled with authoritarian domesticity, ordaining that negligent parents "forfeit their natural claim to [their children] and thereby such children shall be removed from them and placed under better influences, till the claims of the parent shall be re-established by continued sobriety, industry and general good conduct."[12]

The greatest prize that female reformers won in the political arena, the seduction law of 1848, also lent the coercive power of the state to the cause of sexual reform. The effect of the law was to define one species of sexual behavior, seduction, as criminal and to mete out punishment to one class of moral offenders, male seducers, who were faced with up to five years in state prison. By the time the intentions of female reformers were written into law, however, the law's specifications considerably weakened the protection afforded to women. By stipulating that only a woman of "previous chaste character" was liable to seduction, and that the "testimony of the seduced female, unsupported by other evidence" was insufficient for conviction, this statute subjected women to intrusive moral scrutiny that was unlikely to end in their vindication. And once this punitive power had been established, the female reformer could not rely on the state, politicians, or police to enforce it. In most years, the statute led to one or two, if any, arrests in New York City. In the last analysis, the sexual politics of the 1830s and 1840s had provided women with considerable opportunity to express their concerns and even to set public policy. But their claim to that domain was tenuous, circumscribed by their own political inhibitions and constrained by the male citizens and office holders who controlled the political machinery.

The Prostitute and the Politicians: The 1850s

By the time that female reformers had pushed through the seduction law in 1848, the rules of political life had changed markedly. Both the political stewardship of civic elites that held sway early in the nineteenth century and the robust expressions of popular democ-

racy characteristic of the Jacksonian era had been eclipsed by the
two-party system and urban political machines. Contentious but dis-
ciplined Democrats and Whigs squared off against one another in the
local arena until the mid–1850s, when the two-party system splintered around nativist politics and brought Know-Nothings briefly into
power in New York and New Orleans. Whatever the partisan config-
urations of the 1840s and 1850s, public discourse was channeled into
electoral collisions of parties, each with its own platform, stable of
career politicians, multiple interests to accommodate, and enthusiastic support from the male population. This raucous world of the big-
city politicians set the framework for the reemergence of sexuality as
a political issue. In this volatile atmosphere, moral reform lost its
privileged status in the discourse about sexuality and was replaced
by the issue of prostitution as the symbol and the center of sexual
politics.

As early as 1830, the City Fathers of New York inaugurated
campaigns to clean the streets of whores and conducted a few highly
publicized, largely ineffective raids on brothels. In the mayoral elections of 1844, Whig mayor Harper rode into office on promises to rid
the streets of harlots. A decade later, Democratic mayor Fernando
Wood inaugurated his long and tumultuous career with similar promises. This electoral strategy did not lead to major or very energetic
assaults on the rising tide of sexual commerce in Gotham. Of Wood's
antivice efforts, the press reported that "unfortunate women were
arrested for walking the streets and swept off to the Island—while
the houses that lived on their prostitution went untouched. Yet even
these demonstrations absurd as they were, were loudly applauded by
a public too glad to have something done. Even these pretenses at
official vigilance seem to have been relaxed. Broadway swarms with
prostitutes and half the streets of the City are crowded with houses
of ill-fame."[13]

These skirmishes between politician and prostitute provoked only
minor changes in the criminal codes of the city. Sporadic proposals
to change the municipal ordinances to rein in the bustling sexual
commerce of the city seldom got very far. The word *prostitute* was
mysteriously written into the disorderly conduct code in 1833, only
to disappear just as quietly in the next edition of the city ordinances.
In 1844, the vagrancy law was amended to specify sexual offenses,
classifying "all common prostitutes who have no lawful employment
whereby to maintain themselves" as subject to prosecution. Before
1880, the New York criminal code relied largely on the vagrancy and
disorderly conduct statutes to control sexual commerce and did not
outlaw prostitution per se. Further, those city officials who proposed

more explicit restrictions on prostitution in the antebellum period were more concerned about urban economics than sexual behavior. The legislation proposed in 1844 would outlaw drunkenness, gambling, and begging as well as prostitution because the offenders lacked "a visible means of support"; it took the cost-cutting action of confining them to "hard labor" in the almshouse. As Timothy Gilfoyle has demonstrated, the political debates about prostitution were predicated on the emergence of a thriving sexual marketplace, which stuffed the pockets of landlords and the purveyors of salacious public entertainment at the expense of more reputable businessmen.[14]

What was merely a small ripple on the turgid surface of New York City politics became the center of violent civic strife in the fledgling city of San Francisco. The account of the outbreak of vigilantism in the city press in 1856 reads like a deadly, real-life melodrama in which dangerous and endangered women played key roles. The public spotlight focused first on an encounter between a lady, the wife of U.S. Marshal James Richardson, and an infamous whore called Belle Cora, nee Arabella Ryan. On a November evening in 1855, these two representatives of endangered and dangerous womanhood happened to share a box at a local theater. Mrs. Richardson demanded that Belle Cora be expelled from her place amid the respectable classes. Mr. Richardson and Belle's lover Charles Cora quarreled in a saloon two days later, leaving Richardson dead. If the judicial process had led to Cora's conviction for manslaughter, the plot might have ended here. But this was not to be, given the chaotic politics and slipshod justice of gold-rush San Francisco. When Cora was acquitted, after reportedly bribing the jury, an outraged citizenry took action: Charles Cora was the first to wear the vigilantes' noose in the spring of 1856.[15]

The staging of this Western melodrama was actually more calculated than this plot summary implies. In the six months between the encounter with Belle Cora and the hanging of her groom (their wedding had taken place in his jail cell), city officials were embroiled in a campaign to clean the city streets and theaters of prostitutes. The legal focal point of this campaign was a city statute enacted in March of 1854, "To Suppress Houses of Ill-Fame." In keeping with the vague language and haphazard administration of antebellum vice laws, this ordinance stipulated that brothels could be raided on the basis of a citizen complaint and that the inmates and owners were subject to a $50 fine and up to sixty days in jail.[16] Throughout the winter and spring of 1856, the *Bulletin* and the *Alta* badgered local officials under Democratic mayor James Broderick about the inadequacies of the law and the laxity of its enforcement. Immediately after the Cora incident, a special committee of the Board of Supervisors was convened to investigate prostitution. Their recommendations were enacted into law in January, in a statute that mandated harsher penalties against brothel keepers, prostitutes, and "frequentors" of houses of ill fame and appointed a special prosecutor to ferret out and convict these sexual offenders.

Through the spring of 1856, the prosecutor was busily at work drawing up indictments against prostitutes and brothel owners while the press cheered him on and urged citizens to identify sex offenders to city officials. Neither the police nor the judiciary, both under the control of Democrats and Irishmen, were especially cooperative. Convictions were few, and by April the press was bemoaning the fact that efforts to enforce the new statute had been practically suspended. The political rivalries that would erupt into lynch law in May had clearly become entwined with the issue of prostitution.[17]

From November to May, the city newspapers, and especially the *Bulletin*, edited by one James King, played relentlessly on the themes of municipal corruption and sexual immorality. As ballast for his complaints, King printed letters from irate citizens reporting on disorderly houses, disreputable theaters, and negligent public officials. One correspondent described the prostitutes of San Francisco as "beasts that with brazen faces, garments dipped in blood, have ever continued to squat with open doors and windows upon this great artery of the city, exposed to all the good and virtuous who are compelled to pass them." This particular letter to the editor was signed with the feminine nom de plume Ada.[18]

King had expressly invited women to churn up public opinion on the subject of prostitution. When they responded in letters that were usually signed with pseudonyms, he graciously ushered the ladies into the sphere of public discourse. "The above is from a lady," he told his readers, "who has sent it to us with the request that the matter should be made public which we do by publishing the communication as we receive it." There ensued a multivoiced female discourse about prostitution. In addition to Ada's narrative of the dangerous and the endangered, other female correspondents spoke out in a style reminiscent of the female moral reformers of the past; one pointed her finger toward the lecherous males who affronted her in the streets with "licentious stare and meaningless giggle." Yet others proffered a domestic etiology of public vice: "The axe should be laid at the root of the tree of evil in the homes of our family." Finally, one woman, writing under the pseudonym "Sister," introduced a women's rights note into the discussion, expressing some empathy for fallen angels and appealing for better employment opportunities for her sex.[19]

James King did not hesitate to inject his own opinion into this female discourse. In response to "Sister," he opined that woman's place was not in the labor force but at home, under the natural protection of her husband or father. King's efforts to make the streets safe for the female sex proved to be risky as well as gallant and militant. In May of 1856, the editor of the *Bulletin* was himself murdered and made a martyr to the cause of law, order, and sexual morality. A letter to the editor on May 16 displayed how prostitution had fanned the flames of municipal politics to the point of conflagration. A correspondent called C. summoned the vigilantes to arms with an appeal for the hanging not only of King's murderer, James Casey, but also of Charles Cora and his paramour. "Madam Cora and all her class *must*, so help us God *shall* leave *our city* to be hung on a gallows higher than that upon which Haman was suspended. The time for action has arrived. . . . let every Citizen do his duty."[20]

As the vigilantes went about their bloody business through the summer of 1856, hanging Casey and Cora and intimidating and exiling scores of others, the ladies of San Francisco were not silent. They joined in by regularly presenting their hand-wrought banners, taking up their stations at public rallies, and making a ceremonial visit to the headquarters of the Committee of Vigilance. The *Alta* took special note of one of the six hundred ladies in attendance at the last event. This enthusiastic visitor to vigilante headquarters was known to *Alta* readers as "Nellie," the author of four articles in praise of vigilantism. Nellie's epistles acknowledged, endorsed, and orchestrated women's role in the political conflict of 1856. "That we, as women, are vitally interested in the present crisis; that we have been the motive power to animate the brave hearts and manly arms who have sworn to drive corruption from among us, we know and feel." She adopted, at the same time, a peculiarly feminine political role, both to bring peace to the city and to battle municipal corruption from a station in the home. Nellie closed her last epistle with these words: "Keep the hearthstone pure, woman immaculate and the best blessings of liberty are secured." In earlier letters to the editor, Nellie had dismissed more direct political roles for women by referring to women's rights activists as pygmies who would be men, and she recommended, not votes, but good and frugal housekeeping as women's proper political tool. The female chorus in the vitriolic public debates of 1856 took the gender division of the public sphere as its dominant theme. In Nellie's words, "Be ours the task of purifying the social circle, the fireside, while we strengthen with sympathy and prayer those who resolve to cleanse the public ones."[21]

Like Nellie, James King, and most of King's female correspondents, the Committee of Vigilance placed a conservative construction on gender politics: they construed their recourse to lynch law as a manly assumption of their responsibility to protect their wives and children. Their call to arms justified their defiance of elected officials as a defense of their lives, fortunes, and domiciles. The vigilantes were probably closest to the mark when they construed their extraordinary political measures as a defense of property. Astute investigators of the political economy of San Francisco lynch law have identified its perpetrators as a band of merchants acting in defense of their material interests in a local economy that was staggering in the aftermath of the gold rush. Largely native-born Protestants with Whiggish sentiments, the members of the vigilance committee of 1856 mounted a partisan and ethnic coup, usurping the elected government of Irish Democrats.[22]

Despite their rhetoric, concern about either gender or sexuality was relatively low on the vigilantes' list of political priorities. Hence, women's participation in the victory did not reap any notable political spoils for their sex, and public policy about prostitution remained unchanged. Still, the political symbolism so essential to provoking any collective action as decisive and daring as that of the vigilantes placed heavy stock in images of the lady and the whore. These rhetorical devices opened up to ladies an opportunity to express some of their political concerns as they espoused the doctrine of female privacy. The prostitute, however, as symbolized by Belle Cora, who lived out a prosperous life in San Francisco, served largely as a convenient scapegoat for the interests of politicians.

When a vigilance committee was formed in New Orleans in 1858, sexual symbolism was more muted, women's role even more limited, and the issues of gender given even shorter shrift. Municipal reformers allied with the Know-Nothing party placed prostitution on the political agenda early in the 1850s as part of a platform that would both clean up the streets and line the pockets of enterprising businessmen. The New Orleans press occasionally resorted to rhetoric similar to James King's appeals to ladies and their protectors. On March 25, 1854, just before the municipal election, the *Picayune* alerted its readers to a "Disgraceful incident." As they reported it, "one of the most abandoned women of the town" accosted a "respectable lady," committing unimaginable "indelicacies," uttering unmentionable "vulgarities," and, adding injury to insult, "knocking her off the sidewalk into the gutter." The fact that this episode occurred in broad daylight and in the presence of the police gave the editor ammunition against the city government, whose reelection he contested: he asked pointedly, "Do the people of New Orleans not want Reform?"[23]

Some of the reformers, elected to office in 1854 under the Know-Nothing party, took the issue of prostitution and the interests of women seriously. For example, Peter Collins, a leader of the largely Irish Third Municipality, saw control of prostitution as a means of protecting the virtue and interests of his poor countrywomen, who were especially vulnerable to exploitation in the sexual marketplace. For whatever reason, the new city council did amend and strengthen the city's ancient statute against "lewd women." Although some features of the Lorette Act were later ruled unconstitutional, its basic tenets remained on the statute books of the Crescent City for the next thirty years and set the standard of prostitution control for decades to come. There were two central provisions of the 1857 law: that, in much of the city, prostitution would be confined to the upper stories of houses; and that the prostitutes who inhabited a few unrestricted neighborhoods like the waterfront and Creole neighborhoods would be taxed, licensed, and subjected to special restrictions—that is, prohibited from entering cabarets and sharing quarters with women of a different race. With this piece of legislation, New Orleans politicians had defined sexual crime more emphatically than ever before. In the process, however, the politics of sex (and gender) had been reduced to efforts to categorize, control, and punish one class of women, those who made their living by selling sexual services.[24]

It would be myopic, however, to conclude that the architects of this legal innovation were motivated purely or primarily by their concern about sexual immorality. As Richard Tansey has demonstrated, the issue of prostitution galvanized and veiled diverse economic interests. Much as in New York and San Francisco, it pitted respectable businessmen who saw prostitution as an impediment to economic growth and the productivity of the labor force against the landlords and café owners who profited from the trade in sexual favors. The suppression of prostitution served also as one salvo in the campaign of the American sector to wrest control of the city from the Creoles after the three municipalities were reunited in 1852. Just as elsewhere, the combat over prostitution was embedded in the ethnic and partisan rivalries surrounding nativism. Once elected, finally, the reformist politicians turned to other priorities, failing to enforce the new statute and in fact reducing the police force in the interest of municipal economy and lowered taxes.[25]

The war of political rhetoric in New Orleans, New York, and San

Francisco had nonetheless fundamentally reformulated sexual politics; it had shifted and narrowed the terms of public discussion from
the reform of individual morals and the punishment of seducers to
the control of prostitution. While women had contributed to this
process (as early as the 1830s, New York's Female Moral Reform
Society had turned a malicious eye upon the prostitutes and had
endorsed the most draconian measures of controlling sexual commerce), theirs was a small role, cunningly manipulated by big-city
politicians.

The Prostitute and the State: 1860–1880

For the next two decades, prostitution would remain the major
avenue whereby sexuality entered municipal politics. Because the
prostitute had been subjected to municipal scrutiny and control, the
women who plied the trade became the objects of routine governmental surveillance. From the 1860s to 1880, the state's scrutiny was
often capricious, swayed by changes in the political winds, the whim
of policemen, and variations in the zealotry of urban reformers. But
in all three cities it was the effort to control prostitution that brought
women into the closest relationship with government. This relationship between women and politics is revealed in the actions of the
city police, a few decisions by city councils, and aborted attempts,
largely by health officials, to license and regulate prostitution.

Municipal codes changed only subtly after the Civil War, leaving
sexual commerce to thrive in all three cities. As seen in Chapter 2,
the city councils merely tampered with the existing codes of ordinances in order to draw sharper lines between private and public
sexuality. The New Orleans and San Francisco statutes, which min-
utely detailed the spatial boundaries of criminal solicitation, date
from this period, while New York devised a similar law in 1882.
Public places of amusement also came under the jurisdiction of sexual policing after 1860, when dance halls, theaters, and saloons could
be denied a license for permitting sexual improprieties. By this time,
the authors of statutes, politicians, and the press resorted to the term
"public prostitution" to describe the most visible and obnoxious
manifestations of the "social evil"—the territory of the streetwalker,
ribald theatrical performances, and red light districts. With this linguistic device, public leaders conceded that they were powerless to
control the more private expressions of illicit sexuality, such as the
discreet visits of married women to uptown houses of assignation.
The "public prostitute," however, was now fair game for police
harassment.

Police records reveal an erratic system of patrolling prostitutes. Through most of the 1860s, the municipal reports of San Francisco recorded only a handful of arrests for sex crimes annually. The one or two women hauled into the police department as "common prostitutes" were slightly outnumbered by the perpetrators of rape, bastardy, and the crime of "wearing the attire of the opposite sex." All were dwarfed by the several hundreds arrested for the lurid act of using profane or vulgar language. (In 1867, when one prostitute was arrested, the police chief reported 726 cases of using dirty words.) In 1869, when the San Francisco police began to enforce the new ordinance prohibiting solicitation for prostitution in the public streets, the volume of arrests for sexual offenses rose geometrically. In the year ending in 1872, 180 women were arrested for soliciting for a house of ill fame, a figure that doubled ten years later. Although these arrest statistics represented only a tiny fraction of criminal prosecutions, a mere token within the thousands of infractions against public order, they do expose the extreme gender bias of sexual politics. In 1873, for example, arrests of prostitutes outnumbered those of "visitors" to houses of ill fame by a ratio of twenty to one.[26]

Because the city ordinances and state laws of New York incorporated prostitution under the broad statutes outlawing disorderly conduct or vagrancy, it is difficult to determine the extent to which prostitutes were subject to arrest. Statistics on arrests for keeping a disorderly house were recorded by the sex of the offender, however, and reveal that female brothel keepers accounted for forty to a shade more than fifty percent of such arrests during the 1860s. The meticulous reports of the Metropolitan Police Commissioners in the same decade inadvertently revealed the liability of arrest among women directly engaged in sexual commerce. Although prostitution itself was not a punishable offense, the term did appear prominently in a statistical breakdown of the occupations of those arrested. In fact, prostitutes were the third largest category in this rogues' gallery in the 1860s, trailing only laborers and the unemployed. The raw number of prostitutes arrested, around six thousand annually, would account, furthermore, for approximately two-thirds of all the women arrested under the disorderly conduct statute. This estimate was not very far from the total number of prostitutes in the entire city. William Sanger's careful and probably conservative accounting in 1858 estimated the number of public prostitutes at work in New York City at six thousand. Timothy Gilfoyle's meticulous calculation of slightly larger figures for the 1860s would suggest that the working girls of Gotham had at least a fifty/fifty chance of running afoul of the law. Although the district attorney rarely bothered to prosecute those arrested for prostitution, these working women were subject to routine police harassment.[27]

All in all, these spotty records prompt two observations about the relationship between the police and the prostitute. First, despite the fact that prostitution in itself was not explicitly a criminal offense, and contradicting the widespread complaints about the laxity of the police in controlling vice, the women who sold sexual services were subject to thorough public scrutiny and frequent subjugation to state police power. Arrests for prostitution were considerably higher than in the antebellum period in New York and San Francisco and rose significantly in New Orleans as well.[28] Second, the role of the state in monitoring sexual behavior was practically confined to arrests for public prostitution and solicitation, and hence singled out one lowly class of prostitutes, those who peddled their wares in the streets, for arrest.

The enforcement of sexual statutes was riddled through and through with class and ethnic bias. It was common knowledge that upper-class prostitutes, the inhabitants of uptown parlor houses, were protected from prosecution by either the discretion of their operation, their influential patrons, or their hefty payoffs to the police. The poor streetwalker, "the lowest class even in the underworld," was not so lucky, especially if she was not white. The class and ethnic stratification of sexual politics was bluntly exposed in San Francisco in the 1860s. At a time when the police records reported only a handful of routine arrests for prostitution annually, the lawmen launched a separate and more aggressive antivice campaign in Chinatown. The chief of police recorded that in the six-month period ending in June of 1866 he had dutifully enforced a short-lived local statute, number 666, prohibiting Chinese prostitution. He boasted that 137 had been arrested, 124 convicted, and that "over three hundred of these women left the City, and that there remain here less than two hundred at present."[29]

Even such assiduous prosecution of prostitutes, usually pursued against the most vulnerable targets such as San Francisco's Chinese, encountered political difficulties. San Francisco's Ordinance 666 was suspended when the city attorney ruled it unconstitutional on the grounds of its overt discrimination against one ethnic group. Faced with this obstacle, the chief of police adopted an evasive strategy. He transferred jurisdiction over Chinese-American prostitutes to a public institution whose antiseptic purpose and relative distance from democratic politics veiled its coercive and discriminatory intent. The control of Chinese prostitution, recast as a sanitary measure to inhibit the spread of venereal disease, was transferred to the Board of Health.

"A Well-Known San Francisco Chinese Prostitute, 1890s." Photo by Arnold Genthe. Courtesy of Judy Yung.

Under the cover of medical experts protecting the public health, the police chief was confident that "the wretched occupants of these tenements, which are so productive of crime and disease, may be driven to some locality where they may be herded by themselves and not offend public decency."[30]

After the Civil War, the issue of prostitution came under the purview of boards of health in New York and New Orleans as well. This partial transfer of public authority to the state health bureaucracy was but one instance of a more general displacement of the question of sexuality into a new institutional context, one that was distanced from the raucous public discourse and jockeying for influence that characterized partisan politics at the local level. In fact, those police forces that were most vigilant in the surveillance of prostitution were not the creations of local politicians. In New York, the policing of the city had been taken out of the hands of locally elected officials late in the 1850s and entrusted to metropolitan commissioners appointed by the governor. In the 1860s, the Metropolitan Police Commission was also granted state authority over public health. In New Orleans during Reconstruction, superintendence of local health and safety was transferred to an even more remote authority, the military district of Mississippi created by the federal government.

Sexual politics was deeply implicated in this reorganization of state power, which itself was part of a movement both to curtail local autonomy and to enhance the authority of state agencies. The long career of New York police chief George Walling was intimately intertwined with this restructuring of police power. Walling, the first chief of the New York Metropolitan Police, concurred with the opinion of the state legislature in 1857: "the great city was too corrupt to govern itself." The failure to curb the tide of sexual commerce was repeatedly offered as evidence of municipal bankruptcy. Walling's thirty years on the New York police force, where he watched in frustration as the social evil went unchecked, left him cynical about democracy itself. He even came to question the political wisdom of universal white male suffrage. When the democratically elected local politicians failed to suppress vice, state law and professional administration were the favored alternatives. As another reforming police official put it, "Prostitution is a crime against the state, it must therefore be regulated by law."[31]

Once transported to this new jurisdiction, sexual politics generated proposals for major changes in the legal code relating to prostitution. George Walling, along with the boards of health in New York, New Orleans, and San Francisco, proposed that prostitution be legalized and then subjected to stringent state regulation. The possibility of "reglementation" (regulation), through the licensing, taxing, and enforced medical examination of prostitutes, was raised as early as the 1840s and won support from such notable New Yorkers as Judge Charles Daly and Walt Whitman. The First Municipality of New Orleans considered enacting the French model of prostitution control in 1854. Reglementation received a major boost from Dr. William Sanger in 1859. Armed with massive evidence of the extent of both prostitution and venereal disease in New York City, Sanger concluded that while it was utopian to expect to eradicate the rampant social evil, its epidemic health consequences could be controlled by medical authorities. He hedged his proposal for state licensing of prostitution with concern for the economic plight of women driven to prostitution out of destitution and with caveats about the right of privacy. In the last analysis, however, Sanger endorsed the regulation of prostitution as a necessary exercise of the "patriarchal" responsibility of the state. He asked his reader rhetorically, Did he not "seriously believe that it would be a prudent step instead of trying to extirpate the evil to place prostitution under the surveillance of a medical bureau of the police?"[32]

Less than ten years later, in 1867, the newly created Metropolitan Board of Health responded positively to Sanger's daring proposal. A committee composed of three physicians from the board of health recommended a plan of reglementation, to include the registration, sanitary inspection, and forced hospitalization of prostitutes. The colorless, professional prose of the report became more forceful when it invoked the emergency powers of the state: "The question is not a private one, but of great political importance—for the health of the citizens and the wealth and power of the State. The laboring population are ruined in health and made dependent on the public charities." The doctors in the hire of the Metropolitan Board of Health took upon themselves the professional responsibility to make public policy: "Private individuals hesitate to volunteer their opinion, but a public body like the Board of Health can properly urge upon the Government of the State the necessity of enactments to give legal authority to measures which are demanded for the eradication of the venereal diseases." The committee volunteered as well to act as a sanitary police force, seeking state authority "to compel obedience in case of resistance." Although the issue was posed in terms of the larger public interest rather than the "moral status of certain females solely," it was clear that reglementation had honed down sexual politics to a matter of state control over the bodies of women. William Sanger had put it bluntly in 1859: "It cannot be imagined that forcing diseased women to submit to a specific routine of treatment in a special hospital involves any undue interference with her personal liberty. The right to commit a wrong, be it social, moral, or physical, never can exist."[33]

As we shall see later, American advocates of women's rights

would, like England's Josephine Butler, see the flaws in this logic and would question why the men who sinned along with prostitutes were immune from public surveillance and control. Nonetheless, the resistance of feminists was not given much, if any, attention in discussions of reglementation in the New York City newspapers. The press opposed the regulation of prostitution, but for other reasons. Although Horace Greeley was a personal friend of some women's rights advocates who opposed regulation, his *Tribune* couched his objections in more cautious terms. Greeley was unwilling to condone sexual immorality with a state license and preferred private methods of eradicating vice—for example, the wide distribution of tracts extolling the benefits of social purity. Although the *Times* pilloried the *Tribune*'s tactics as a laughable exercise of reforming zeal ("watching school girls in the public streets and urging upon them the 'moral' tracts"), its editor was no more willing than Greeley to endorse the radical proposal of the board of health. The *Times* identified the root cause of prostitution as a wage scale that would not permit young women to make a living in more savory occupations. The editor did not linger near this feminist argument very long, however, hastening to link the issue with his favored political cause. To abolish poverty, eliminate prostitution, and stamp out venereal disease, said the *Times*, one need only return to specie currency. But a few days later the *Herald* put the whole issue to rest with this obituary: "We wish to hear no more about it. Legislative committees are the proper persons to hear and read statements of facts which are not only of no importance to the public, but very disgusting and should not be paraded in the daily press."[34]

While state agencies like New York's Metropolitan Board of Health were able to place prostitution on the agenda of municipal politics, they did not succeed in either provoking a broad public debate on sexuality or enacting new laws. Bills to regulate prostitution were defeated in New York in 1867 and again in 1871 and 1875. Similar attempts were defeated in a dozen cities across the nation, including San Francisco. The physicians and reformers who sponsored such legislation were as doomed as Sisyphus. Their assiduous exertions were repeatedly stopped short of governmental implementation, stymied by resistance to the public discussion of sexuality, impeded by the priority given other political issues, and blocked by the cumbersome process of local politics. They were omens, however, of the politics of the future, which would place the public interest, the power of the state, and sexuality under the jurisdiction of experts and bureaucrats.

The Private Vice Patrols: The 1870s

Without state regulatory legislation to control it, public vice seemed to grow ever more audacious and ribald in the 1870s. Those who wished to stem the tide of immorality had to work within an inefficient administrative and legal structure. They were dependent on vague statutes that exacted small penalties, a graft-ridden police force, an unreliable judicial system, and ingenious prostitutes capable of evading the law. Frustrated at this impasse, tenacious bands of reformers took direct and militant action against the sexual vice they saw running rampant in city streets. Acting essentially as private citizens, bands of New Yorkers and San Franciscans took the matter of arresting brothel keepers, proprietors of unsavory dance halls, and prostitutes into their own hands.

Occasionally private citizens resorted to violence to achieve their sanitizing goals. San Franciscans, dissatisfied with the actions of police and health commissioners, periodically took direct action against Chinese brothels in the 1860s and 1870s, assaulting houses of ill fame and their occupants. The city press was not above using prostitution to inflame opposition to the Chinese. The *Chronicle* reporter who submitted an article in 1869 entitled "Horrors of a Great City, Chinatown by Day and Night" lingered around the brothels to provide his readers with especially off-color images of "Mongolian females." "In company with the police officer, who kindly offers to protect our feeble frame from the assaults of these Mongolian sirens, we again pass through the alley. At the corner stand a few of the miserable things who hope to seduce some opium-crazed Chinese man or drunken white into their dens. At a word from the police officer they run into their hovels, for it is against the law for these women to appear outside their door, or in any manner endeavor to attract custom."[35]

The ordinances that intimidated the working women of Chinatown were not enough to satisfy those who wished to prohibit Asians from even residing in the United States. Prostitution was also a leitmotif in the movement to restrict Chinese immigration in the 1870s, led by the Workingmen's Party of San Francisco. The visibility of brothels and the prominence of bachelors and prostitutes in the Asian quarters of the city were translated into slogans like "no virtuous women in Chinatown" and carried into rallies that ended in anti-Chinese riots. Other, more reputable citizens, including the Reverend Gibson of the Methodist Church, put their energies into a more benign private method of policing prostitution. The chief of police thanked the Reverend Gibson for assisting him in the round-up of

Chinese prostitutes in 1865; again, in 1874, Gibson was to be found instigating the arrest and detention of thirteen Chinese women suspected of being imported by brothel keepers.[36]

It was in the city of New York, however, that the private policing of sexuality became most forceful and well organized. The most notorious practitioner of this species of sexual politics was Anthony Comstock, who lent his name to the national statute prohibiting the transmission of obscene materials through the mails and who, as special agent of the post office, acted as the United States censor, without portfolio. Comstock's career began in New York City with the founding of the Society for the Suppression of Vice in 1872. Comstock and a small band of elite New Yorkers who joined and financed the SSV were outraged at the failure of established procedures to prevent the corruption of the nation's youth by an avalanche of salacious books and "articles of immoral and indecent use." The jaded sex reformers of the 1870s had lost confidence in the police, the law, the government, and public opinion. The annual reports of the SSV bemoaned "the absence of a healthy public sentiment to sustain the law" and ranted about the "interference of citizens" in their operations. The SSV, like a number of other reform groups that Timothy Gilfoyle has called preventive societies, stepped into this moral and political vacuum and constituted themselves as a private police force.[37]

Although the preventive societies welcomed the sobriquet "vigilantes" and even invoked the name of San Francisco's Committee of Vigilance, they took pains to win the imprimatur of the state. The charter of incorporation secured by the SSV in 1872 gave legal sanction to their enterprise, described as "the enforcement of the laws for the suppression of the trade and circulation of obscene literature, advertisements and articles of indecent and immoral use as it or may be forbidden by the laws of the state or of the United States." The act of incorporation also made the society an arm of the local police, invested with the power of arrest. Section Five stipulated that "the police force of the city of New York, as well as of other places shall as occasion may require, aid this corporation, its members or agents." Section 6 permitted the society to confiscate property and pocket half the fines procured through their actions. The society's publications described their police functions in more colorful language, as "voluntary detectives and complainants" and operators of a "system of espionage."[38]

Those trapped in Comstock's net were primarily the producers and distributors of obscene materials—that is, male entrepreneurs, and they were usually foreign-born. In 1875, when the SSV made

193 arrests, they happily reported that only 50 were "our country-men." Yet, by the 1870s, a variety of other preventive societies had adopted Comstock's methods and applied them regularly to female offenders. Groups like the Society for the Prevention of Cruelty to Children made forays into the homes of the poor and led mothers off to jail, charged with intoxication, child abuse, and exposing their offspring to sexual danger. The reports issued by the Five Points House of Industry in the 1870s read like a cross between a social worker's casebook and a police blotter. "At a late Hour" on March 9, 1878, agents of the House of Industry entered the home of Sara Wilson, two of whose children were beggars and the third "an older girl who had been in the habit of peddling flowers on the streets, and shared the fate of the majority of these girls and was arrested a few months previous for disorderly and indecent conduct." The whole family was carted off to court, where the father was sentenced to three months, and the mother to six, in the penitentiary, and the children were "disposed of" at public charities or with relatives.[39]

During the 1870s, the agents of the Five Points House of Industry often conducted their moral espionage not in tenements but in the dance halls. Their investigations of places of amusement were sanc-tioned by a municipal ordinance that required that certain proprieties be maintained on the premises in order to secure a license from the city. By authority of their state charter and in order to enforce the public amusements ordinance, which banned the employment of children, agents of the House of Industry raided the Bowery Varieties in 1878. They found within a ten-year-old girl named "Little Ida," whose singing and dancing, "however harmless in themselves, threw her in contact with the most depraved elements, as she was permitted to remain in the 'wine room' where women of the town were in the habit of congregating." Ida was removed from the theater posthaste despite the protests of her mother, an actress. In the same year, a girl of seventeen was removed from the Tivoli Theatre, where the inhab-itants of the wine room had reputedly attempted to "induce her to commit immoral acts." In this case, the young woman, an orphan, was said to welcome her rescuers, and went happily into the care of the ladies of the Home for the Friendless.[40]

Whether such policing of sexual commerce offered women a wel-come escape from sexual exploitation or constituted a brutal "dispo-sition" that tore children from their parents, the women who worked in places of popular entertainment were ensnared in a tangled net of sexual politics. The rough political sea that such women had to navi-gate is revealed by a few police records that have survived in New

York City, namely the extensive paperwork generated by investigations of places of amusement specified by Chapter 863 of the 1872 ordinance. Occasionally the theaters investigated were owned by women, like Barbara Weisner of the Variety Theater, 106 Bowery. Her place of business was singled out neither by complaining neighbors nor by the policeman on his beat but by the Society for the Prevention of Crime, which asked that "no license shall be granted to said place as we believe it to be an immoral place and a resort of improper persons." First, Mrs. Weisner's ownership of the theater was disputed, prompting her to testify that she had owned the mortgage for 106 Bowery for some time and had recently foreclosed and taken up occupancy. She was well connected enough, furthermore, to secure letters testifying to her sound character from both her attorney and eight of the neighboring businessmen. The neighborhood police captain who visited the Variety Theatre concurred in this positive opinion of both Mrs. Weisner and her place of business. A contradictory judgment was lodged by an Inspector Murray, who summarily dismissed the Variety Theatre because it "has recently been frequented by a class of people of questionable character." The latter opinion was decisive to George Walling, chief of police, and Mrs. Weisner was denied the license. Even a female property owner with recourse to a lawyer and the support of the police and her neighbors could not escape the long arm of the law, especially when it was extended by a zealous private police force.[41]

Women poorer and less well connected than Mrs. Weisner were in an even more difficult position. Since the presence of prostitutes was a prima facie cause for denying an amusement license, those women who frequented dance halls were the target of especially intense policing by both private and public agents. Their vulnerable position was graphically recorded in the report of Inspector William Waite who, on April 1, 1879, entered Number 23 Bowery and sat down at a table where there were "about twelve girls and women with a number of men engaged in drinking and conversation." Waite was soon "approached by a woman and asked what he would have to drink and if she could drink with him." After accepting an invitation to go with her to a upstairs room where privacy and a bottle of wine could be procured for three dollars, the inspector inquired what other services might be offered for so high a price. Her answer: "They would have a glad time that she would give him a nice diddle, pulled up her dress, showed her leg above the knee and made use of every persuasion and said she would get one dollar of the money and the other two would go to the proprietor." At this point, the inspector had accumulated sufficient evidence to rule that "the females present were all of a low character and easy virtue and the license should therefore be denied."[42]

Such ignominious episodes as this represent one of the closest and most treacherous encounters between nineteenth-century women and their government. Those women who frequented concert saloons for pleasure or profit were subject to police surveillance and liable to lose their livelihood or end up in police court. The politics surrounding sexuality had lodged women in a powerful vise by 1880. First, they were placed in the grip of a few municipal statutes that subjected prostitutes and the habitats they frequented to close police surveillance. Then, the vise was tightened by zealous bands of voluntary law enforcement officers who roamed through the tenements and the red light districts ferreting out sexual immorality. While the righteousness of these moral policemen might be unswerving, the cop on the beat could often be counted on to be more indulgent of lower-class mores or deterred by bribery. By 1880, prostitutes were paying hefty initiation fees and monthly tithes for police protection.

In the end, most common prostitutes, streetwalkers, and dance-hall girls were hard-pressed by the vise of sexual politics. Paying off the police, eluding the vice inspectors, sharing earnings with landlords and dance-hall proprietors, facing the complaints of neighbors, and cajoling and serving their johns—such was the realpolitik of the prostitute. The sexual had become political by 1880, but hardly in a way that contemporary feminists would applaud.

Women as Sexual Politicians: 1860–1880

The *modus vivendi* of sexual politics proved to be less hospitable to women in the latter half of the nineteenth century than a generation earlier. After 1850, women were rarely found among the key players when sex appeared on the municipal agenda. The membership of the city councils, the Know-Nothing party, the boards of health, and the preventive societies was entirely male. Urban politics turned into narrow channels to which women had little access. The major female roles in this civic drama were played by prostitutes—objects, not subjects, of sexual politics. Those women who on a few occasions did became active agents in the domain of sexual politics, moreover, were often found on the margins of the fray or in a defensive position.

Female sexual politicians generally eschewed the aggressive police practices of the preventive societies. The Women's Christian Temperance Union, for example, forged an alliance with Anthony

Comstock on behalf of the cause of social purity but preferred to use the older, more benign methods of moral education. Some women could still be found among the moralistic sex reformers, operating homes for the reform of prostitutes and missions for fallen women. These benevolent institutions, however—exemplified by the Midnight Mission, sponsored by an Episcopalian parish in New York in the 1860s—were rather modest affairs serving a small clientele. In the Midnight Mission, women found a congenial, if archaic, way of expressing their sexual politics. The male leaders of the mission distributed invitations to attend prayer meetings, which commenced at 11 P.M. near a red light district. When, to their surprise and gratitude, a few streetwalkers accepted these invitations, the Midnight Missionaries delivered their guests into the hands of the ladies' committee, who "lovingly welcomed" the fallen angels, trained them in virtue, and secured them more morally salubrious jobs, usually as domestic servants. The ladies no doubt found some urban excitement in their mission, having "left home in inclement weather at late hours of the night to mingle with and minister to the poor lost ones of their sex." The ladies' committee also raised funds for the cause, amounting to a few hundred dollars a year—not including the pies, cranberries, and calico dresses they contributed to the annual Thanksgiving festival. The Midnight Mission was a moral and political midget among the aggressive and coercive sex reformers of the 1870s, however, measuring its annual successes in the reform in a handful of prostitutes, most of whom shared their own Episcopalian background.[43]

The women of San Francisco also entered the realm of sexual politics through religious channels. In the 1870s, both the Presbyterian church and the YWCA opened homes for destitute women, including those whose careers might have been sullied by prostitution. The Presbyterian Mission Home, founded in 1874 and directed by female officers, had "for its especial field of labor the evangelization of heathen women of the pacific coast." By 1890, the Presbyterian Mission Home also advertised the following service: "Chinese Women in cases of persecution afforded shelter in the Home." In the 1870s, under the direction of the superintendent of the home, Margaret Culbertson, these female urban missionaries had quietly begun to secure the release of women from the brothels of Chinatown. In the process, the pious ladies of San Francisco entered onto the most volatile terrain of San Francisco politics after the Civil War—the bitter, often violent conflict over Chinese immigration. They encountered angry opposition from male politicians. By daring to provide services to Chinese women, they incurred the wrath of workingmen, who rioted outside the Presbyterian Mission Home. Neither did these female reformers win the support of the men of their own class; the bulk of the Protestant clergy opposed their involvement in the unseemly world of Chinese prostitution. The women of the Presbyterian Mission Home, although they shared some of the same racist assumptions as the most virulent opponents of the immigrants from the Far East, never endorsed their legislative remedy, acts to exclude the Chinese from the United States.[44] Rather, these female interlopers in the public debate about prostitution developed their own brand of sexual politics.

The female missionaries of the Presbyterian church were propelled into this municipal conflict by distinctly female concerns. Like female sexual reformers before them, these women perceived the prostitute as a particularly vivid symbol of female powerlessness. They dwelt on images of an Oriental sexual despotism, manifested in bound feet, dominated wives, and, above all, young women sold to the brothel keepers of San Francisco—into "a Slavery worse than death." The lines of sexual politics were drawn in familiar strokes, setting off female victims from male oppressors—the Chinese Tongs, greedy entrepreneurs of sexual commerce, the lascivious clients, the indifferent city politicians. On the strength of such portraits of besieged womanhood, the ladies of the Mission Home had recruited some twelve hundred local volunteers to their cause.[45]

San Francisco's female reformers of the 1870s also adopted their own characteristic methods of combating this rampant sexual oppression. They eschewed the legislative remedy of Chinese Exclusion, the favored techniques of control enacted by police commissioners and public health officials, and the militant private policing of the preventive societies. As Peggy Pascoe has observed, the feminine method of moral reform was summed up in the name of the institution they built, the "Rescue Home." First, their efforts to retrieve women from the clutches of vice were acts of rescue rather than arrest. They identified those in need of protection not by search and seizure but by the quiet intelligence of "house-to-house visits." Second, once they had secured the release of Chinese women from the brothels, the female missionaries provided them not with a prison or a hospital but a "home." That home was constructed according to the Victorian blueprints of domesticity: it was a place to socialize young women into habits of cleanliness, industry, and piety; it was carefully sequestered from the world outside, into which the "inmates" could not venture without an escort; and it was governed by loving, maternal control rather than brute coercion.[46]

In general, the ideology and methods of the ladies of the Presbyterian Mission Home of San Francisco steered a straightforward, separate course of women's politics. They circumvented the official center of the male political arena, built separate institutions on a domestic model, and even eschewed the more combative and direct sexual politics that had been used by New York's Female Moral Reformers decades earlier. Rather than asking the legislature to enact a law against male seducers, they rescued women and trained them in domesticity.

Nevertheless, although their methods were privatized, San Francisco's sexual missionaries did embrace some political techniques characteristic of the late nineteenth century. Acting without an official mandate from the public, they armed themselves with state power: they colluded with police to extradite women from brothels, harbored women arrested for illegal entry into the United States, held under house arrest prostitutes rounded up in police raids, and took in women and children delivered to them by preventive societies. In the 1890s, moreover, under the legendary leadership of Donaldina Cameron, the women of the Presbyterian Mission Home mimicked the aggressive methods of sexual policing pioneered by Anthony Comstock. Cameron was known to go in disguise to investigate conditions in brothels and to personally lead policemen wielding axes and sledgehammers to extricate the less fortunate of her sex from "Chinese Slavery." Cameron was the commander of another private police force, acting without publicly sanctioned authority and upon a vulnerable ethnic minority. The residents of Chinatown, denied citizenship regardless of sex, were ill equipped to defend themselves even in that parapolitical arena which was the chosen turf of female sexual missionaries.

The peculiar course that these female sexual politicians took toward public influence, their brand of privatized politics, proceeded at a safe distance from the male political arena. The ladies of the Presbyterian Mission Home never spoke up on the issue of female suffrage, even at a time when women's rights conventions met regularly in San Francisco. However, the advocates of women's rights, dubbed "strong-minded women" by the local press, steered another political course, which led them directly into the public conflict about sexuality. These circles of women stood up defiantly, in the robes of feminists, to resist the regulation of prostitution. Attempts to write the double standard into law were an outrage to women's rights advocates, including the California Woman's Suffrage Association, which publicly opposed the policy in San Francisco in 1871.

Susan B. Anthony led the fight against regulation nationally. In a public address delivered in Chicago in 1875, Anthony provided a tough-minded feminist response to the regulation movement. She led off her oration with a conventional portrait of sexual politics. Citing the alarming number of prostitutes in such places as New York, San Francisco, and New Orleans, Anthony evoked the image of "a holocaust of the womanhood of this nation sacrificed to the insatiate Moloch of lust." She cast licentious males opposite "wretched women . . . discouraged, seduced, deserted unfortunates." Yet she did not attribute this pattern of male lust and female victimization to universal causes innate in the two sexes. The "tap-root" of the social evil, according to Anthony, was "woman's dependence . . . woman's subjection." Therefore, she maintained that sex reform would not be achieved through the easy fix of regulating prostitution but only as part of a thoroughgoing feminist transformation: women must be accorded equal economic resources, equal education, equality in marriage, full citizenship—in sum, "all possible rights and powers to control the conditions and circumstances of their own and their children's lives." Other women's rights stalwarts such as Elizabeth Blackwell also translated prostitution regulation into a simple issue of gender justice: "All legislation applied to one sex only, in relation to an evil in which both sexes are concerned is radically unjust; and unjust legislation is the profoundest immorality—the greatest crime that a government can commit against its people."[47]

The tactics of the suffragists were at one with their feminist ideology. Political injustice demanded direct political action. Accordingly, women's rights activists in both New York and San Francisco went directly to the legislature to redress their grievances. The California Woman's Suffrage Association sent a delegation to the city clerk's office, where they deposited a critique of the reglementation bill, which was read before the San Francisco Board of Supervisors and printed in the local press. A Mrs. Churchill produced a broadside that satirized the legislative debate. She countered the reglementation bill, written by a Doctor Holland, by placing her own mocking piece of legislation before the "wise men of the City of Cloudy Water." In this simple but effective burlesque, Churchill inserted references to the male visitors to brothels wherever the term "prostitute" appeared in the official social evil bill. Male readers were enticed into imagining themselves subjected to such indignities as surveillance in the public streets, medical examinations by male and *female* doctors, and consignment to a public hospital for enforced treatment for venereal disease.[48]

The California Woman's Suffrage Association responded to the proposed legislation more soberly and directly. Their communication to the Board of Supervisors summoned up a wide range of arguments against reglementation, from the "high moral grounds" of refusing to condone evil, to the "inexpediency" of enforcing such draconian procedures, to a xenophobic allusion to the Chinese. Although the members of the California suffrage club depicted themselves as "matrons of the state" and pled for "our dear sons and daughters," they made the argument based on sexual equity patently clear. "There seem to us, also, to be points of great injustice involved in the bill. As for instance the penalties are ALL IMPOSED ON THE VICTIMS." The California Woman's Suffrage Association was one of the most vocal and best organized opponents of the Holland Bill, which, like similar proposals in New York, went down to a crushing defeat.[49]

When the New York State Assembly had considered prostitution regulation a few years earlier, the stalwarts of nineteenth-century feminism, Susan B. Anthony, Elizabeth Cady Stanton, and Lucretia Mott, all brought their objections before this body of male politicians. Anthony rose to the challenge of legislative action in an unobtrusive but nonetheless effective way, by privately making her objections known to a prominent legislator. According to her biographer, Anthony "immediately protested to Judge Folger who told her that such a bill should not be publicly discussed by women. She assured him that if such a bill were presented she would see that it was discussed from one end of the state to the other. Knowing her 'word was as good as her bond' the bill was not presented."[50]

This vignette from the sexual politics of the 1870s suggests that even the feminist sexual politicians were turning in a somewhat more privatized direction. Anthony used a mere warning of public agitation as a means of pressuring public policy makers. She and her colleagues rarely mounted public podiums or convened public meetings during the anti-reglementation campaign of the 1870s. Their chief organizational base was in fact a small group of citizens of both sexes called the American Committee against the Legalization of Vice, a short-lived organization whose leaders included the veteran of abolitionism and women's rights Abby Hopper Gibbons. By the 1870s, Gibbons had beaten a well-worn trail from her home in New York City to Albany, where she enlisted state support for her favorite charities and reforms. It was from her experience in what she called "hobnobbing with the politicians" that Gibbons acted expeditiously to prevent the licensing of prostitution. She preferred lobbying legislators to mounting campaigns to sway public opinion.[51] In this she was not unlike Susan B. Anthony and the California Woman's Suffrage Association. By the late nineteenth century, those feminists who ventured into sexual politics had resorted to narrower channels of influencing governmental policy, such as lobbying the legislature. In this process, furthermore, they conducted a holding action, battling primarily to defend their sex against a draconian measure to control prostitution. Although they conducted themselves like adept and seasoned politicians and used the opportunity to project a powerful feminist ideology, theirs was largely a defensive action on the single issue of prostitution, a discrete and narrow definition of gender politics.

Because women did not convert the nineteenth-century political sphere into a feminist forum about sexuality does not mean that they were merely pawns in a male-dominated sexual politics. While clearly second-class citizens, women did batter away at the urban political system, winning concessions here and there, imprinting their ideas on public debates, and adding their perspective to the array of conflicting interests that influenced policy decisions. Even the prostitutes, the most beleaguered objects of the urban political economy, displayed some political savvy. Some prostitutes, as Rachel Bernstein has demonstrated, found a space for maneuverability and even a modicum of power in the role of prostitute by deploying their illicit contacts in City Hall and the police station during disputes with their neighbors or their clients. The more powerful Manhattan madams were even known to appear in court with Tammany Hall leaders and former mayors acting as their attorneys. One San Francisco madam was so well connected with the city's leaders that her house of illustriously ill fame was dubbed the Municipal Club. Dangerous women as well as feminists had a taste of the new political techniques of the late nineteenth century: a delegation of New York City dance hall girls journeyed to Albany to lobby against the public amusements bill in the 1860s.[52]

Women who occupied the least powerful positions in the scheme of sexual politics often proved to be vigilant protectors of their own legal rights. Some met the accusations of being "disorderly persons" with suits against their accusers. Others like the San Francisco prostitute told to vacate a "respectable locality" on Kearny Street in 1857 claimed the privileges and immunities of a citizen, brazenly telling the city authorities to "go to ———" and then demanding a jury trial. One prostitute of Chinese origin adapted quickly to American politics; the affluent San Francisco madam Ah Toy sued in the American courts to protect her rights as a taxpayer. Other women scoffed at the values and resisted the authority of the private policers of morality. A woman whose two children were employed as singers at a drinking saloon on Christie Street in New York refused an offer of a more respectable job for her offspring with this retort: "They could coin more money in a single night than they earn in a whole week singing in the church." She and her daughters took flight every time the policemen and do-gooders approached, and when they were finally captured she promptly secured a writ of habeas corpus. Almost of necessity, the thousands of city women who trod close to the borders of sexual deviance had to become wise to the ways of politics. The prostitutes of New Orleans, for example, were neither ignorant of nor indifferent to local politics. When the Lorette Act was ruled unconstitutional in 1857, they reputedly celebrated with a bawdy parade down Canal Street.[53]

Women who subscribed to quite another code of sexual morality, both purity reformers and feminists, had their own political victories to celebrate. They contested mightily and often cunningly in the political arena and had such prizes as the New York seduction law of 1848 and the defeat of prostitution reglementation to show for it. Women were critical if not decisive parties to the complex negotiations that made sexual policy in the cities of New York, San Francisco, and, to a lesser extent, New Orleans, where the sexual propriety of Victorian Protestants was constrained by Gallic and Catholic mores. The stand-off that characterized sexual politics as of 1880, the failure either to fully outlaw or to officially condone sexual commerce, owes much to the political exertions of women. Theirs was not an unimpressive record, given the handicap of their sex in a political system that placed such great stock in votes and elections.

Summary and Conclusion

Despite the constant factor of women's disenfranchisement, the structure of urban women's politics was not uniform throughout the nineteenth century. Women's place in sexual politics tilted and shifted with the changing political system and in synchrony with their own heroic and ingenious efforts. Women were key parties to the induction of sexuality into the political arena in the 1830s, riding the high tide of democratic and participatory politics. In this political atmosphere, women exploited the opportunity to express their own construction of sexual propriety and even to write it crudely into public law. The seduction statute enacted in New York defined the exploitation of women by men as that species of sexual behavior which especially required governmental intervention and punishment. By midcentury, when competition between political parties for local offices and influence had been routinized, the issue of sexuality became posed largely as a measure of the efficiency and honesty of local government as displayed by streets clean of crime and vice. In this context, the prostitutes who swarmed the streets and the places of public amusement became the symbol of urban political corruption

"The Women's Night Court, before Her Makers and Her Judge, 1913." Whitney
Museum. From John Sloan, *Spectator of Life*, Delaware Art Museum, 1988.

and the target of reform. Once prostitutes became the centerpiece of
sexual politics, their control and confinement became the focus of
legislative debate. Ordinances that permitted the surveillance of
brothels, the confinement of sexual commerce to certain areas, and
the rounding up and jailing of prostitutes were the chief political
results. Coercion and control of prostitutes was a prime example of
an increasingly hierarchical division of the political landscape. In
New York City and San Francisco, private police forces led by elite
citizens and invested with state power meted out punishment against
the most vulnerable urban populations, the foreign-born, racial minorities, the women who sold sexual services on the streets. In the
1870s, the elite and privatized policemen, along with the public health
officials who wished to regulate prostitution, and even feminist lobbyists, experimented with those expert, regulatory, and bureaucra-
tized political methods that would have wider currency in the Progressive era. Sexual politics, in short, both reflected and anticipated
major changes in the structure and process of American politics.

All this is also to suggest that in the latter half of the nineteenth
century, sexuality and gender were caught up in an increasingly
narrow political vortex. Statutes that targeted a specific population—
in this case, women suspected of prostitution—as subject to state

interference applied a highly constricted definition to the wide range of human behavior that might be termed sexual and judged worthy of public discussion and action. This narrow definition of the sexual also tended to set the boundaries of gender politics. Ordinances regarding lewd women or prostitutes constituted a primary example of municipal policies that dealt specifically with the social relationships and differences between the sexes. In short, the politicians of the nineteenth-century city were swiftest to acknowledge women as bodies in a sexual marketplace. They risked reducing gender to sexuality. The female sexual politicians of the nineteenth century had waded into the quagmire that feminists often encounter in the political arena even to this day. Like feminists who have battled against pornography from the 1970s to the present, their necessary efforts to protect the most oppressed of their sex placed them in a defensive political position and situated them at a place in the gender system where women are easily defined in narrow biological terms and portrayed as victims.[54] The relationship between gender and public life was not, however, even in the nineteenth century, confined to the points where women intersected with government. The people as a whole, then as now, were perhaps more hospitable to females than were the politicians, and more latitudinarian in their interpretation of gender issues. This more commodious public sphere, not restricted by the priorities of politicians nor confined to the institution of government, will set the wider political boundaries of the next essay.

4
The Public Sphere
*Of Handkerchiefs, Brickbats,
and Women's Rights*

I n the spring of 1862, Secretary of State William Seward received
an official rebuke from the Parliament of Great Britain. The action
that provoked this international squabble was General Butler's
infamous General Order Number 28, which held that those women
of New Orleans who insulted Union soldiers in the city streets were
liable to prosecution as common harlots. All the themes of the previous essays come together in this single episode, which placed women
at the center of sectional conflict and of national and international
politics. General Butler expected women "calling themselves ladies"
to live up to the prescriptions of gender culture—to act decorously in
public. When he found that the females of New Orleans used their
position in the public streets in contrary and politically motivated
ways, he rudely exiled them to the lowest realm of the dangerous—
prostitution. The defiant woman was to be regarded as "a woman of
the town plying her avocation." The woman who snubbed and even
spat upon Yankee soldiers in the streets of New Orleans experienced
firsthand the common fate of the dangerous of her sex before urban
political authority as described in the last chapter: by order of the
government, she was reduced to a sexual being and subjected to
public controls.

In the process, however, women were implicated in a political
struggle of larger proportions and greater import than merely local
efforts to control public sexuality. They were the center of public
controversy, provoked a high-level policy decision, and participated
in the fratricidal politics of the Civil War. Women on the streets of
New Orleans in 1862 took up stations in nineteenth-century America's unseemly manifestation of what Jürgen Habermas called the
"public sphere," that place between the state and the private citizen

where "the public organizes itself as the bearer of public opinion." This essay will take the question of gender to a variety of places where this wide-ranging public discourse transpired. Throughout the nineteenth century, much of the most febrile public debate and decisive public action took place outside the voting booths and the halls of government. In the municipalities of New York, New Orleans, and San Francisco, the power to speak about and act on the fate of the whole people did not rest solely in the hands of the executive, judicial, and legislative branches of government. Public opinion was formed in the streets, in the struggles of political parties, and in the popular press. Public policy was made by political machines, committees of vigilance, and urban crowds. While this rough-and-tumble public life of nineteenth-century cities seems worlds apart from the Olympian notion of the public sphere as theorized by Hannah Arendt or Habermas, it nonetheless set the historical conditions for a multi-voiced, often discordant deliberation on questions that concerned the people as a whole, including women.

Habermas derived his typology of the public sphere from the political theory and practice of Western Europe during the eighteenth century. He conceded that even this idealized public sphere originally extended only to the bourgeoisie, and that with the onslaught of popular movements early in the nineteenth century it quickly began to degrade into the bastardized form of "mass democracy." Habermas's truncated social history of the public sphere would suggest that the period between 1825 and 1880 and the locality of the United States provide a critical test of his theory. Such "American exceptions" as the early provision of universal white male suffrage and the two-party system helped generate an especially vigorous sphere of public debate in the Jacksonian period, one that was hospitable to a wider constituency than the bourgeois sphere as manifested in Western Europe. The most cursory examination of the politics of the Jacksonian era reveals that public opinion was generated by working-men and propertyless immigrants as well as by the bourgeoisie. It expressed itself not just in sedate debates in the bourgeois press but in raucous public meetings and popular political institutions—at the conventions of workingmen, Locofocos, and Jacksonians. The particular political jurisdiction of this study, the city, admits into evidence especially exuberant public politics. As Tocqueville first observed, it was local politics that galvanized the American citizen's attention and provided the conditions for democratic practice in the 1830s.

Transferred to America, the public sphere seems to have been slightly longer-lived as well as more pluralistic than it was in Western Europe. Politics remained vigorously and broadly public through the antebellum period and the beginnings of the two-party system. By the late nineteenth century, however, as a number of political historians have suggested, democratic institutions and practices were constrained and fractured by the rise of state bureaucracies, organized private interest groups, and mass methods of political persuasion.[1] Less attention has been given to the place of women and gender in this elusive but critical transformation from the bourgeois public sphere to its remodeled, perhaps ersatz form, interest-group politics.[2] A survey of nineteenth-century newspapers, urban institutions that occupy a critical place in Habermas's history and theory, reveals numerous occasions when women and gender entered the public discourse. This essay will show, in a preliminary manner, how women found access to a universe of public discourse that resembled, in always imperfect and ever-changing ways, the ideal of the public sphere.

Femininity and the Male Public Sphere: 1825–1860

Between 1825 and 1840, the public spaces of New York and New Orleans offered men of nearly every class and ethnicity a place to express all varieties of opinions, in all manner and ill-manner of discourse. Newspapers were peppered with calls for "public meetings," and sometimes whole columns of newsprint were devoted to listing the congregations planned each evening in halls, saloons, and public squares and on street corners. The very language of these announcements expressed a public politics. The Jacksonian revolution was ushered in by summonses to familiar public places. On November 3, 1827, for example, the Evening Post invited New Yorkers to Tammany Hall for a "General Meeting—a meeting of the Citizens of New York friendly to the election of General Jackson." Early in the decade, workingmen were expressly invited to a "Great public meeting on Wooster Street." In New Orleans, the explosion of public discourse onto the streets occurred later in time but was just as vigorous in expression. By the 1830s, citizens of the Crescent City were invited to a "great democratic meeting," a "public convocation of the citizens," and "meetings of democracy." When San Francisco's civic life commenced in the wake of the forty-niners, a public congregation in open space established popular sovereignty. On February 15, 1849, the Alta California called the citizenry together in Portsmouth Plaza, to consider a "plan of organization of government." Enrollment in the public life of the city would come later for Americans of African ancestry, but it would still take the same form of open, outdoor politics. In New Orleans during reconstruction, black men were summoned to conventions, ward meetings, and public assemblages in Lafayette Square with a frequency and seriousness that recalled the Jacksonian era. The *New Orleans Tribune* championed the cause of public outdoor meetings: "The streets and squares of New Orleans should be open and free" to all. Such meetings were especially critical cradles of democracy for black men, who were often illiterate and unschooled in political practices.[3]

These conventions of the public were constituted with great seriousness and forethought in the 1820s and 1830s. Both newspaper editors and the popular bodies themselves carefully monitored the procedures for convening meetings of the citizenry. A meeting called in New York in 1835 for the uncontroversial purpose of providing relief for the veterans of the Revolution and the War of 1812 conformed to the preferred procedures. First, the Common Council asked that the mayor "be respectfully requested to call a meeting of our fellow citizens at such time and place as he may designate." The mayor promptly obliged, issuing a public notice saying that "I now respectfully invite the citizens of New York to meet in front of the City Hall." A nominating convention of Jacksonians in New Orleans in 1837 prefaced its resolutions with the statement that "whereas such a decision cannot be obtained unless the people meet in their primary assemblies and give free and full expression to their opinions—therefore, this meeting is so assembled." Those who attended public meetings were equally scrupulous in establishing their legitimacy. A meeting of Locofocos at the Merchant Exchange in the same city was aborted when the *Picayune* discovered that it had been instigated at "the suggestion of a correspondent of the *Bulletin* and not an understanding among citizens generally."[4]

A meeting of Locofocos in October of 1835 enforced the procedures for convening the public sphere with the greatest panache. When a "monopoly force" tried to impose its chair and its policies on the "Great Democratic Republican County Meeting" and, failing, tried to abort the proceedings by turning off the lights, the assemblage ignited candles with locofoco matches. As the "cheers of the democracy blazed in her . . . resplendent glory," the meeting passed a score of resolutions that outlined the Democratic platform for the next decade. Resolution 6 pledged allegiance to the public sphere: "That the people have a right at all times and it is their duty to assemble together to consult for the common good, to give utterance to their sentiments, to give instructions to their representatives, and to apply to the Legislature for redress for wrongs and grievances, by address, petition and remonstrance." The Locofocos, like other antebellum Americans, had convened and actualized their own robust public sphere, committed to open discussion of controversial issues that concerned the popular classes as well as the bourgeoisie.[5]

Participation in this public sphere was, however, a masculine prerogative. Only a few radicals, most notably followers of Thomas Paine, even considered that women were to be counted among the public. While open to the propertyless and newly arrived Irishmen, membership in the public sphere was an extension of suffrage, for which only men need consider applying. Convened in the halls of Tammany, or at saloons and at twilight, public meetings were often spatially remote for women as well. The gender restrictions that underpinned the public sphere in the 1820s and 1830s were, however, occasionally articulated. Commenting on a contingent of school children in a Whig procession honoring Henry Clay in 1845, for example, the *New Orleans Bee* observed, "The boys will reach manhood in the age that leads to moral and social excellence, and the girls will make helpmates for the sons of the Republic."[6] The *Bee* had dusted off the doctrine of republican motherhood available since the eighteenth century to place women on the margins of the public domain. Even such rhetorical allusions to the second sex were rare during the halcyon days of the Jacksonian public sphere.

On several conspicuous occasions, however, the masculine border of the public sphere had to be more forcefully patrolled. The most aggressive assault on that border was made not by an American woman but by the English radical Fanny Wright. In 1836, Wright was granted an audience in the citadels of the partisan public sphere at both Tammany and Masonic halls. Her appearances, however, were soon exploited by the press to tarnish the opposition with charges of Jacobinism and free love. Invitations to female speakers were promptly rescinded. On September 23, at the Masonic Hall, masculine outrage rudely dismissed this female interloper in the public sphere. Wright's speech on that evening was interrupted by hisses halfway through. Cane pounding, stink bombs, and a "volley of expressions of the most vulgar and indecent kind" drove her from the meeting. The mob outside called her a whore and harlot, while one commentator dubbed her a "female man." As the paradox of gender in public would have it, Fanny Wright was simultaneously barred by her sex and desexed by her politics. By 1838, Fanny Wright was no longer welcome in the major public halls of New York City. To find a public podium, she had to purchase her own small, saloonlike building on Broome Street.[7]

During the same period, women abolitionists mounted another assault on the public sphere. The presence of women at the abolitionist meetings in New York City in 1834 was especially grating to the editorial spokesmen for the public. The press tarnished abolitionism with sexual innuendos as well as gender impropriety: rumors of "amalgamationism" and lechery among the promiscuous antislavery ranks were circulated by the daily press. As the abolitionists met in Chatham Street Chapel in July, the city was astir with talk about "sexual passion, with a vehemence of manner, and in a tone of earnestness, utterly abhorrent from the generally received notions of propriety."[8] In Boston, female abolitionists had provoked rebukes in pastoral letters, which drove many women from the public sphere; New Yorkers took a less decorous but equally effective action, a riot that drove the abolitionists from their meeting place, injuring one black woman and one white member of the mob. The violent and visceral response to daring women like Fanny Wright and the abolitionists made the gender limits of the public sphere emphatically clear. When in the 1840s both abolitionists and the temperance movement turned to electoral and legislative methods of achieving reform (the Liberty party and the Maine Law), another door to the public sphere was closed to the disenfranchised woman.

The rise of the common man and the political exclusion of women proceeded in tandem between 1825 and 1840. By the 1840s, the American public sphere presented a relatively one-dimensional gender picture. Any females along its border were decisively shunted aside, and the composition of the public became masculine. At the same time, the border of the public sphere was decorated with a few symbols of femininity. When Jacksonians or Whigs dined to celebrate their partisan loyalties, they customarily raised at least one of many glasses to women. Even the Workingmen's party was not immune to the genteel image of womanhood. At a public dinner on July 8, 1830, the last of twenty-four official toasts (the thirty-three voluntary toasts that followed cast some doubt on the sobriety of the assembled citizens) read, "The Fair—when pain and anguish wring the brow / A ministering angel thou." But such accolades to the fair were minor and perfunctory exercises and hardly the central concerns of the public men of the 1820s and 1830s. Political energies were focused on building a masculine fortress in the public sphere.

Once that sphere had been well established and popular participation in politics had been channeled into two well-organized parties, women's presence became more visible, if only through their symbolic representation as emblems of femininity. The debut of femininity occurred at the national level, along with the first direct confrontation of two mass parties, in the Harrison-Van Buren campaign of 1840. The same political strategists who created the popular iconography of Tippecanoe and log cabins pioneered in drafting feminine archetypes as well. One Democratic partisan observed that "this way of making politicians of their women is something new under the sun but so it is the Whigs go to the strife." Before audiences that included large numbers of ladies, the Whigs recited paeans to "our mothers, sisters, daughters, now, as in the days of the Revolution. All Whigs. Locofocoism and Fanny Wrightism find no response from them." Others appealed to party stalwarts to "shield the fairest flower that blooms, by staying the hand and resisting the blows that would destroy its sweetness and its beauty." The Whigs introduced women into politics as passive and respectable representatives of femininity, carefully distinguished from radicals such as Fanny Wright. They dwelt upon sexual difference, not political commonality, including among the "resplendent charms" of the Whig hearers their "graceful fans" and "exquisitely molded arms." The bosoms of Whig ladies also commanded attention. Tennessee belles wore sashes proclaiming "Whig Husbands or None," which offended their Democratic opponents: "I am sorry to say that I have seen ladies too joining in [Whig songs] with them and wearing ribands across their breasts with two names printed upon them."[9]

The Democrats were only slightly tardy in adding feminine political symbolism to their campaign. In New Orleans, partisans of Van Buren, concerned about growing enthusiasm for Harrison, brought Andrew Jackson to the city in 1840. Of the welcoming ceremonies the press pointedly noted that the "balconies were groaning with their fair burdens" as women waved their handkerchiefs in unison with the popular support for the Democrats. By the end of the decade, feminine symbols and female audiences were commonplace in the political rallies of both parties. When the Whigs welcomed Zachary Taylor to the Crescent City in 1847, women were invited to the festivities and public halls rang out both with toasts to the ladies and strains of "Home Sweet Home." Local elections two years later featured ornate political pageants with honored female guests. When the Whigs met at the St. Louis Exchange in November of 1849, "The galleries were graced by the presence of a goodly number of ladies, who added greatly to the interest and enthusiasm manifested on the occasion." Women as audience and symbol, pronouncedly feminine in iconography and action, had appeared in all three cities by 1850. While the Democrats remained less ardent in their courtship of the fair, even Tammany Hall was opened to ladies in 1848 when four hundred women heard speeches honoring the anniversary of Jackson's triumph in the Battle of New Orleans.[10]

The induction of femininity into politics cannot be understood apart from the strategies of electioneering that sanctioned it. The feminizing of the public sphere was less a part of the insurgent democracy of the 1820s and 1830s and more a by-product of campaign practices designed a decade later to attach partisan loyalties to the designated nominees of the mass parties. Femininity entered politics not during the era of the public meeting but along with partisan pageantry, calculated to "bring out the masses for a last grand demonstration before the election." Femininity was surrounded by spectacle, the "monster mass meetings," complete with torchlight processions, bands, bonfires, and fireworks. The ladies joined the Whigs of New Orleans, not in public deliberation but as symbols: they looked on as their menfolk "turned out strong in procession and with music, Chinese lanterns, banners etc, and marched through the principal streets making a fine exhibition of their strength and enthusiasm." While the Democrats remained relatively indifferent to feminine symbolism, their partisan ceremonies were just as spectacular, featuring firecrackers, cannons, balloon ascensions, and a procession in which the "principal feature was an artificial chicken cock of gigantic dimension." This theatrical rather than participatory style of politics could also spotlight masculine symbols, and by inviting men and women to experience public life as passive but passionate viewers had a tendency to "feminize" the political process for both sexes. The *Picayune* described the audience for such a political pageant, which honored the Whig idol Zachary Taylor, in almost sheeplike terms: "The streets through which the procession moved were densely thronged with patient masses waiting for a sight of the old hero."[11]

The feminization of party symbolism was also rooted in the changing social base of partisan affiliation. The Whigs, who took the initiative in constructing feminine political symbols, had a particularly strong base in the Yankee middle classes, the same constituency that, during the same period, spawned a domestic ideology celebrating both femininity and private virtue. When the Whigs sang "Home Sweet Home," they honored the wives, daughters, and mothers of their own class and ethnic group who were recent subscribers to the cult of domesticity. In grafting this privatized ideology onto public symbols, the Whigs joined ranks with parapolitical associations like the temperance movement, whose popular meetings were especially well practiced in the new language and pageantry of femininity. Temperance meetings in all three cities were effusive in their invitations to women, who were granted special seats in the galleries and invited even to sing songs and recite odes at indoor ceremonies. Women in the temperance movement played more instrumental roles as well. Temperance meetings in the 1840s in both New York and

New Orleans passed public resolutions endorsing women's activism. In April of 1847, a New York temperance meeting resolved "that we solicit the influence of female laborers of every description and that we will make their interests our own." Earlier in the same year, ladies were a large part of the audience at a "Great Temperance Demonstration," where it was resolved "that thanks of this meeting be tendered to the ladies of this city who by their labors and contributions have assisted the committee in circulating petitions." Those petitions were direct appeals to legislators and a sure link between women and politics.[12]

Another overtly political movement of the Yankee middling ranks was an early and enthusiastic promulgator of political femininity. When nativists organized in New York in the 1840s in order to restrict the political participation of Irish immigrants, the leaders invited their kinswomen to participate and honored feminine symbols. Meetings of the United Americans in 1847 featured goddesses of Liberty, enrolled large contingents of women, and encouraged men to bring their families along. In the 1850s, the Know-Nothing party was especially concerned to recruit women to its festivities as its members clothed themselves in the mantle of domestic propriety. Nativists instructed partisans of the cause, furthermore, to visit families in their domiciles rather than simply to churn up support from men in the public streets and places of New York City.[13]

While Democrats were at first hesitant about using this strategy of winning partisan loyalty, their affiliates among the Irish and the working class soon incorporated gender into their own political symbolism. When the Young Friends of Ireland met on St Patrick's Day in 1850, they invited women to endorse their foreign policy of a united Ireland. They toasted "Woman ever an ingenious advocate of Union: may it be her happy lot to enlarge and purify the patriotism of the land, by excluding all Disunionists from her favor." Women had a central role in the ceremonies of Irishmen and the public meetings of Fenians ever after.

The leaders of Irish societies were likely to represent the middle classes, who, regardless of national origin, would find the images of purifying ladies congenial. Working-class voters, less receptive to this construction of gender, devised another symbolic relationship between their politics and their kinswomen. This rhetorical strategy was in use as early as the 1830s, when workingmen's parties justified their public protests as a means of securing a family wage, capable of sustaining their wives and children. After 1850, workingmen pushed this ideology more to the foreground in the public presentation of themselves and their grievances. The banners of workingmen carried in rallies demanding public relief for the unemployed in 1857 demanded, "Work—that our wives and children may not starve." Like their social superiors, the workingmen were careful to distinguish between the symbolic (and dependent) political status of women and actual female participation in the public sphere. The needs of women workers were rarely addressed, and female speakers who asserted themselves in public meetings were gruffly put in their place. One Madam Ranke, who "edged her way out of the crowd and commenced talking to a circle of men" at a meeting of the unemployed in 1857, was driven from Tompkins Square by a band of two hundred boys. She was escorted to safety by two protective elderly women and a contingent of city police. The sorry case of Madam Ranke notwithstanding, women had secured at least a symbolic foothold in the public life of workingmen. They were symbols not so much of private virtue as of the private needs of impoverished families.[14]

Be they workingmen or middle class, native-born or Irish, the male actors in the tumultuous local politics of the 1850s were dividing up the public sphere into contentious social groups distinguished by national origin and class position. This reformulation of political identity was not always conducted in an orderly fashion, nor within legitimate political institutions. In all three cities, ethnic and class politics exploded into a form of vigilantism in the 1850s. This peculiar American species of extralegal government was inaugurated by the vigilance committees that ruled the streets of San Francisco in 1851 and again in 1856. When city merchants usurped the power of democratically elected officials, who were of Irish ancestry and reputedly connected to New York's Tammany Hall, they draped themselves in feminine symbols, some of which were supplied directly by women. The first onslaught of the vigilantes in 1851 was a self-proclaimed defense of the life and property of businessmen. Yet the ladies of the city quickly championed the cause. The women of Trinity Church presented the Committee of Vigilance with a banner and an address giving thanks for protecting their fragile ranks. When the vigilantes rose again in 1856, feminine symbolism was at the forefront: James King had orchestrated a campaign to protect endangered females; the banner from the ladies of Trinity Church was carried in parades; and the call to arms on May 15 of that year was issued for "the protection of our families." A committee of vigilance also took up arms in New Orleans' Jackson Square in 1858, and a year later the steps of New York's City Hall were the site of a bloody battle between Mayor Fernando Wood's local police and the Metropolitans, newly appointed by the state commissioners. In both cases, the battle lines of urban strife were drawn between the native and the foreign-born and were inscribed with gender symbolism. Women also joined directly and at times violently in the volatile ethnic politics of the 1850s. One Irish woman in San Francisco ordered her children, "Don't Look at them dirty Know-Nothings," while another in New York was more belligerent, chanting, "Kill the bloody Know-Nothings."[15]

Femininity was inducted into politics hand in hand with the ethnic partition of the public sphere, which was manifested both in partisan rivalries and in violent civic strife. Gender, therefore, was deeply implicated in critical changes in the American political process. Gender rose to the surface of political culture just as politics was transformed into the interplay of select groups within the population, identified as much by their ethnicity and religion as by their opinions on specific questions of public policy. The kinship bonds represented by women were, of course, specific signals of ethnic identity. The fellow travelers of the 1840s and 1850s—the Whigs, temperance reformers, and nativists—not only shared Yankee, Protestant, middle-class allegiances, but also embraced a particular construction of private and public life. They honored not so much the individual citizen acting in a public capacity as they did a political reference group based in private associations and virtues—native birth, family bonds, temperate habits, domestic propriety. Horace Greeley's *Tribune,* the New York paper partisan to all these constituencies, articulated this new political philosophy in his customary July 4 sermon, delivered in 1845. "Let men feel in their private lives more than in public measures must the salvation of the country be. . . . They have not deepened and purified the private lives from which the public must spring."

Using New York State as his testing ground, Lee Benson argued long ago that by the 1840s electoral politics had become a contest between segments of the population with different ethnic, religious, and symbolic allegiances. More recently, Amy Bridges has demonstrated a similar rearrangement of working-class political identifications in the machine-ridden public sphere of New York City.[16] The foregoing should illustrate that gender was a party to this decisive turn in American politics. Women had entered the public realm as symbols and as accomplices in the transformation of the political process. First, feminine symbols accompanied the transition from democratic participation to theatrical techniques of molding partisan loyalty. Second, references to gender and family ate away at the older definition of citizenship, replacing individual action in pursuit of the public good with appeals to the private loyalties and values of differ-

ent social groups. Third, those social groups especially eager to recruit females as symbols into the new politics displayed certain anti-
democratic tendencies: nativists would restrict the franchise,
temperance reformers would use state power to enforce private sobriety, and vigilantes subverted the elected authorities. These multiple
linkages between women and politics in the years before the Civil
War may have been merely coincidental and marginal to male control
of public life. Yet the pattern of association is sufficiently widespread
and consistent to accord women a place within political history, and
to implicate gender in the reformulation of the public sphere even
before 1860.

The Civil War and Sexual Strife

The acceleration of sectional conflict and the outbreak of the Civil
War brought these incipient relationships between gender and politics into tense and often explosive prominence on the public stage.
Even before the shots were fired at Fort Sumter, the stage of sectional
politics was strewn with a profusion of the now-familiar feminine
symbols that had taken root in party politics twenty years earlier.
When fourteen thousand San Franciscans congregated at the junction
of Market, Montgomery, and Post streets on February 22, 1861, the
women took up their stations in windows and on balconies to endorse the Union cause. Simultaneously, the plans for rallies in support of secession in New Orleans specified that the ladies would be
"politely cared for by the committee of reception" and provided a
separate grandstand for their sex. Once war broke out in April,
women took honored seats at demonstrations of sectional solidarity
in all three cities. By one accounting, the "Immense Demonstration"
assembled in New York's Union Square on July 16, 1862, to proclaim
"The Union Forever" included thirty thousand adult men and twenty
thousand women and children.[17]

On these ceremonial occasions, essential to maintaining political
solidarity in a time of crisis, women edged their way toward greater
political visibility, at times almost to the center of the public stage.
The war years gave new prominence to the ceremonies wherein
women presented their hand-wrought banners to militia companies
preparing for battle. The February 20, 1861, issue of the *Picayune*
reported on three such ceremonies. In one of these, a Southern lady
went daringly public to present a banner from the women's auxiliary
to the Washington artillery; she delivered "a brief speech in their
own name" as her compatriots formed an honor guard through which
the battalion passed. Similar presentations made headlines in New

York, where they featured the doyennes of the highest social circles. When Mrs. Augusta Astor presented a banner to the elite Seventh Regiment, her speech was delivered by the commanding general. She did, however, make one audacious public gesture: she "stepped down from a carriage and took a position in front of the regiment." The ladies of the Crescent City were not to be outdone in their patriotic bravado: after presenting their own banner, two women "took up positions on each side [of the Confederate General] to lead a procession through the city streets."[18]

The most immediate impact of women's presence at the rallies of Unionists and Rebels was to fill the air with cloying gender stereotypes and recruit women to traditional roles on the sidelines of the public sphere. The *New York Herald* was typical: its pages offered women exalted political status with one hand and took back its liberating promises with the other. Women would "share the danger and privations of war . . . in defense of the liberties secured them by our constitution," but they would do so in "charity and meekness, without the prospect of fee or reward."[19]

Thousands of women, North and South, responded appropriately. Within days of hearing the shots at Fort Sumter, they called their own public meetings and organized fairs to raise money and supplies for the soldiers. The press honored such efforts, like the congregation of some three thousand women at the Cooper Institute in New York, with front-page stories about "Mass movements of the Ladies," or "Another Ladies Movement." At such public assemblages women displayed their respectable status, feminine appearance, and patriotic ardor. The chair and the speakers at such ladies' meetings were usually men. Woman's role in the war effort was more public than ever, in both style and organization, but still domestic in substance— to fold bandages, sew clothing, and weave blankets.

The course of the war, on the home front and in the wake of extreme civic conflict, was to complicate and significantly expand women's political roles. The public sphere was especially volatile in the cities of New York and New Orleans. The citizens of the first city were deeply divided on the issues that provoked the war, and the Union cause was challenged throughout the 1860s by the protests of Copperhead Democrats, who called for an early cessation of hostilities. The majority of New Orleans voters had not supported secession candidates in the presidential election of 1860, and the citizenry tepidly embraced the Rebel cause after the Confederates fired on Fort Sumter. Then one year later the Union army marched into the Crescent City to preside over a largely hostile white population. In all three cities, mobilization for mass warfare impelled women as well as men into heightened political awareness and heroic patriotic service. In this highly unstable and charged atmosphere, the tension between gender and politics came to the surface of public life.

The city of New Orleans became the setting for the particularly vivid dramatization of the contradictions in gender symbolism that featured star performances from Benjamin Butler and the ladies. The peculiar demographics of war-torn New Orleans influenced the casting of this drama. With thousands of men at the battlefront, the population of the city was predominantly female. With military officers from the North at the helm of local government, male Rebels were placed in a feminized political position, as passive supplicants before the conquering Yankees. Consequently, much of local civic life was expressed in symbolic gestures rather than active participation in self-government. For the duration of the occupation, local public opinion often spoke in a feminine voice and through the actions of women.

Benjamin Butler, who had won a reputation in Massachusetts as a republican champion of working men and women, had hardly landed in the Crescent City when he met resistance from feminine quarters. He recalled that "complaints of women, of all states and conditions and degrees in life, came pouring in on me." Women Rebels made use of every opportunity to flaunt their political allegiances. Schoolteachers trained their pupils to sing Rebel songs, female parishioners refused to pray for the Union, ladies at the theater exhorted the orchestra to play a stanza of the "Bonnie Blue Flag," sewing bees crafted Rebel banners, and, by one account, prostitutes placed pictures of Ben Butler in their "tinker pots."

The women of New Orleans committed the most flagrant and annoying acts of resistance in the public places to which they had the easiest access, the streets. The more timorous Rebels went abroad with small Confederate flags pinned to their dresses. An otherwise demure young lady announced that her compatriots "had a pistol in their pockets" for any man who would dare to remove these badges from their bodices. Others greeted Union soldiers by crossing the street, turning around, or raising their skirts in a gesture of repugnance. The most brazen daughters of the Confederacy launched a barrage of saliva at their conquerors. Soldiers complained to General Butler that they could not "walk the streets without being outraged and spit upon by young girls." Butler was not about to take such offenses lightly. When some women did an about-face to avoid encountering the general in the street, he shot back, "These women evidently know what end of them looks best."[20]

Butler was determined to act the statesman if not the gentleman

"The Ladies of New Orleans before General Butler's Proclamation and after
General Butler's Proclamation." *Harper's Weekly* (c. May 15, 1862).

and set his mind to designing a strategy that would subdue this
female mutiny. Yet nothing in his experience prepared him to deal
with such a widespread female revolt. In Boston, he recalled, such
acts were committed only by drunken viragos, who could be summarily arrested. But what was a public official to do when the offender was reputed to be a Southern lady? After pondering the conun-
drum for some time, Butler determined that he needed a law that
would "execute itself," rather than embarrassing its promulgators or
the policemen charged with enforcing it. The strategy he devised was
issued as the infamous General Order Number 28, on May 15, 1862.
Quoted at the outset of this book, it repaid women's lack of courtesy
with the charge of prostitution.

Butler had deliberately snared the female Rebels in a trap wired
together by the contradictions of sex and class. His reasoning went as
follows: "All the ladies of New Orleans forebore to insult our troops
because they didn't want to be deemed common women, and all the
common women forebore to insult our troops because they wanted
to be deemed ladies, and of those two classes were all the women
secessionists of the city." Butler's stratagem seems to have worked.
It provoked a battle in the consciousness of at least one Southern lady
named Sarah Dawson, who recorded the episode in her diary. On
May 11, 1862, just four days before Order Number 28 was announced, Dawson reported that she had journeyed to the State House,
accompanied by some young female friends who wore Confederate

insignia on their bosoms. When they met up with some Union soldiers, she refused to "strike my colors in the face of the enemy."
Still, she paid some psychic cost for such unladylike behavior: "I am
disgusted with myself for being there and everyone for seeing me."
A few weeks later, after Order Number 28 was in force, Sarah Dawson had tempered her rebellion against the Yankees and focused her
criticism on her own sex. She asked, "Do I consider the female who
would spit on a gentleman's face, merely because he wore United
States buttons, as a fit associate for me?" The answer was a resound-
ing no: "Such things are enough to disgust anyone, 'loud' women
what contempt I have for you. How I despise your vulgarity." Other
women reported that Butler's strategy had produced widespread fear
and temerity among the ladies of the city. Butler appeared to have
won his first skirmish with the gentler sex.[21]

But the war of symbols went on and achieved a national and
international audience. Order Number 28 provoked Jefferson Davis
to put a price of ten thousand dollars on Butler's head; the ladies of
New York proposed a reception in the general's honor at the Academy of Music, and the incident was discussed in the English Parliament. Before the war was over, two more skirmishes between the
Union army and the ladies of New Orleans made their way into
Southern folklore. The first was the "Battle of St. Paul's," fought on
October 1, 1862, when Butler sent troops to expel a minister and his
largely female congregation for refusing to pray as ordered for President Lincoln. But to the vanquished belonged the symbolic victory,
as exemplified by this stanza from a popular song:

Up rose the congregation—
We men were all away
And our wives and little children
Alone remained to pray
But when has the Southern woman
Before a Yankee quailed?
And these with tongues undaunted
The Lincolnites assailed
In vain he called his soldiers
Their darts around him flew
And the strong men then discovered
What a woman's tongue can do.

The second battle, fought on the levee in February of 1863, was
a replay of the first. The forcible removal of thousands of women
who had gathered to bid farewell to Confederate prisoners inspired a
ballad called "The Great Victory of the War: La Bataille des Mou-

choirs," which rendered the public life of New Orleans as a satiric warfare between masculine bayonets and a feminine arsenal of parasols and handkerchiefs. Such mythology both clothed women's politics in feminine garb and solaced the vanquished Southern man by ridiculing Yankee masculinity.[22]

The Civil War on the Southern front brought women into the symbolic center of the public sphere. But while the occupation of New Orleans turned gender symbolism topsy-turvy, it did not dislodge patriarchy. Rather, women fought the Yankees from their customary informal and symbolic places on the margins of public life, using their feminine weaponry of etiquette and attire, snubs and handkerchiefs. Even then they were disarmed by the volley of sexual innuendo in Order Number 28. The gender battles in New Orleans in 1862 and 1863 merely brought into the open the explosive potential of the ladies' ceremonial role in politics. They did not break the masculine monopoly on the formal public sphere.

The legacy of slave society and the tensions of military occupation which kept women's political action within narrow bounds in New Orleans restricted the political expression of African-American women with particular severity. Their voices were scarcely audible in public, even in the vortex of a civil war that emancipated their race. Even Radical Republicans of both races construed the political emancipation of New Oreans blacks in male terms, sometimes gilded with references to the ladies. The historian can hear the political concerns of African-American women only in muted tones, expressed in contorted ways and emanating from unusual places. Some intriguing suggestions of the suppressed politics of African-American women can be dimly surmised in one cultural institution of New Orleans, voodooism. The political import of congregations of conjurers was not lost on the leaders of the city of New Orleans. When a dozen women of the First Municipality were found assembled to practice African rituals in 1851, the press reported that "nothing tends more to demoralize the servile population than gathering for such purposes, and the police are doing well to break them up wherever they find them." With the intensification of sectional conflict leading up to civil war, such assemblages loomed more ominous and prosecutions for voodooism increased.[23]

Such practices had long been a female domain in New Orleans, presided over by voodoo queens like the famed Marie Laveau. Slaves and free women of color could take their personal politics to the conjurer, seeing magical power as leverage in their volatile relationships with black and white—kinsmen, masters, mistresses, and par-

amours. Civil war gave increased political importance to these rituals, which did not recede with Yankee occupation. The *Daily True
Delta* sounded the alarm in 1863 when nineteen women were arrested for "having formed an unlawful assemblage, with voudous
[*sic*] practices and disloyal sinister purposes, in using heathenish
incantations to cause the return of the rebels." The tangled relations
of race and gender in New Orleans gave a byzantine cast to the
politics of this assembly of women, most of them identified as free
persons of color rather than newly emancipated slaves and including
one white female. The *Delta* reported the political objectives of this
meeting as follows: "to cause the return of the rebels, to assuage their
hatred and disgust against those persons who had lately been slaves
and were now their equals." Such shards of evidence, their meaning
hopelessly obscured by the biases of the reporters, point to the unex-
plored depths of the women's politics that for African-American
women still lay buried beneath the surface of the public sphere.[24]

In the North, where female symbols became currency not only in
sectional conflict but also in fratricidal local politics, women's stake
in the public sphere was easier to discern. Early in the war, women
became more prominent appendages to the rallies of both Republicans and Democrats. In New York, the spring and summer of 1863
was a particularly feverish period of outdoor politics, featuring nearly
weekly public meetings of both Republicans and several factions of
Democrats, including Copperheads. The Copperheads were led by
former mayor Fernando Wood, who had proposed that the city of
New York secede from the Union if peace were not declared. The
press scrutinized the crowds at these meetings to determine whether
women were party to the often incendiary proceedings. Although the
ladies were most prominent among the Republicans, women were
also spotted in the audiences at the Democratic and peace rallies,
which threatened to undermine the Union cause.

The women who planned to attend the "Grand Rally of the Democracy" to be held at the Cooper Institute on April 7, 1863, were
to be party to a public action in which "the people will assemble in
their might to express their sentiments on the public questions of the
day." Those sentiments included such rallying cries as this: "Let all
those come who are opposed to the Conscript Act, opposed to War
for the Negro in favor of the Constitutional Rights of the Poor."
Throughout the spring, Democratic rallies played on discontent with
the war's cost to the poor and working classes and directed that rage
in racist channels. The women who heard such turgid political discourse in public places would have the point driven home by paeans

to white femininity. One Democratic rally in San Francisco, for example, rang out with hurrahs "for white men, and repeated cheers for white women."[25]

During the spring of 1863, when the Copperhead offensive placed the Union cause in greatest jeopardy, New York women were parties to vitriolic public discourse. The fearful possibility that women might not compliantly support local war efforts became transparently clear on April 8 when the *New York Times* reported on a bread riot in Richmond. The headlines read, "3000 Hungry Women Raging in the Streets"—"armed with clubs, guns, stones broke into government stores." In the same issue, the *Times* looked nervously toward the women closer to home. Of the Copperhead rally staged at Cooper Union to protest similar wartime austerity just the day before, the *Times* reported, "Amidst the vast concourse one—and only one—of the gentler sex was observed." Others disputed the *Times*'s tally of female attendance and later reported significant numbers of women at similar meetings in May and June. Perhaps ladies could be counted upon to act out the role of the gentler sex among Republicans and Union loyalists, but the actions of women of the lower classes, especially those who chanced to hear the incendiary antiwar political slogans of the Democrats, were more unpredictable, and worrisome.[26]

This brand of women's politics would be spelled out on the streets in July, when for three days the opponents of the conscription law battled the Union army, called up to repel them. If the presence of women at Democratic rallies was disputed, their sex was not hard to find amid the small circles of anxious individuals who witnessed the first selection of conscripts on Saturday, July 10. The *Herald* reported that "a large number of workingmen's wives, etc., began also to assemble along the various avenues, and if anything, were more excited than the men." The *Herald* also pointed to women as instigators of the political violence soon to follow. Its editor noted that on the following Sunday, when an eerie calm hung over the city, families had time to consider the fate of sons who were drafted two days before. "It must be said by way of explanation of the extraordinary resistance that marked the draft, that the female relatives of the conscripts mingled their wildest denunciations against the conscription law, and thus gave the people a 'cavalier' motive to enact the terrible scenes."[27]

Although women were clearly a small minority of the combatants during the July Days of 1863 (less than 10 percent of those arrested), this incident was one of the more sexually integrated political actions of the nineteenth century. Every account found women among the rioters. Even the archbishop of New York warned Catholic parents to "watch over their daughters as well as their sons, and keep them at home" for the duration of the riots. The scores of women who did not stay home but expressed their politics through violent street action were attempting to implement a political program they might have learned at the Copperhead rallies in the spring, or even a week earlier. One woman reportedly announced her political allegiance as she entered the fray by challenging a group of black women to combat, saying, "I am a copperhead and I can fight too by ———: who will take me up?" Others acted out the racist ideology that pervaded Democratic rhetoric. Women were reputedly well represented in the crowds that assaulted and abused Negroes, besieged the Colored Orphan Asylum, and attacked the homes of abolitionists. They were rallied by ditties like this: "Go in for the nigger / the sweet-scented nigger / The wool headed negro / and the abolitionist crew."[28]

Yet, a closer look at both the women who participated in the draft riots and the targets of their wrath indicates something else as well. It provides a glimpse of the covert political agenda of poor and working-class women. In this unseemly public appearance, women gave vent to concerns that had been addressed only elliptically, if at all, by either the Republican government or the Democratic opposition. The outdoor, protest politics of the Copperheads came closest to articulating a women's interest in the war and the draft by invoking the doctrine of the family wage. In the days before the riots, for example, the Peace Democrats issued a call to the laboring population to "assemble peacefully in Mass meeting" to protest a conscription policy that would "compel a white laborer to leave his family destitute and unprotected while he goes forth to free the negro, who being free will compete with him." Women of the laboring poor could surely understand this summons. As Christine Stansell has demonstrated, the loss of a male wage earner was the most devastating fate to befall the poor wives and mothers of New York, a sure sentence to poverty given the dearth of women's employment opportunities and the paltriness of their wages. By proposing to remove young male wage earners with the highest potential earning power from the family, and at a time of extreme inflation induced by the war, the effect of the conscript law would be to ruin many women of the lower classes.[29]

Faced with this dire possibility, some women did not wait upon the political deliberations of voting men but acted directly and violently in their own interest. The majority of the women arrested during the riots were in their forties or fifties, and thus likely to have several children to support as well as adolescent, wage-earning sons

"The Rioters Dragging Col. O'Brien's Body through the Street." From Joel Tyler Headley, *The Great Riots of New York, 1712–1873* (Indianapolis: Bobbs-Merrill, 1970).

who were placed in immediate jeopardy by the draft law. Mary Kennedy, 44, arrested for stealing from one of the looted houses, was typical. Born in Ireland and illiterate, Kennedy told her prosecutors, "I do nothing except wash, got four children." Most of the crimes of which arrested women were accused were, like Mary Kennedy's offense, economically motivated. Women were found looting the riot area for objects of domestic utility: dry goods, soap, and starch. Others reputedly expropriated some feminine luxuries: "dresses of brocade, moire, antique merino and other fine and costly materials." However paltry this redress of economic grievances, women rioters, along with their kinsmen, had effectively made policy in the public streets. In the wake of their violent expression of opinion, the city of New York suspended the draft and, when it was reinstated, set aside $2.5 million to purchase exemptions for the city's most destitute families.[30]

In other instances, rioting women were acting in immediate retaliation against wrongs against themselves and their families. A Captain Howell, attacked in his carriage, was remembered for the fury with which he had fired into a crowd of women and children. Weeks after the riot, another "Savage woman" physically assaulted a police-man who she identified as the murderer of her husband. One of the most grisly incidents of the July Days, the pummeling to death of one Colonel O'Brien, was also the scene of gender politics. O'Brien's attackers reputedly included many women, who were provoked by his order to fire a volley in which "one woman, with her child in her arms, fell pierced with a bullet." When O'Brien was left a mass of gore in the streets, it was said that women "committed the most atrocious violence on the body." Finally, some of the rioting women selected targets that represented an ugly combination of sexual, ra-cial, and economic antagonism. Another group of women singled out a white woman who had married a black man as their victim, "beat her, tore her hair and divided her property." In yet another case, women's rage was expended on one Black Sue, the proprietor of a low dive where the sons and husbands of poor women might forfeit the family wage, not to the war effort, but to sexual commerce.[31]

For three full days in July of 1863, New York's contentious poli-tics broke outside the boundaries of legitimate authority, opening to women the chaotic space in which to make their claims upon the polity public. Yet, understandably, when those pent-up grievances finally exploded, the force was violent and the devastation fell mostly on innocent and inappropriate targets. The victims in New York in 1863 were frequently black men, women, and children, or institu-tions like the Colored Orphan Asylum.

But the racism of the draft riots did not entirely disguise other items on the implicit agenda of women's politics. By assaulting char-itable associations like the Colored Orphan Asylum, for example, rioting women took oblique aim at urban institutions (described in Chapter 1) that provided for the public welfare in ways that rankled poor and especially Irish Catholic women. The asylum was one no-table example of the private system of providing poor-relief, one usually sponsored by middle-class, native-born Protestants, who dis-pensed their beneficence most magnanimously to those they deemed the "worthy poor," and rarely to Irish Catholics. The Catholic immi-grants who were so well represented among the rioters might have chafed at this private, niggardly, prejudicial, and condescending method of providing for the public welfare. A few months after the riots, in November of 1863, striking seamstresses made similar objec-tions explicit by repudiating private philanthropy as a means of re-dressing the grievances of their class. During the riots, such concerns were expressed more obliquely. Two Protestant missions situated in poor neighborhoods were attacked and looted in the July Days.

Women also rampaged through the house of Postmaster Wakeman, whose wife "was noted for kindness to the poor and wretched, who repaid her by sacking and burning her home." Poor women made their opinions about these voluntary parapolitical activities of charitable men and women dimly but violently public in the course of the draft riots.

On one July evening, the free fire of women's rage happened to fall nearby another faction of politically active women, the women's rights movement. Residing just a block away from the Orphan Asylum on the night it was ransacked was none other than Elizabeth Cady Stanton. From her base in New York City, Stanton interjected a feminist perspective into the central political debates of the Civil War period. Working in a celebrated feminist partnership with Susan B. Anthony, she added a clarion and uncompromising voice of women's rights to the febrile local politics of 1863. Stanton and Anthony's organizational base was the National Loyal Women's League, which met weekly (even during the week of the draft riots) at the Cooper Institute, scene of Republican, Democratic, and Copperhead rallies, as well as conventions of suffragists.

The Loyal Women's League exhibited the increasingly and concertedly political posture of the women's rights movement. As described by Lori Ginsberg, the advocates of women's rights had become disenchanted with the informal and indirect methods of influencing public opinion typical of antebellum reformers.[32] Stanton and Anthony had close ties to the Radical Republicans in Washington, including Senator Charles Sumner, who recruited Anthony to mobilize public support for the total and unqualified emancipation of the slaves. As the first act of that campaign, Anthony journeyed to New York City, where she and Stanton drew up a "Call for a Meeting of Loyal Women of the Nation." The opening meeting of the Loyal Women's League on May 14, 1863, began with salvos to the politics of femininity. Stanton invoked the familiar image of domestic sacrifice: "when a mother lays her son on the altar of her country . . . nursing the sick and wounded, knitting socks, and making jellies." She also paid homage to womanly privacy: "To man common consent has conceded the forum, the field and the camp." These loyal women proceeded immediately, however, without title to the vote, to act as if they were full citizens of the public sphere. Stanton demanded for her sex "an object equal to the sacrifice" and surmised that "woman is vitally interested and responsible with men for the final settlement of this problem of self-government." Both she and Ernestine Rose delivered forceful criticisms of Lincoln's timorous steps toward emancipation, and the league resolved to circulate petitions to that effect, to men as well as women. By 1864, when some four hundred thousand signatures had been delivered to Congress, the Radical Republican leadership expressed its deep indebtedness to the league and to its leadership.[33]

The members of the Loyal Women's League were well schooled in the language of partisan politics, and their opinions were in fact heard. All the major papers were attentive to their meetings in 1863, and only occasionally resorted to the sophomoric humor that had greeted suffrage meetings in the past. While the *New York Herald* found recollections of "the funny women's rights conventions of former days," made jokes about the bonnets of the lady politicians, and characterized Angelina Grimké Weld as "an ancient spinster with an inexhaustible flow of talk," it also printed a full account of the league's deliberations.[34]

In the process of lending their support to the Radical Republican cause and directing their seemingly inexhaustible energies toward the goal of freeing the slaves, Stanton and Anthony propounded a distinctive theory of the relationship between gender and politics. They never lost sight of the special agenda that women took into the public sphere. At the very first meeting of the Loyal Women's League, Susan B. Anthony put the issue of female suffrage to a vote. In Resolution 5 she included among the goals of the war that of securing the "rights and privileges of women" to "equal citizenship." The current mode of acting in the public sphere was not satisfactory to Anthony, who chafed at being "placed at the mercy of legislatures in which [she was] not represented." Anthony and Stanton called for women's suffrage in tones reminiscent of the Founding Fathers. They claimed their "birth right of freedom" as "daughters of the revolution" and members of "a Christian republic." The franchise, said Anthony, "is the fundamental principle of Democracy and before our Government can be a true democracy—before our republic can be put on true and enduring foundations—the civil and political rights of every citizen must be practically established."[35]

However impeccable this rendition of democratic theory, not even all the members of the Loyal Women's League were willing to extend it to their own sex. Mrs. Hoyt from Wisconsin led a concerted opposition to Resolution 5, calling it "obnoxious to most Americans" and therefore likely to jeopardize the abolitionist goals of the league. Although the resolution was passed over such opposition, it proved a pyrrhic victory for the Loyal Women's League. The attendance at the weekly meetings fell off precipitously thereafter. The league met regularly to perfect its techniques of circulating petitions, but it never recaptured public attention. For the remainder of the war and in the quiet after the storm of the draft riots, the public forum in New York City was dominated by the rallies of Republicans and Democrats, with their condescending appeals for the support of ladies.

The clearly articulated but quickly stalled cause of female suffrage was indicative of the hamstrung status of women in the public sphere in the 1860s. Stanton and Anthony had based the political claims of women on democratic principles. Yet most Americans, male, and female, were not ready to admit women directly into the liberal mechanisms of government. The call for citizenship without gender distinctions fell on ears that had been deafened by the glorification of woman's private place and her ceremonial position in the public sphere. At the same time, the veneration of the suffrage rang a bit hollow at a time when citizenship was exercised through highly ritualized and masculine partisanship. As popular political action increasingly took the form of torchlight processions and symbolic endorsements of party nominees, the franchise no longer seemed to translate automatically into effective participation in self-government.

Nonetheless, by focusing their efforts on winning the vote, advocates of women's rights made direct and independent claims on the public sphere on behalf of women. The suffragists added their sex to the growing list of social groups, based on ethnicity, class, and race, that vied for power in the public sphere. They both invoked universal democratic principles and singled out women as a group with specific claims on the public domain. In this early stage in the development of the women's rights movement, however, the category of gender was drawn in highly abstract terms that obscured the many social differences among women. The advocates of women's suffrage did not act on behalf of all women. The meetings of the Loyal Women's League, for example, did not concern themselves with the issues raised in the same city, at the same time, by working women. When seamstresses and umbrella workers met publicly in the fall of 1863 to demand higher wages, the women's movement did not rise to support them. The women's movement was also deaf to the clamorous politics of the women rioters. Elizabeth Cady Stanton rose from writing a speech on that July night in fear that her home would be ransacked by the mob. Her mind was not put at ease until, as she coolly put it, "a squad of police and two companies of soldiers soon came up and a bloody fray took place near us which quieted the neighborhood."[36] Stanton failed to hear or to champion the strained political voices of women less fortunate than herself. Rather, she acted very much the part of a middle-class property owner, calling on the state to protect her interests. The women's rights movement was entering the public sphere in a manner that reflected the political possibilities of the times. Its advocates proclaimed themselves champions of the political rights of all women—and, indeed, they were especially attentive to the condition of African-American women— but they gave voice to only a select few of the many substantive grievances that stemmed from gender inequality. They had only begun to identify the specific interests that a diverse citizenry of women might take to the halls of government.

Women Take Their Stand: Gender in a Fractured Public Sphere, 1865–1880

After the Civil War, women's political agenda would grow significantly but would be put forth in a remodeled public arena. Two parties resumed their electoral rivalries, battled over the reconstruction of the South, and contested for the prizes at stake in a more activist federal government. Simultaneously, the social groups that were visible within the public sphere before the war proliferated, acquired higher definition, and exposed class as well as ethnic tensions within the polity. Dim premonitions of interest-group politics were visible within the still exuberant party politics of the late nineteenth century. The shifting ground of American politics was apparent at the local level in the changing language of political mobilization. The public meetings that had given way to mass rallies before the war were now supplanted by calls to assemble as "committees" rather than as constituents. The "Central Executive Committee" of the Republicans called meetings in New Orleans. New Yorkers were advised of "mass meetings of influential citizens," and San Franciscans were informed of the deliberations of a "Committee of 25 Citizens." Committees, whether of twenty-five, seventy, or one thousand, spoke the language of political bureaucracy and introduced a new terminology to designate the individual's stake in the public sphere as well. They began to call themselves not citizens but taxpayers and intimated that they were linked to the commonweal by a private monetary function. The machinery of city government was also being renovated: its expanded operations were increasingly conducted by appointed commissioners rather than elected mayors, aldermen, and supervisors.[37]

Within this remodeled political organization, women expanded the political base that had grown up in earlier decades and had acquired particularly strong definition during the war. Their symbolic place in partisan politics had been securely established. In addition, some women became active agents of the parties themselves; gender still commingled with ethnicity, sometimes in violent ways; working women appeared more prominently in the protests of trade unions; and the call for women's suffrage became more distinct and voluble. Women and their interests, in other words, became more visible and more diverse, but competed for attention in a fractured and factious public sphere.

The end of the war did not halt women's participation in political ceremonies. Ladies were cordially invited to partisan rallies in all three cities. When Reconstruction brought black men into the public sphere, their womenfolk were also installed in the galleries and the balconies. At the increasingly perfunctory but elaborate and massive partisan rallies, women regularly added a feminine filigree to the rubber stamp that these meetings affixed to party nominations. At a "Grand Impromptu Union Mass Meeting" held in San Francisco in 1867, "front seats were principally occupied by ladies, who during the present campaign, more perhaps than any other, invest the hustings, if the expression may be used, with the charm of their presence." With the resurgence of the Democratic party in the South in 1877, white ladies were restored to their former seats of honor. Gathered at the inauguration of the first Redeemer mayor in New Orleans, they were told that Democrats acted not just for their own sex, but on behalf of the "feminine portion of the population, its better half who share also their property and liberty." The handkerchief battles of the Civil War left at least this rhetorical legacy.[38]

A few women had secured more instrumental roles in partisan politics. Throughout the war and thereafter, the Republicans had employed women such as Anna Dickinson of New York as lecturers. When Horace Greeley, long a champion of the less controversial women's causes, announced his candidacy for mayor in 1872, a host of women flocked to his campaign. Even Southern Democrats were made aware of a female presence in the electioneering process. A native New Orleansian and correspondent to the *Picayune* reported in 1880 that her sex was deeply involved in the fall presidential campaign. Although the author of "Women in Politics" disguised her name with the pseudonym "Drift," she was hardly shy about displaying her partisan fervor. She waded deep into partisan issues and was not above racist allusions and mudslinging. But most of Drift's report was devoted to describing the energy that seasoned political women like herself were expending on behalf of the Democrats, chiefly through their writing and public speaking. The biographical sketches drawn by Drift identified some of the public avenues that led women to the campaign trail. The suffrage movement, municipal

"The Inauguration of Governor Nicholls, on the Balcony of St. Patrick's Hall, New Orleans, January 8th," drawn by S. W. Bennett. Historic New Orleans Collection, Museum/Research Center, acc. no. 174.25.9.321.

reform, and even a stint in the theater steered these women to the public and partisan platform.[39]

One of these politicians, a Miss King, presented an especially colorful vignette of a nineteenth-century female on the hustings. A native of Maine, Miss King said she was "always a politician," or at least since age nine when she participated in the Clay-Jackson campaign. She dated her political initiation from a Whig procession in her native village, recalling, "I did not know why a girl should not hurrah for a president as well as a boy." So she crafted her own Jacksonian banner and carried it into the parade of the opposition. The leader of the rally rescued Miss King from a band of men who tried to evict her from the public sphere, and "so I was installed, with my flag, in the place of honor and permitted to start three cheers for Jackson." The guardians of the male bastion in the public sphere might have been forewarned that admitting females into even this ceremonial political role might nurture aspirations of a higher order.

After the Civil War, as before, women were loyal not only to their party but also to their ethnic group. Although they most often expressed allegiances in the decorous manner of the Maid of Ireland, on at least one occasion they became accomplices to bigoted and violent ethnic conflict. In New York in July of 1870, a group of

Thomas Nast, from *Civil Rights, The Hibernian Riot, and the "Insurrection of the Capitalists."*

CALIBAN "THIS ISLAND'S MINE BY SYCORAX MY MOTHER WHICH THOU TAK'ST FROM ME" Shakspeare.

Protestant immigrants from Ireland paraded to a picnic ground to celebrate the anniversary of the Battle of the Boyne. By invoking particularly ugly symbols of the Orangemen's victory over the Catholics some two hundred years before, the parade sparked a violent encounter with some Irish Catholics working on the construction of Central Park. Accounts of the mayhem dwelt on the attackers' disdain for gender distinctions; they engaged in fisticuffs and fired stones into crowds of men, women, and children. When the anniversary of the Battle of the Boyne drew near the following year, the prudence of permitting another such provocative celebration was debated in the state and local governments. After the governor invoked the rights of public assembly and countermanded the mayor's prohibition of the Orange parade, the stage was set for a bloody holiday on July 12, 1871. The Orangemen, facing a hostile audience along the parade route, voted to expel women and children from the parade. Nonetheless, women maintained their rights to the public streets by making a prominent and provocative appearance in the crowd of angry bystanders. According to the *Tribune,* "Women were most conspicuous by the vehemence with which they denounced Orangemen, police and soldiers alike." Accounts of the mayhem that followed dwelt on female provocateurs, the Catholic woman who stripped an Orangeman of his national colors, and the Protestant who donned orange skirts and teased the ethnic opposition by dancing a ribald can-can. In this charged atmosphere, the regiment of militia called up to protect the march of Orangemen lost control. The soldiers fired into the crowd, leaving forty persons dead, many of them women and children.[40]

This bloody incident, and women's roles within it, also played into major struggles for power in the municipality of New York. To some, the Orange Riots provided a frightening example of the cost of machine politics. The press, even the supposedly nonpartisan *Herald,* attributed the violence to the Irish domination of city politics. As middle-class, Protestant New Yorkers organized in the name of taxpayers to oust the Tweed Ring, they found rhetorical ammunition in bloody recollections of July 12, 1871. The pamphlet that inaugurated the anti-Tweed campaign, entitled *Civil Rights, the Hibernian Riot, and the "Insurrection of the Capitalists": A History of Important Events in New York in the Midsummer of 1871,* reveled in gender imagery. The strongly Irish city government's ruling to prohibit the Orange march was construed as an act to "emasculate the American." The crowd's unruly passions were personified by a "ferocious looking woman who rushed out from the sidewalk seized the regalia of one of the Orangemen, attempted to pull them from his shoulder . . . spit in his face and reproached her country men for their cowardice." The forces of reform, like the Hibernians, were represented by female symbols. The frontispiece of *Civil Rights* was adorned with two classic female allegories drawn by Thomas Nast to represent Liberty and Reform. Another cartoon portrayed municipal virtue as a terror-stricken female, who was besieged by a rapacious-looking personification of the rioters and the city machine, his features drawn in the standard simian caricature of an Irishman. Behind these feminine images and sexual innuendos stood male reformers from the elite classes, a "committee of 1000" who pledged not to pay municipal taxes until the city government opened its books for their review. By posing municipal contention as a confrontation between a "hibernian riot" and an "insurrection of the capitalists," the reformers of the 1870s construed politics as a volatile alloy of class and ethnic rivalry. They also used females to symbolize both contending parties.

The lower-class contingent in this rivalry also resorted to gender symbolism. In the 1870s in both New York and San Francisco, workers occupied public places to make demands on both their employers and their government. Tompkins Square on the Lower East Side of New York was the site of especially vocal lower-class politics during the depression of the seventies. The poor and unemployed who met there in 1877, a year of violent class conflict across the nation, marched on City Hall to demand public relief. At the same time, workers in San Francisco camped directly outside City Hall, which was under construction. Every week for over two years these "sand-lot meetings" drew thousands to the threshold of city government, and under the aegis of the California Workingmen's Party (CWP) they injected a potent brew of ethnicity, class, and gender into local and state politics.

The party's charismatic leader, Denis Kearney, downplayed his own Irish origins but nonetheless channeled class interest into ethnic and racial bigotry. The keystone of the party platform was the restriction of Chinese immigration. To better the position of white working-men, the CWP sought to exclude Chinese competitors from the American labor force. Kearney deftly orchestrated the political symbolism of racism and played on gender themes with special virtuosity. The women of the working class were key players in the CWP parade through the streets of San Francisco on Thanksgiving Day in 1877. This event and the party's weekly rallies were littered with slogans and banners evoking gender relations—appealing for the family wage, deriding Chinese bachelors, and raising the fear that your daughter "might marry one."

Working women were a key to Kearney's particular construction of political economy, for as domestic servants and laundresses they often bore the brunt of Chinese competition. This theory was inscribed on placards reading "Women's Rights to No More Chinese Chamber Maids" and acted out by men and women who dismantled Chinese wash-houses during the riots of July 1877. The party later organized a "Working Woman's Protective League," which defined women's interest as the suppression of Chinese domestic labor. The wife of an unemployed man, on the other hand, betokened her consort's right to a job. Unlike Chinese bachelors and prostitutes, the white male worker was portrayed as a respectable family man with children to support. (This picture, incidentally, did not conform to the actual household economy in the working-class districts of San Francisco, where bachelors abounded.) Finally, gender was used to fan the flames of opposition to capitalists as well as immigrants from China. The CWP staged burlesques of the higher social circles in which the ladies played central comic roles. (For example, the wife of Charles Crocker, a tycoon who employed the Chinese, was dubbed Mrs. Croaker.) Kearney was also upbraided in the press for his insulting public references to the wives of San Francisco's prominent citizens.[41]

The political strength of workingmen in San Francisco, like the Irish machine in New York during the same period, provoked a political resurgence among the middle and upper classes. As in New York, their political offensive was clothed in the rhetoric of gender. When a vigilance committee formed once again in San Francisco (this time to impose order in the wake of the small riot that followed a workingmen's rally in July of 1877), the assembled merchants took up arms to "protect wives, children and fortune." They condemned the profanity of the workingmen's meeting and the women who would be party to such vulgarity. Again, as in New York, San Francisco's municipal reformers focused on themselves as taxpayers, thus taking their private financial interests into the public arena. Gender and family were central to the taxpayers' political stance: they labeled themselves "citizens with land, wives and children."

Not just gender symbols, but women themselves, acquired an unprecedented prominence in the ethnic and class conflicts of the 1870s. The strident class antagonism of 1877 also brought lower-class women to the threshold of politics. Women appeared regularly at both the sandlot meetings of the CWP in San Francisco and on the rough-hewn public podiums in Tompkins Square. At both these rugged conventions within the public sphere, women were formally elected to positions of leadership. A Mrs. Heisler (or Hausler or Hansler, depending on the whim or accuracy of the reporter) assumed a central public place in the most militant New York protests in 1877. She spoke repeatedly, sometimes even for half an hour, and was elected a vice-president of this worker's parliament. Mrs. Heisler was of foreign birth and delivered her public addresses in Bohemian. Bohemia, by way of the cigar makers' union, was a major contributor of women activists. One-third of the striking cigar makers in 1877 were said to be Bohemian girls, who announced their public presence by actually marching through the streets: "Men, women and children came singly and in groups from shops, each shop bearing a flag and banners with inscriptions."[42] The women who gathered on the sandlots in San Francisco could not be dismissed as foreigners and communists quite so easily. The regular speakers bore names such as Mrs. Smith, Mrs. Greenwood, Mrs. Andrews, and Mrs. Sargent. Mrs. Anna Smith was the most familiar female speaker at the sandlots. Her tenacity and eloquence were officially acknowledged in 1880 when she was elected to chair the weekly meeting. In so honoring their comrade, the workingmen praised Mrs. Smith as a "mechanic" rather than a woman.[43]

If the women active in the working-class protests of the 1870s spoke to the special concerns of their sex, their words were seldom heeded either by their kinsmen or by the press. For example, after Mrs. Laura Kendrick called on San Francisco workers to share their wages with wives and children suffering from the depression, her husband took the floor, not to second this demand, but to propose resolutions relating to the corporations and the police. The few snippets from women's speeches that found their way into the newspaper either echoed the party line or couched women's interests in appeals to the welfare of family and community. "We ask these things in behalf of the peace and order of this community," said Anna Smith, "and also for the women and children who are well nigh desolate." In general, women appeared among the protesting workers to personify the extent of class needs and the respectability of worker claims, that is, to endorse the appeal for wages that would support the family. One workingman in New York, for example, took to the podium to explain that his earnings would not support his wife and five children. Appropriately, the New York workers called their movement a "Breadwinner's League." In symbol and in actuality, the interest of working-class women was still bound up with the family economy.[44] Women were more visible than ever in the sphere of class politics, but still clung to the shirttails of their husbands and fathers.

In sum, the principals in the political contests of the 1870s remained men, and they used gender references to shore up the position of their class and ethnic group. All parties to these public combats employed a Janus-faced image of woman. Her good face represented a kinswoman and confirmed the legitimacy of claims upon the public. Her bad face represented the irrationality of the opposition and vented sexual as well as class and ethnic antagonism. Either way, representations of women were liberally bandied about in the ethnic and class rivalries that buffeted the public sphere in the 1870s.

Predictably, then, gender would leave its mark on the most bitter political struggle of the time, the aborted reconstruction of race relations in the postwar South. Feminine symbols were especially prominent when the conquered Rebels attempted to reclaim local government from Radical Republicans, black and white. The first electoral effort to regain Democratic control of the city government of New Orleans in 1866 was called the White Camelia Campaign. That effort failing, New Orleans ladies practiced politics in time-honored feminine ways. They celebrated white supremacy by presenting flowers and banners at the graves of Rebels and at the major local institutions that survived occupation and reconstruction, such as the fire company and elite Mardi Gras clubs. One woman took direct action to restore the racial hierarchy: she had black children removed from a reception for the archbishop when they infringed on the territory claimed by white ladies. Southern ladies seemed poised to advance into politics on the strength of their experience as guardians of civic pride during the occupation.[45]

The initiation of congressional reconstruction was to delay the restoration of local authority for almost ten years. In the interim, black women had the opportunity to play the lady in politics. They were invited into the galleries and the balconies during political ceremonies like the anniversary of emancipation in 1869 called "to make the most of our manhood suffrage." As recounted elsewhere, black women played more effective and instrumental roles in reconstruction as well, helping to desegregate the streetcars, for example. In 1874, they took aim at another segregated institution, the public schools. In December of that year, three young scholars along with their teacher, a Miss Wood, appeared at the Girls Upper High School to demand admittance. Their efforts were rebuffed, however, by a reassertion of white women's politics. The first result of this attempted desegregation was to produce a flutter of offended honor among the white scholars of the girls' high school. But quickly, led by a teacher by the name of Mrs. McDonald, the girls took organized political action to maintain school segregation. They wrote, signed, and delivered a petition to the school board, threatening to withdraw from the academy should African-Americans be matriculated. When they found an account of their actions in the Republican press offensive, the same young women lodged a protest at this public institution as well and secured a public apology. Soon, young white men joined the segregationist campaign. They patrolled both the girls' and boys' high schools, driving out any pupils whose complexions did not pass their scrutiny.

The opponents of reconstruction, poised in 1874 to resume control of the city government, greeted this female political action with approval. They praised the young scholars who "stood out in bold defense of their dear rights as ladies. Bravo Mesdemoiselles." The *Picayune* went on to thank the ladies for defending "the honor of your race." These phrases seem a fitting epigram for the gender politics of New Orleans in the 1870s. Although the city had not spawned a women's rights movement, it was populated with women who were expert in waging symbolic political battles in defense of their race and class. That oxymoron the "rights of ladies" aptly characterizes this influential feminine mode of women's politics. And in New Orleans, women entered the public realm by proudly patrolling the racial divisions of the body politic, "to the honor of their race." Thus, it was not unexpected that when in September of 1874 the members of the White League of New Orleans took up arms to put an end to reconstruction, they posed their actions as a response to a written "Appeal of the Women to the Men of New Orleans."[46]

The Suffrage Movement: Defining the Political Interests of Women

Long before the centennial of the American Revolution, gender politics had been defined not just as the privileges of ladies but also and alternatively as a movement to advance the rights of women. By the 1870s, the second meaning of women's claim on the public sphere was familiar to most Americans. Both New York and San Francisco hosted woman's rights conventions whose deliberations were now accorded an almost respectful hearing in the press. The convention that nominated Victoria Woodhull for president in New York in 1872 was greeted with the least seriousness—for example, it was ridiculed by the *Herald* as a gang of long-haired men and short-haired women. But still the *Herald* printed a bold manifesto of woman's claim on the public sphere. Woodhull excoriated the "lordly arrogance of man" in presuming to determine the "sphere" of her sex, and then called for the "full participation of women in political affairs." The conventions in San Francisco in 1871 and 1880 made the franchise the center of their platform. One speaker made this demand with a peculiarly Western flourish. She boasted that her husband would "protect her with a six shooter when she went to deposit her ballot and thought that any man who would not do the same thing was not possessed of brains." A Mrs. Gordon put the case for the vote broadly in 1880: "All questions of reform were affected by and rooted in that of woman's suffrage."[47]

The story of how the nineteenth-century women's movement came to focus on the single issue of the franchise is a familiar one. A related, more complex and equally consequential reconfiguration of the movement has been charted with special care and insight by Ellen DuBois. By the close of the 1860s, catalyzed by bitter debates within the first civil rights movement, suffragists came to distinguish their interests as a sex clearly from those of African-Americans, once their allied claimants on the public sphere. According to DuBois, the Equal Rights Association was the chrysalis of an independent women's movement. When, in May of 1866, Stanton and Anthony convened the first meeting of the association in New York City, there were few harbingers of the conflict to come. Anthony's address at that meeting was uncompromising in its commitment to a conjoined movement to secure the rights of both women and African-Americans. It was her intention to "broaden our woman's rights platform and make it in name what it has ever been in spirit, a human rights platform. As women we can no longer claim for ourselves what we do not for others, nor can we work in two separate movements to get the ballot for the two disenfranchised classes, negroes and women." Stanton seconded this commitment at the next annual meeting. Denying that "sex or complexion should be any ground for civil or political degradation," she took her stand with the broadest, most hallowed interpretation of the public sphere: "that our government may be republican in fact as well as in form: a government by the people, and the whole people; for the people and the whole people."[48]

But in 1869 the Equal Rights Association disbanded in acrimony when Stanton and Anthony refused to condone a political strategy that seemed to place the civil rights of African-American males ahead of those of women, regardless of race. Only when the Radical Republicans' "negro first" strategy had succeeded in enacting the Fourteenth Amendment, which also attached the adjective *male* to constitutional privileges, did the advocates of women's suffrage set a new and separate political course. Stanton and Anthony formed an independent organization, the National Woman Suffrage Association (NWSA), for the single and express purpose of advancing the political cause of their sex.

Historians have plotted the course of the independent women's movement from 1869 forward, along several paths: the narrowing focus on suffrage, the byways into racism and xenophobia, the increasing recourse to domestic and feminine rhetoric. Most recently, Ellen DuBois has sketched a critical intervening chapter in this history, the attempt of the NWSA during the 1870s to base women's suffrage on the guarantee of national citizenship implicit in the Constitution. Only when the courts had rejected this interpretation did the suffrage movement focus on both amending the Constitution and justifying female enfranchisement in the language of gender difference and class exclusion—arguments to the effect that the votes of middle-class women would purify politics and counteract the influence of illiterate males.[49] Attention to women's voices in the public discourse of nineteenth-century cities introduces another theme into the history of the newly independent women's movement. In the 1870s, after women's rights advocates had staked out an independent women's politics, they began not only to elaborate gender differences but also to define the interests specific to women, and to employ expressly political methods of representing them.

The special interests that women took to the political arena in the 1870s were many and various. The women's rights movement, despite its focus on the franchise, placed a variety of measures on the public agenda, including married women's property rights, women's stake in temperance legislation, demands for equal access to public institutions of higher education, a single standard of sexual conduct, and equal pay for equal work. The suffrage conventions held in California recurrently appealed for higher remuneration for women's work; they documented their case by describing the needs of their own members, especially schoolteachers and a few seamstresses.

Working women's special interests were presented in the daily press with some regularity. The political demands of schoolteachers were front page news in San Francisco in 1870 when 120 teachers, mostly women, met, elected women officers, and appealed to the state legislature to defeat a bill that would reduce their pay. Susan B. Anthony appeared at a meeting of the National Labor Union in 1868, thereby extending her definition of gender politics to include the economic interests of working women. While this alliance would be brief, and although the suffragists seldom won support outside the ranks of middle-class, professional, or highly skilled women, an independent women's movement had begun to identify a range of issues that were the specific and exclusive interest of their gender.[50]

Advocates of woman's rights took these issues directly into the public sphere, not just to the press and along the lecture circuit but to the statehouse. One convention of the California Woman's Suffrage

Association, meeting in San Francisco, dispatched a delegation to Sacramento to plead their cause. Stanton and Anthony were familiar if not always welcome personages in Albany, where they aggressively and tenaciously worked to represent women's interests in the revisions of the state constitution. Horace Greeley called them the "most maneuvering politicians in the State of New York." While intensely political, these suffragists eschewed partisanship. Their experience with the Republicans in the 1860s destroyed their faith in national parties, and they ceded municipal politics to the noxious maneuvering of machines. More commonly they took women's interests as they had defined them to the state legislatures. In this they prefigured the interest-group politics of the twentieth century as they lobbied for their special interests. Although the women's movement was not a public sphere unto itself, and while suffragists avoided the major parties, which tried at least to accommodate multiple constituencies within the public, they were indeed seasoned politicians, ever-attentive to women's interests and indefatigable in voicing them before the government.[51]

Among the groups of women who clustered in and around the public sphere during the 1870s, the suffragists were the most intently conscious and single-mindedly attentive to the interests of their sex. Although their numbers may have been small, women were deployed all over the political map by the late nineteenth century. Their multiple stations in public life included the following: ladies waved their handkerchiefs in enthusiastic approval of the partisan actions of men; a few even took to the hustings themselves; another class of women mounted public podiums at the outdoor demonstrations of workingmen (only to find their economic needs and political interests buried in appeals for a family wage); a tenacious band of suffragists stepped forth to demand full and equal political participation for their sex. Gender also became more visible in the midst of militant, often violent political struggle outside the halls of government. These confrontations—the Orange Riots, the sandlot campaign, and the battles of segregationists—pitted one racial or ethnic group against another. Women were more active, visible, political, and public than ever before. Yet defining woman's politics as a focus of public debate, independent of men and united across race, ethnicity, and class, was still an unfinished business. Women's places were still marginal to a fractured public sphere, whose faultlines were ethnic and racial, and whose confusing interface was littered with troublesome gender symbols. But clearly women were in public life to stay, establishing a lineage and accumulating experience which we cannot ignore and from which we might take some instruction.

Summary and Conclusion

From the 1830s through the 1870s, women had clamored relentlessly and with ever-increasing vehemence and ingenuity to make their voices heard in the public sphere. Admittedly, neither their voices nor the concerns specific to their sex commanded the amount of attention or the degree of power enjoyed by men. To conclude that women were poorly represented in the public sphere, however, is not to say that politics was untouched by gender difference. The relationship between gender and politics was far more significant than the number of female actors on the public stage and the weight of explicit gender issues in public debate. At the very dawn of the Republic, as historians such as Linda Kerber and Ruth Bloch have demonstrated, citizenship was associated with manliness.[52] The rise of the party system and the age of the common man were accompanied by an elaboration of distinctly masculine rituals of partisanship. Gender symbolism and a ceremonial role for women became more elaborate in the 1840s and 1850s, just as the public sphere began to unravel into conflicting ethnic allegiances. Accomplices in the ethnic division of the public sphere in the antebellum period, gender symbolism and female politicians helped give stronger definition to class differences in the years after the Civil War.

If women and gender were accomplices in the fragmentation of the supposedly seamless public sphere into contending social groups identified by ethnicity and class, they were also agents of the reformulation of political practice. Female moral reformers, elite philanthropists, and suffragists pioneered the methods of interest-group politics and bureaucratic government that would mature into the welfare state and mass democracy of the twentieth century. All these female politicians were compelled by their disenfranchisement to devise alternate means of affecting public policy, including the direct lobbying of state officials and the placement of "private" family and gender issues on the public agenda. As historians such as Paula Baker have shrewdly pointed out, women's politics was a major factor in the transformation of the American political system that took place in the Progressive era.[53]

There is, in sum, considerable evidence to support the hypothesis that women politicians and the politics of gender were midwives to the birth of the welfare state and mass democracy. Jürgen Habermas and others paint this transformation of politics as the decline of the public sphere, but in the United States it might be evaluated in other ways as well. The articulation of social differences within the polity—ethnic, racial, class, gender—can also be seen as the making of

American pluralism, and as a step above and beyond the disembodied abstractions of republicanism and liberalism that had disguised the public's limited constituency of white male property owners. As long as class, race, ethnicity, and gender remain the bases of inequality, the political articulation of these divisions in the public, the representation of these "special interests," and the empowerment of marginal groups are positive steps in the expansion of the public sphere.

Yet pluralism came, haltingly and at a cost. First, the new configuration of American politics obscured some social differences as it highlighted others. To declare the political identity of an Irish Catholic, for example, might be to occlude consideration of injustices based on class or gender. Second, in the context of social and economic inequality, the politics of identity and difference could provoke bitter, violent, and racist confrontations, as the nativism, draft riots, and segregation of the nineteenth century repeatedly attest. Gender, and women too, were complicitous in these more troublesome aspects of an evolving interest-group politics. The exclusion of women from the Republic constituted a primary and fundamental fissure in the public sphere. Symbols of femininity inflamed racial and ethnic antagonism. The advocates of women's rights were hardly immune to the politics of exclusion—usually neglecting, sometimes disdaining, at other times competing against, the Irish, the illiterate, the poor, and the nonwhite.

Finally, a politics that becomes preoccupied with contests between special (that is, "private") interests can lose sight of the larger (that is, "public") good. It distracts attention from the commonality of the public sphere, "the explicit, reflective, achieved consensus reached by unconstrained discussion under conditions of freedom, equality and fairness," or, as Hanna Pitkin expresses it, "that shared, collective deliberate intervention in our fate."[54] The task of working out a common public purpose was often obscured by the ritual, the rancor, and the divisiveness of nineteenth-century politics.

Put simply, the nineteenth-century political system was not notably successful at balancing the legitimate needs of contentious social groups with the larger, overarching concerns of the people as a whole. Yet, the conflict, the irrationality, the tawdriness and sheer rambunctiousness of urban public life should not be confused with the breakdown of the commonweal. Hanna Pitkin puts the goal of the public sphere in less Olympian and more generous terms: "Although citizens must certainly share some degree of commonality to be and remain one community, there is room for much difference and conflict among them; and the mutuality politics requires is a recognition of similarity with difference, a peerhood that does not presuppose total equality, a capacity to continue to live together and act with others who are substantially, even offensively, different from oneself."

If the object of the public sphere is to ally difference and mutuality, then the politics of gender puts that idealistic formulation to a critical test. Because women often serve to represent the master "other" in the scheme of social differences, their place in the public sphere is a good measure of its viability. Pitkin, in the course of demonstrating how misogyny blemished the republican theory of Machiavelli, notes that "the relations with the opposite sex are perhaps the most common and certainly the most intimate example of this encounter with the 'other,' of the difficulties in achieving mutuality with difference." The plane of gender politics, therefore, might be the strategic place to work out the political alliance between difference and mutuality. If men and women can honor both sexual difference and human mutuality, the public discourse of the whole multifarious society might become more harmonious. Certainly the removal of the dualistic and oppositional gender symbols so ubiquitous in the nineteenth century might have reduced the distortion and perhaps some of the violence of public debate.

Since the days of Stanton and Anthony, the women's movement has not only demanded that men recognize their political commonality with women but has wrestled with the whole question of social and sexual difference. From the very outset, the women's movement worked to balance claims for equal and unbiased inclusion in the public with the need to represent the interests specific to their sex. In their struggles to define gender as a political and social category, feminists have repeatedly confronted differences within their sex—of race, class, ethnicity, religion, age, and sexual preference. In the last century, most notably in the debates of the Equal Rights Association and the brief efforts of Susan B. Anthony to include workingwomen in the suffrage coalition, women's rights advocates first confronted the ambiguity and volatility of gender identity, and dimly recognized the many social divisions that are fragilely accommodated within the term *woman*.

The history of women's entry into public life, begun so ardently and energetically in the last century, at least alerts us to the possibilities, the difficulties, and the importance of carrying forward the project that they initiated. We can take courage and wisdom from the energy, skill, and intelligence often demonstrated by our foremothers and forefathers; their activist's determination, their politician's perspicacity, their utopian dreams. The goal set by the founders, as amended by Elizabeth Cady Stanton in 1867, still remains before us: to remove "all discrimination on account of sex or race . . .

that our government may be republican in fact as well as in form: a government by the people, and the whole people; for the people and the whole people." The whole people has expanded to include a far wider constituency than when Stanton penned these lines, but convening the people, assessing our differences, and working out a just and shared fate still requires that women and men work together in time and place, in the public as history presents it. The search for the public continues, and for the same high stakes: as Hanna Pitkin puts it, "Only in public life can we jointly as a community exercise the human capacity to think what we are doing and take charge of the history in which we are all constantly engaged by drift and inadventure."[55]

Epilogue

Handkerchiefs, brickbats, and votes; prostitutes and politicians; the dangerous and the endangered; ladies, goddesses, and benevolent matrons, all strewn across the seemingly boundless space of the public. To set all these actors and props neatly on the stage of the public is an impossible, perhaps wrong-headed enterprise. By way of conclusion I shall merely juggle these motley relics of women and the public in the last century for a bit longer. Herewith, exploration gives way to speculation about the possible meanings that the placement of women in public holds for historians and citizens: its contribution to American historiography, its implications for theories of the public, its location in the contemporary debates about feminism and postmodernism. But first I shall briefly indulge in the historian's presumptuous predilection to construct a narrative and sketch the progression in which gender was inserted into public ceremony, space, politics, and discourse a century ago.

In 1825, at the arbitrary but heuristic beginning of my story, the urban public was the testing ground for republican notions of the common good. It was a public still overseen by elite and virtuous citizens, presented in pageantry strewn with classical images, and experienced in the quotidian mingling of the walking city. Gender, whose clearest mark was the female other set apart from universal man, appeared in public life in 1825 in evanescent and abstracted guises. Personified by the classical goddesses honored in public ceremonies, gender was at once the symbol of the Republic and a sign of the exclusion of women from its universal, rational, and disembodied plane of public deliberation. Barred from politics and government, denied the autonomous claim on property that girded the citizen for independence, yet mingling anonymously in everyday public life, women were a phantomlike public presence during that auspicious time when the Republic was planted on American soil.

Between 1825 and the outbreak of the Civil War, gender made a progressively more distinct and consequential impression on a remodeled public life. The female gender stood out in sharpest relief on ceremonial occasions, where she paraded not simply as a sexualized mark of exclusion but as a symbol of newly feminine civic values—chastity, sobriety, passivity, domesticity. The new gendered typography of public culture evolved at a time of democratic insurgency when a fuller array of citizens planted themselves in politics and in public space. The vast majority of the new political actors were male and emphatically masculine—the soldiers on parade, the manly Democrats of Tammany Hall, the breadwinners out on strike. But the elaboration of public politics also opened up territory for the expression of women's opinions, most fully enunciated by the female moral reformers of New York in the 1830s and 1840s. The issue that brought female reformers into the public arena, the protection of women from male seduction, was indicative of the most facile way of placing gender on the public agenda, by identifying women with their sexuality.

The increasing visibility of women in public was not, however, a discrete display of pure sexual difference. Rather, women as a category were tightly linked with other social groupings, political identities, and cultural categories. First, women and gender symbolism propped up ethnic and religious differences in the polity. Simultaneously, womanhood was subdivided along the axis of sexual propriety and social respectability into the dangerous and the endangered. By the 1850s, gender difference was distinct and public enough to figure prominently in the most vitriolic local conflicts—it became intertwined with the nativism, class antagonism, and partisanship that characterized vigilantism in New Orleans and San Francisco and the Wood machine of New York. By 1860, gender had appeared on the public stage as something far more complicated than the simple representation of the female sex.

At that epochal historical moment when American national politics erupted into civil war, public culture was crosshatched with gender differences, politics was riddled with the contentions of discrete interest groups, space was divided by sex, and women were beginning to add their voices to public discourse. The unprecedented politicization of life during wartime spotlighted and entrenched women in public. At the level of ceremony, gender paraded ever more bluntly and boldly—represented by the ladies who graciously championed Union and Confederate soldiers. At the same time, women

found room to maneuver in the contested urban spaces: they confronted Benjamin Butler, draft officials, and policemen in the streets.
These reconfigurations of gender in the public sphere would gain
coherence and definition after the war.

In the late 1860s and the 1870s, women took clearer if more
various stands in the public arena. Gender was posed in ever more
dualistic and naturalized guises—for example, in the comely forms of
goddesses of Liberty and maids of Erin—and attached itself to bolder
class and race distinctions, such as were seen in the rites of rich
women feeding poor children and the confrontations of black and
white during reconstruction. At the same time, women brought their
own concerns closer to the seats of power—to the platforms of workers in New York's Tompkins Square, to the sandlots outside San
Francisco's City Hall, to legislative debates regarding prostitution, to
state constitutional conventions, to women's rights conventions in
New York and San Francisco, and to the local battleground of reconstruction in New Orleans. In the last quarter of the nineteenth century, under the cover of a public language that recognized and acclaimed the private virtues of females, women were entering the
public carrying interests of their own and armed with a full stock of
political tools, from the symbols of feminized politics (e.g., handkerchiefs) to access to the ears of legislators (e.g., as lobbyists) to the
street weapons of the disenfranchised (e.g., brickbats) to a share of
state power (e.g., public funds for private charities). In this way,
women participated in, and sometimes pioneered, a reconstruction of
the public. Once seen as an Olympian citadel of virtuous and idealized male citizens, the American urban public had become a wide-
open arena of political contention.

No single part of the process that drew and redrew the borders
between public and private, male and female, can be isolated as a
first cause or primary structure. Men as well as women, elites as
well as the marginal, held genuine agency if unequal power in the
public arena. No single location in this diffuse and decentered public—neither the cultural, the spatial, the political, nor the discursive
stands out as the foundation and initiator of these wholesale changes.
Yet the men and women who lived in a concrete time and place, in
New York, New Orleans, or San Francisco, wove together a public
modus vivendi that was more diverse and vigorous than the founders
of the Republic could have anticipated.

The story of the making and engendering of the public amplifies,
if it does not answer, a number of questions that occupy historians
of the United States in their more contemplative moments. First, it
provokes some observations about the setting of these explorations,

the nineteenth-century city, and warrants a quick foray into urban historiography. Without engaging in the debate about the essence of the urban—whether it inheres in geopolitics, social and economic processes, administrative functions, or cultural vitality—it may be said that the search for the public in New York, San Francisco, and New Orleans highlights a unique aspect of urban history. When the city is seen as the testing ground for the viability of the public sphere, urbanism assumes a particular meaning often overlooked in historiography, which paints the city as space where teeming social problems meet the beleaguered forces of political and administrative containment.

Through the lens of this investigation the city appears at times so inveterately disorderly, so ridden with riot, vigilantism, and political conflict, that it lacks any center of indisputable authority. Yet, with a slight shift of perspective, the big city seems a miracle of human social organization with a magnanimous capacity to withstand diversity and conflict. My brief and oblique encounter with three unique urban landscapes paints the city as a historical location which, rather than concentrating social problems, distills possibilities for cultural exchange, social creativity, and political ingenuity. The jostling of differences in urban space, the concentration of immigrants from many shores, representatives of many cultures, different races, and disparities of wealth, created not just disorder but immense political possibility, not just problems of governance but potential for reading new meaning into the term *public*.

This potential of urban settings provokes speculation about "the American political tradition," the historiographic concern that has spun off schemes of liberalism and conservatism, consensus and conflict, and, of late, a serpentine interpretive thread called republicanism. From the vantage point of the urban public, the thread of republicanism appears as a thin rhetorical trace of the classical theories of the eighteenth century. Although invocations of the virtuous citizen as the mainstay of healthy public life echoed through the public discourse of these nineteenth-century cities, they were soon drowned out by the practice as well as the language of democratic insurgency. The public record surveyed here suggests that the practices labeled Jacksonianism should be restored to a central place in the American political tradition, as it calls attention to their social and cultural as well as partisan meaning. In the 1830s and 1840s, democracy appeared on urban turf not just as a party formation but as a civic culture intent on incorporating and representing the distinct social groupings within the urban populace (the proud divisions in the parades) and convening different constituencies around distinct interests and issues (the ubiquitous public meetings).

The recognition of this democratic and increasingly diversified public raises other thorny historiographic questions as well, namely the notions of American exceptionalism and pluralism. This exploration seems to give credence to the argument that American politics, in contrast to some European model, fostered ethnic and partisan rather than class divisions of the public. Ethnicity appears to be an especially potent solvent of the universalized and Olympian public. At the same time, this reformulation of the public, a simultaneous splintering of the commonweal and specification of the social constituents of the polity, did not create a simple pluralism, measured either in the equal political valences among individuals or in discrete boundaries between social groups. The distribution of power in the urban public was always measured by the varying degrees of political mobilization, economic resources, ingenuity, and aggressiveness of different groups. The process of creating political identities, furthermore, amputated or ignored some social characteristics as it selected others as the focus of solidarity.

To acknowledge and proceed to investigate this broad and colorful palette of American politics is to disrupt, but not to invalidate, the very concept that inspired this exploration. The idea of a public sphere, from Aristotle through Jürgen Habermas, is surrounded by an aura of unity and rationality, which the robust and contentious politics of nineteenth-century American cities seemed to hold in contempt. The closest intellectual kin of the Aristotelian notion in nineteenth-century American cities was the republican ideal, which installed the public good on an abstract plane where its presumptions of universality were belied by flagrant social exclusion on the basis of class, race, and gender. The early Republic too often sacrificed the colloquial meaning of the public as accessible, inclusive, and open to the normative standard of a virtuous, selfless responsibility for the good of an abstract whole.

My reading of nineteenth-century American cities locates the public on a historical plane where alone the common good can be allied with social diversity, albeit in a contentious and imperfect way. Here the public becomes the potential to put differences face to face, where they may be recognized, represented, and counted in publicly binding decisions. Nineteenth-century American public life was not enacted in some ideal hall of rational deliberation, in no modern-day acropolis or small town meeting, but on a fluid field of cultural, social, and political mobilization. In the big city, the historical, if not intrinsic, good was worked out at multiple points of public access. This process of creating a diverse and democratic public, begun over a century ago, has hardly been concluded. Given the recent wave of immigration to the United States and the global interdependence of the late twentieth century, it has only been transplanted to an even more diverse and global theater.

The shifting and problematic place of gender in the public sphere and the American political tradition leaves a particularly telling imprint on the history of democracy and pluralism. At the outset of the American experiment, women were insulated from republicanism, dismissed by classical theory, debarred by custom, frozen in sexualized symbols. As Linda Kerber has demonstrated, the ideology of the early Republic detoured women away from the public arena into the domestic responsibilities of "Republican Mothers."[1] Scholars of woman's sphere and the middle-class culture of the antebellum period have chronicled the progressive expansion and elaboration of this private domain of womanhood. Indeed, my own earlier work has argued that much of women's extra-domestic energy was invested in building up and out from this private realm.

But these essays should make clear as well that the public sphere itself was more than a netherland in the history of nineteenth-century women. When women appeared in public, however, they were easy game for incorporation as ornaments, dependents, or pawns of other identities—goddesses of Liberty, the nativist's "happy wife," or hostages to the "honor of her race." For women, moreover, a politics of identity posed some unique problems (at least from feminists' hindsight). On entering the public arena, women risked being categorized according to either sexual biology or gender stereotypes—as hapless victims of male vice or pure custodians of domestic virtue. Yet women's efforts to enter public life on their own terms were just as tenacious as the forces that excluded or occluded them. In fact, their political exclusion, particularly when combined with the relatively high economic and social status enjoyed by some classes of their sex, also made women especially resourceful and innovative in storming the public sphere—assembling, persuading, lobbying, reinterpreting the Constitution, and rioting. This legacy of women in public between 1825 and 1880 must be taken into account in any attempt to foster a heterogeneous and democratic public.

The place of women in the public, as theorized and promoted by feminism, helps us understand the nature of this ever-contested and changing sphere. The difficulties that women have encountered in their attempts to claim the right to enter that sphere illuminate the complexity and contradictions of stitching together a public out of social diversity. First, the problematic relationship between women and the public exposes the unstable and arbitrary elements of any social and political identity. In going public as a sex, nineteenth-century women inevitably obscured other salient stakes they held as individuals in the polity, based most predominantly on class, race, and ethnicity. The most politicized female claimants on the public realm, the advocates of women's rights, encountered these contradictions head-on. For example, while leaders of the women's movement such as Elizabeth Cady Stanton remained oblivious to working-class women in New York, they did, as Ellen DuBois recounts, give unprecedented attention to black women during the 1860s, only to retreat into white middle-class privileges and a politics of blunt sexual difference when their hopes of support from Radical Republicans were shattered.

The urban public of the nineteenth century also exposed the tendency of gender politics to decompose into essentialism and sexual reductionism. Those gender-specific issues that were especially likely to become formulated as issues of political interest in the municipalities of New York, New Orleans, and San Francisco focused on the specifically sexual behavior of women. The sexual reformers of the nineteenth century, from female moral reformers to anti-prostitution activists, have been justly acclaimed for their militant defiance of the double standard and their effective exercise of political power. This expressly sexual politics proved to be one of the easiest ways of translating gender into politics. But by virtue of its close links to reproductive biology, it also tended to reinforce essentialist definitions of women, cast the relations between the sexes in dualist and oppositional terms, obfuscate other issues, and objectify some women as sexually aberrant. These snares of sexual politics continue to haunt feminists, as is exhibited in the politics of pornography in the 1980s.[2]

In the late twentieth century, however, it is easier to decipher the intricate warp and weft of sex, gender, and social difference in the fabric of public life. In 1920, the Constitution was amended to grant women access to formal politics. Then the social movements of the 1960s, conjoined with the massive entry of women into the public labor force, began to actualize that promise of participation in the public sphere. It is now possible to see women clearly as political actors and to identify the interests of gender in public debates on a wide range of issues. Everything from the private conflicts between men and women, to women's personal rights to their own bodies, to the sexual inequality that lurks in the private sector of the economy has become the subject of public debate and public policy. In 1988, even the presidential campaign paid heed to those issues.

Yet, as women enter the public arena more directly than ever, they still encounter obstacles reminiscent of the nineteenth century: the manipulation of gender symbols, the obfuscation of gender justice by the bonds of kinship and family, and the occlusion of complex social differences in the politics of simplified and oppositional ethnic, racial, or gender identity. Contemporary men and women do not go blindly into the public arena which is still mined with the contradictions of gender politics. Since even before World War I, feminist thinkers have been suspicious of the cultural category *woman;* the new wave of feminists directly challenged gender identities and is now joined by deconstructionists in a frontal and concerted attack on the false universalism of the generic man and the categorization of woman as "other." To Jacques Derrida, "woman" designates the disruptive element in the whole system of Western logocentrism: "out of the depths, endless and unfathomable, she engulfs and distorts all vestige of essentiality, of identity, of property. And the philosophical discourse, blinded, founders on these shoals and is hurled down these depths to its ruin." In a recent synthesis of feminism and poststructuralism, Linda Alcoff illuminated some of the ways in which women might accrue political power and represent their gender without obscuring social heterogeneity or reverting to essentialism. Her epistemological guidelines are simple: to construe gender as a malleable historical creation, to represent women's interests as concrete and specific historical needs (and not extensions of roles decreed by biology), and to choose a social identity as a place of political action rather than an inherent quality of being and a decisive boundary with others.[3]

But a postmodern theory of difference is a relatively fragile building block of practical politics, and a weak foundation from which to assault the continuing inequity and injustice that clings to gender differences even amid the transformations of a postindustrial economy. For these refined conceptions to become guidelines for feminist change, they need to be grounded in political practices and social spaces, in some approximation of a public sphere. Here the countless women who began to make gender public in the last century offer guidance and hope. Against great political odds and despite emphatic cultural prohibitions, these citizens of New York, New Orleans, and San Francisco defied the boundaries of the public sphere to assert, however imperfectly and conflictually, the claims of a heterogeneous population for public consideration. The massive entry of women and of gender issues into the public sphere in recent times is a major sign of vitality in a public life that seems at times to have been reduced and distorted until it is little more than a domain of personalities, "public relations," and private greed. As women, those persons who from the outset of the democratic project have been the most patently and forcefully excluded social group, become fully and freely public they not only represent one gender but also challenge the unwarranted and outdated process of constructing others and consigning them to marginality. In such a broad and heterogeneous public, we set about the same painstaking tasks that confronted the urban citizenry over a century ago. Like the Locofocos in 1835, we must "assemble together to consult for the common good, to give utterance to our sentiments, to give instructions to our representatives, and to apply to the legislature for redress for wrongs and grievances, by address, petition and remonstrance." The search for the public still challenges the inventiveness of the people.

Notes

Introduction: In Search of the Public

1. Benjamin F. Butler, *Autobiography and Personal Reminiscences of Major-General Benjamin F. Butler; Butler's Book* (Boston: Thayer, 1892), 418.
2. Michelle Zimbalist Rosaldo, "Woman, Culture and Society: A Theoretical Overview," in *Woman, Culture, and Society,* ed. M. Z. Rosaldo and Louise Lamphere (Stanford, Calif.: Stanford University Press, 1974), 17–42.
3. Michelle Zimbalist Rosaldo, "The Use and Abuse of Anthropology: Reflections on Feminism and Cross-Cultural Understanding," *Signs,* suppl. 5 (1980): 389–417.
4. See Joan Wallach Scott, *Gender and the Politics of History* (New York: Columbia University Press, 1988). Scott boldly states that gender and politics "dissolve the distinction between public and private" (26).
5. Nancy F. Cott, *The Grounding of American Feminism* (New Haven: Yale University Press, 1987).
6. For the high valuation of privacy, see Barrington Moore, Jr., *Privacy: Studies in Social and Cultural History* (Armonk, N.Y.: M. E. Sharpe, 1984), and Jean Bethke Elshtain, *Public Man, Private Woman: Women in Social and Political Thought* (Princeton, N.J.: Princeton University Press, 1981).
7. See, for example, Richard Sennett, *The Fall of Public Man* (New York: Knopf, 1976).
8. Rosaldo, "Use and Abuse," 395; see also Martin King Whyte, *The Status of Women in Preindustrial Societies* (Princeton, N.J.: Princeton University Press, 1978), 57.
9. Sherry Ortner and Harriet Whitehead, eds., *Sexual Meanings: The Cultural Construction of Gender and Sexuality* (New York: Cambridge University Press, 1981).
10. Paula Baker, "The Domestication of Politics: Women and American Political Society, 1780–1920," *American Historical Review* 89 (1984): 620–47; Anne Firor Scott, "On Seeing and Not Seeing: A Case of Historical Invisibility," *Journal of American History* 71 (1984): 7–21.
11. For a brilliant and pioneering investigation of women in public life in Europe,

see Joan B. Landes, *Women and the Public Sphere in the Age of the French Revolution* (Ithaca: Cornell University Press, 1988).

12. Martin Krygier, "Publicness, Privateness, and Primitive Law," in *Public and Private in Social Life*, ed. S. I. Benn and G. F. Gaus (London: Croom Helm; New York: St. Martin's Press, 1983), 337.

13. For especially good maps through this territory, see Benn and Gaus, *Public and Private in Social Life* (cited in n. 12, above), and Anna Yeatman, "Gender and the Differentiation of Social Life into Public and Domestic Domains," *Social Analysis* 15 (August 1984): 32–50.

14. Hannah Arendt, *The Human Condition* (Chicago: University of Chicago Press, 1958), 48, 53.

15. Jürgen Habermas, "The Public Sphere: An Encyclopedia Article (1964)," *New German Critique* 5, no. 2 (1974): 49–55; see also Stephen K. White, *The Recent Work of Jürgen Habermas: Reason, Justice, and Modernity* (New York: Cambridge University Press, 1988).

16. Nancy Fraser, "What's Critical About Critical Theory? The Case of Habermas and Gender," *New German Critique* 35 (Spring/Summer 1985): 97–133; Hanna Fenichel Pitkin, "Justice, On Relating Private and Public," *Political Theory* 9, no. 3 (1981): 327–52.

17. Iris Marion Young, "Impartiality and the Civic Public: Some Implications of Feminist Critiques of Moral and Political Theory," in *Feminism as Critique*, ed. Seyla Benhabib and Drucilla Cornell (Minneapolis: University of Minnesota Press, 1987), 56–76.

18. The ongoing work of Joseph Logsdon provides a refined analysis of New Orleans Creole culture. My apologies to him and other scholars in this field for so glibly passing over their insights and distinctions for the time being.

19. Hendrik Hartog, *Public Property and Private Power: The Corporation of the City of New York in American Law, 1730–1870* (Chapel Hill: University of North Carolina Press, 1983); Jon C. Teaford, *The Municipal Revolution in America: Origins of Urban Government, 1650–1825* (Chicago: University of Chicago Press, 1975).

20. William M. Sullivan, *Reconstructing Public Philosophy* (Berkeley: University of California Press, 1982), 13.

1. *Ceremonial Space: Public Celebration and Private Women*

1. *Daily Alta California* (San Francisco), November 27, 1855.

2. For a compendium of theories on public ceremonies, see Clifford Geertz, *The Interpretation of Cultures* (New York: Basic Books, 1973); John Skorupski, *Symbol and Theory: A Philosophical Study of Theories of Religion in Social Anthropology* (Cambridge: Cambridge University Press, 1976), 84; Victor Turner, ed., *Celebration: Studies in Festivity and Ritual* (Washington, D.C.: Smithsonian Institution Press, 1982); John J. MacAloon, ed., *Rite, Drama, Festival, Spectacle: Rehearsals toward a Theory of Cultural Performance* (Philadelphia: Institute for the Study of Human Issues, 1984); Frank E. Manning, ed., *The Celebration of Society: Perspectives on Contemporary Cultural Performance* (Bowling Green, Ohio: Bowling Green University Popular Press, 1983); Mikhail Mikhailovich Bakhtin, *Rabelais and His World* (Bloomington: Indiana University Press, 1984), 255.

3. Susan G. Davis, *Parades and Power: Street Theatre in Nineteenth-Century Philadelphia* (Philadelphia: Temple University Press, 1986); Sean Wilentz, *Chants Democratic: New York City and the Rise of the American Working Class, 1788–1850* (New York: Oxford University Press, 1984).

4. Nellie Wetherbee, Diary, Bancroft Library, University of California, Berkeley, July 4, 1860; Anne Fader Haskell, Diary 1, Bancroft Library, July 4, 1876; Jane West Benedict, Diary, Louisiana Division, New Orleans Public Library.

5. Edgar Ewing Brandon, ed., *A Pilgrimage of Liberty: A Contemporary Account of the Triumphal Tour of General Lafayette through the Southern and Western States* (Athens, Ohio: Lawhead Press, 1944), 168, 173, 178; *Visite du Général La Fayette à la Louisiane, contenant les discourses qui lui ont été addresses. Les réponses qui'il y a faites. Par un citoyen de la Nouvelle-Orléans* (New Orleans: M. Cruzat, 1825), 52, 53; Mayors' Messages, Louisiana Division, New Orleans Public Library, January 26, 1825; Cadwallader D. Colden, *Memoire, Prepared at the Request of a Committee of the Common Council of the City of New York, and Presented to the Mayor of the City, at the Celebration of the Completion of the New York Canals* (New York: By Order of the Corporation, 1825).

6. Colden, *Memoire*, 30, 184.

7. Brandon, *Pilgrimage of Liberty*, 163–64; Colden, *Memoire*, 342, 229, 232, 254, 253.

8. Colden, *Memoire*, 129.

9. Colden, *Memoire*, 220.

10. *Evening Post* (New York), January 2, 1825; *Daily Picayune* (New Orleans), February 28, 1838; Leonard V. Huber, *Mardi Gras: A Pictorial History of Carnival in New Orleans* (Gretna, La.: Pelican, 1977), 8; Natalie Zemon Davis, "Women on Top," in *Society and Culture in Early Modern France: Eight Essays by Natalie Zemon Davis* (Stanford, Calif.: Stanford University Press, 1965), 124–51.

11. Gabriel Furman, "Winter Amusements in New York City," *New-York Historical Society Quarterly Bulletin* (1939): 3–18; Lucy Jones, Diary, Bancroft Library, January 1, 1875; *New York Tribune*, January 1, 1853; *Daily Alta California*, January 3, 1853; Frank Soule, John H. Gihon, and James Nisbet, *The Annals of San Francisco; Containing a Summary of the History of . . . California and a Complete History of Its Great City* (New York: Appleton, 1855), 673.

12. See Mary P. Ryan, "The American Parade Representations of the Nineteenth-Century Social Order," in *The New Cultural History*, ed. Lynn Hunt (Berkeley: University of California Press, 1989).

13. Jean Gould Hales, " 'Co-Laborers in the Cause': The Women in the Ante-Bellum Nativist Movement," *Civil War History* 25, no. 2 (1979): 119–38; *New York Herald*, October 15, 1842.

14. *New York Herald*, September 1, 1858.

15. *Irish American Weekly*, March 23, 1861, March 28, 1857.

16. *Irish American Weekly*, March 28, 1857, March 27, 1858.

17. *Irish American Weekly*, March 23, 1862, March 28, 1863.

18. *New York Tribune*, December 25, 1841.

19. *New York Tribune*, December 25, 1844.

20. *Daily Alta California*, January 3, 1853.

21. *New York Tribune*, December 25, 1859; *Daily Alta California*, December 24,

1859; *New York Tribune,* December 26, 1853, December 4, 1855.

22. Glenna Matthews, *"Just a Housewife": The Rise and Fall of Domesticity in America* (New York: Oxford University Press, 1987), 43.

23. *The Old Brewery, and the New Mission House at the Five Points. By the Ladies of the Mission* (New York: Stringer and Townsend, 1854), 273.

24. *Brewery,* 276–77.

25. *Brewery,* 275–76.

26. *Brewery,* 277–78.

27. *New York Tribune,* July 3, 1848.

28. See MacAloon, *Rite, Drama, Festival,* and also Lawrence W. Levine, *Highbrow/Lowbrow: The Emergence of Cultural Hierarchy in America* (Cambridge: Harvard University Press, 1988).

29. *New York Herald,* July 6, 1875.

30. *Daily Picayune,* March 5, 1872.

31. *Daily Picayune,* September 5–15, 1877.

32. *New York Herald, New York Tribune,* May 18–25, 1883.

33. *Irish American Weekly,* March 24, 1866.

34. *Daily Picayune,* February 23, 1871. The kind of ceremonial reversal of sex roles described by Natalie Davis in her classic essay "Women on Top" may have operated in early New Orleans carnivals but was no longer appropriate in the gender economy of the late nineteenth century.

35. *New York Times,* May 18, 1877.

36. *L'Abeille de la Nouvelle Orleans [New Orleans Bee],* November 5, 1866; *Daily Picayune,* November 26, 1877.

37. Records of the Ladies Benevolent Association, Louisiana Historical Association, Tulane University Archives; *New Orleans Bulletin,* April 11, 1874; Gaines M. Foster, *Ghosts of the Confederacy: Defeat, the Lost Cause, and the Emergence of the New South, 1865 to 1913* (New York: Oxford University Press, 1987), 37–46.

38. Samuel MacKeever, *Glimpses of Gotham, and City Characters* (New York: National Police Gazette Office, 1880), 29–32.

39. Lynn Hunt, *Politics, Culture, and Class in the French Revolution* (Berkeley and Los Angeles: University of California Press, 1984), 61–66; Maurice Agulhon, *Marianne into Battle: Republican Imagery and Symbolism in France, 1789–1880* (New York: Cambridge University Press, 1981); Joan B. Landes, *Women and the Public Sphere* (Ithaca: Cornell University Press, 1988).

40. See Mary P. Ryan, *The Cradle of the Middle Class: The Family in Oneida County, New York, 1790–1865* (New York: Cambridge University Press, 1981).

41. Victor Turner, *"Carnaval* in Rio: Dionysian Drama in an Industrializing Society," in Manning, *Celebration of Society,* 103–24.

2. *Everyday Space: Gender and the Geography of the Public*

1. Henry James, *The Speech and Manners of American Women,* ed. E. S. Riggs (Lancaster, Pa.: Lancaster House Press, 1973), 15, 31.

2. Guillermo Prieto, *San Francisco in the Seventies: The City as Viewed by a Mexican Political Exile,* trans. and ed. Edwin S. Morby (San Francisco: J. H. Nash, 1938), 8; the Italian visitor to Boston at the turn of the century is quoted in Gunther Barth, *City People: The Rise of Modern City Culture in*

Nineteenth-Century America (New York: Oxford University Press, 1980), 121.

3. Emrys Jones and John Eyles, *An Introduction to Social Geography* (New York: Oxford University Press, 1977); Samuel B. Halliday, *The Lost and Found; or, Life among the Poor* (New York: Blakeman and Mason, 1859).

4. Kenneth Alan Scherzer, "The Unbounded Community: Neighborhood Life and Social Structure in New York City, 1830–1875" (Ph.D. diss., Harvard University, 1982); Steven Philip Erie, "The Development of Class and Ethnic Politics in San Francisco, 1870–1910: A Critique of the Pluralist Interpretation" (Ph.D. diss., UCLA, 1975); Lewis William Newton, *The Americanization of French Louisiana: A Study of the Process of Adjustment between the French and Anglo-American Population of Louisiana, 1803–1860* (New York: Arno Press, 1980).

5. Junius Browne, *The Great Metropolis: A Mirror of New York* (Hartford, Conn., 1867), 28–29.

6. Lyn H. Lofland, *A World of Strangers; Order and Action in Urban Public Space* (New York: Basic Books, 1970), 19.

7. Philippe Ariès, "The Family and the City," *Daedalus* 106 (1977): 227–35. Quotations in this paragraph appear in Grace Elizabeth King, *New Orleans: The Place and the People* (New York: Macmillan, 1895), 264.

8. Henry C. Castellanos, *New Orleans as It Was: Episodes of Louisiana Life* (New York: L. Graham, 1895), 145–47; Marion Southwood, *"Beauty and Booty": The Watchword of New Orleans* (New York: for the author by M. Doolady, 1867), 223; George Washington Cable, "The Dance in Place Congo," *Century Magazine* 31 (1886): 517–32.

9. Helen Throap Purdy, "Portsmouth Square," *California Historical Society Quarterly* 3 (1924): 30–44; George Tays, "Portsmouth Plaza," typescript, Works Progress Administration, 1936, Bancroft Library, University of California, Berkeley; Charles H. Haswell, *Reminiscences of an Octogenarian of the City of New York (1816–1860)* (New York: Harper, 1896), 18.

10. *Daily Picayune* (New Orleans), November 9, 1837; Judge E. D. Crosby, "Statement of Events in California as Related for the Bancroft Library," 1870, Bancroft Library, 123; Thomas F. De Voe, *The Market Book, Containing a Historical Account of the Public Markets in the Cities of New York, Boston, Philadelphia, and Brooklyn, with a Brief Description of Every Article of Human Food Sold Therein* (New York: for the author, 1862), 584–85; Christine Stansell, *City of Women: Sex and Class in New York, 1789–1860* (New York: Knopf, 1986).

11. Celia Morris Eckhardt, *Fanny Wright: Rebel in America* (Cambridge: Harvard University Press, 1984), 258–67.

12. Tyrone Power, *Impressions of America; During the Years 1833, 1834, and 1835* (London: Bentley, 1836), 72–73, 180; Lewis A. Erenberg, *Steppin' Out: New York Nightlife and the Transformation of American Culture, 1890–1930* (Westport, Conn.: Greenwood Press, 1981).

13. Thomas Bender, *New York Intellect: A History of Intellectual Life in New York City from 1750 to the Beginnings of Our Own Time* (New York: Knopf, 1987), 36–38.

14. *Daily Alta California* (San Francisco), July 9, 1855.

15. *Daily Picayune*, December 15, 1851.

16. Augustine E. Costello, *Our Police Protectors: A History of the New York Police*

(1885; Montclair, N.J.: Patterson Smith, 1972), 116, 216; *Daily Picayune,* February 4, 1867.

17. Isaac S. Lyon, *Recollections of an Old Cartman* (New York: New York Bound, 1984), 27–33; *New York Tribune,* September 28, 1857; *Daily Alta California,* June 3, 1855.

18. George Ellington, *The Women of New York; or, Social Life in the Great City* (New York: New York Book Co., 1869), 207; Rev. E. H. Chapin, *Humanity in the City* (New York: DeWitt and Davenport, 1854), 21.

19. *New York Tribune,* July 5, 1869.

20. Browne, *Great Metropolis,* 439; Ellington, *Women of New York,* 261; Edward Crapsey, *The Nether Side of New York; or, the Vice, Crime, and Poverty of the Great Metropolis* (New York: Sheldon, 1872), 122.

21. Crapsey, *Nether Side,* 138; Thomas L. Harris, *Juvenile Depravity and Crime in Our City: A sermon . . . Preached in the Stuyvesant Institute . . . Jan. 13th, 1850* (New York: C. B. Norton, 1850), 4; Browne, *Great Metropolis,* 274; George Foster, *New York by Gas-light: With Here and There a Streak of Sunshine* (New York: DeWitt and Davenport, 1850), 15.

22. J. W. Buel, *Mysteries and Miseries of America's Great Cities, Embracing New York, Washington City, San Francisco, Salt Lake City, and New Orleans* (San Francisco: A.L. Bancroft, 1883), 43, 85.

23. Browne, *Great Metropolis,* 129, 276, 507; Marie Louise Hankins, *Women of New York* (New York: by the author, 1860), 9; *Daily Alta California,* June 1, 1855; *Daily Picayune,* April 22, 1846.

24. Mary Douglas, *Purity and Danger: An Analysis of the Concepts of Pollution and Taboo* (New York: Praeger, 1966), 4.

25. Harry E. Resseguie, "A. T. Stewart's Marble Palace—The Cradle of the Department Store," *New-York Historical Society Quarterly* 48 (1964): 131–62.

26. Ralph M. Hower, *History of Macy's of New York, 1858–1919: Chapters in the Evolution of the Department Store* (Cambridge: Harvard University Press, 1943); Robert Hendrickson, *The Grand Emporiums: The Illustrated History of America's Great Department Stores* (New York: Stein and Day, 1979); *Daily Picayune,* November 1, 1868.

27. Charles Lockwood, *Manhattan Moves Uptown: An Illustrated History* (Boston: Houghton Mifflin, 1976), 150, 296; M. Christine Boyer, *Manhattan Manners: Architecture and Style, 1850–1900* (New York: Rizzoli, 1985), 42–46; Ellington, *Women of New York,* 388.

28. Benjamin Lloyd, *Lights and Shades in San Francisco* (San Francisco: A. L. Bancroft, 1876), 115–20; *Daily Picayune,* September 26, 1862.

29. Frederick Law Olmsted, *Public Parks and the Enlargement of Towns* (Cambridge, Mass.: for the American Social Science Association, at the Riverside Press, 1870), 6–7; *San Francisco Newsletter,* August 28, 1869.

30. *Report of the San Francisco Park Commissioners* (San Francisco, 1874), 78–79; *Statutes, Ordinances, and Laws Relating to the Park Commissioners of the City and County of San Francisco,* comp. Harold Wheeler (San Francisco, 1894), 73; Charles E. Beveridge and David Schuyler, eds., *The Papers of Frederick Law Olmstead* (Baltimore: Johns Hopkins University Press, 1983), 3:279.

31. Galen Cranz, "Women in Urban Parks," *Signs* suppl. 5 (1980): 79–95.

32. Browne, *Great Metropolis,* 123; Melvin Leonard Adelman, "The Develop-

ment of Modern Athletics: Sport in New York City, 1820–1870" (Ph.D. diss., University of Illinois at Urbana-Champaign, 1980), 623.

33. Foster, *Gas-light,* 88.
34. Peter George Buckley, "To the Opera House: Culture and Society in New York, 1820–1860" (Ph.D. diss., State University of New York at Stony Brook, 1984), chap. 6.
35. *Daily Picayune,* January 9, 1858; *Irish American Weekly,* March 24, 1850.
36. *Daily Picayune,* February 13, 1872.
37. Adelman, "Modern Athletics," 623.
38. Ellington, *Women of New York,* 301; George Foster, *New York in Slices: by an Experienced Carver: Being the Original Slices Published in the N.Y. Tribune* (New York: Wm. H. Graham, 1849), 99.
39. Lydia Maria Child, *Letters from New York* (1844; New York: C. S. Francis, 1850), 96–99, 167.
40. Lucy Jones, Diary, Bancroft Library, University of California, Berkeley, 1874.
41. Stansell, *City of Women;* Foster, *Gas-light,* 106–8.
42. Fredrika Bremer, *Homes of the New World: Impressions of America,* trans. Mary Howitt (New York: Harper, 1854), 325; *The Old Brewery, and the New Mission House at the Five Points. By the Ladies of the Mission* (New York: Stringer and Townsend, 1854), 45–55; Helen M. Sweeney, *The Golden Milestone, 1846–1896: Fifty Years of Loving Labor among the Poor and Suffering, by the Sisters of Mercy of New York City* (New York: Benzigan, 1896), 44.
43. Anne Fader Haskell, Diary 1, Bancroft Library, February 11, June 30, 1877.
44. *Journal of Julia Le Grand, New Orleans, 1862–1863,* ed. Mrs. Morris L. [Agnes Browne] Croxall (Richmond, Va.: Everett Waddey Co., 1911), 286–87.
45. Nellie Wetherbee, Diary, Bancroft Library, May 4, 1860.
46. Samuel MacKeever, *Glimpses of Gotham, and City Characters* (New York: National Police Gazette Office, 1880), 13.
47. Child, *Frugal Housewife,* 96–99; Sarah Morgan Dawson, *A Confederate Girl's Diary* (Boston: Houghton Mifflin, 1913), 82–83.
48. Wetherbee, January 9, December 22, 1860; Haskell, June 16, 1876.
49. Timothy J. Gilfoyle, "City of Eros: New York City, Prostitution, and the Commercialization of Sex, 1790–1820" (Manuscript), chaps. 2, 7, 9.
50. Scherzer, "Unbounded Community," 324–25; Foster, *Gas-light,* 6.
51. Ellington, *Women of New York,* 171.
52. George Walling, *Recollections of a New York Chief of Police* (New York: Caxton Book Concern, 1887), 479–84.
53. Ellington, *Women of New York,* chap. 40; Walling, *Recollections,* 484.
54. *A Digest of the Charters and Ordinances of, and relating to, the City of New York* (New York, 1866), 2:654, 658.
55. *Digest of Ordinances* (New Orleans, 1866), 278.
56. *Digest of New York Ordinances,* 455.
57. New Orleans *Digest of Ordinances,* 274; *A Compilation of Parts of the Consolidated and Other Acts Now in Force relating to the Powers and Duties of the Police Department of San Francisco* (San Francisco, 1870).
58. M. Gottdiener, *The Social Production of Urban Space* (Austin: University of Texas Press, 1985).
59. Cited in ibid., 153.

60. James M. MacPherson, *The Struggle for Equality: Abolitionists and the Negro in the Civil War and Reconstruction* (Princeton, N.J.: Princeton University Press, 1964); *New Orleans Tribune*, May 4, 9, 1867.
61. Alcée Fortier, *A History of Louisiana*, vol. 3 (New York: Goupil Co., 1904), 139–57.

3. Political Space: Of Prostitutes and Politicians

1. *New York Evening Post*, July 9, 1831.
2. Barbara Meil Hobson, *Uneasy Virtue: The Politics of Prostitution and the American Reform Tradition* (New York: Basic Books, 1987), 5.
3. Arthur B. Spingarn, *Laws Relating to Sex Morality in New York* (New York: Century Co., 1915); *Revised Statutes of New York* (New York, 1829), 1:638; Larry Howard Whiteaker, "Moral Reform and Prostitution in New York City, 1830–1860" (Ph.D. diss., Princeton University, 1977), 30.
4. *Digest of Ordinances* (New Orleans, 1846), 92; Mayors' Papers, New Orleans Public Library.
5. Timothy J. Gilfoyle, "City of Eros: New York City, Prostitution, and the Commercialization of Sex, 1790–1920" (Manuscript), 157–60.
6. Whiteaker, "Moral Reform," 36.
7. *New York Evening Post*, August 22, 1831.
8. From the Magdalen Report, as cited in the *New York Evening Post*, July 11, 1831.
9. Carroll Smith-Rosenberg, *Disorderly Conduct: Visions of Gender in Victorian America* (New York: Knopf, 1985).
10. Whiteaker, "Moral Reform," 255.
11. Ibid., 255.
12. Ibid., 276.
13. *New York Daily Times*, September 22, 1855. See also James F. Richardson, "Mayor Fernando Wood and the New York Police Force, 1855–57," *New-York Historical Society Quarterly* 1 (1966): 5–40.
14. City Clerk's Approved Papers, Document no. 44, 1833, Municipal Archives of the City of New York; Gilfoyle, "City of Eros," chap. 3.
15. Jacqueline Baker Barnhart, *The Fair but Frail: Prostitution in San Francisco, 1849–1900* (Reno: University of Nevada Press, 1986), 36; Robert M. Senkewicz, *Vigilantes in Gold Rush San Francisco* (Stanford, Calif.: Stanford University Press, 1985).
16. *Ordinances and Joint Resolutions of the City of San Francisco* (San Francisco, 1854), 264–65.
17. *Daily Alta California*, November 23–29, 1855; January 22–23, 29, February 2, 11, March 24–25, April 11, 1856.
18. *San Francisco Bulletin*, January 16, 1856.
19. *San Francisco Bulletin*, June 21–24, February 1, 16, 1856.
20. *Daily Alta California*, May 16, 1856.
21. *Daily Alta California*, June 8, 11, 13, 15, 19, July 9, 19, August 2, 19, 22, 23, 1856.
22. Robert W. Cherney and William Issel, *San Francisco, Presidio, Port, and Pacific Metropolis* (San Francisco: Boyd and Fraser, 1981); Cherney and Issel, *San Francisco, 1865–1932: Politics, Power, and Urban Development* (Berkeley:

University of California Press, 1986); R. A. Burchell, *The San Francisco Irish, 1848–1880* (Berkeley: University of California Press, 1980); and Mary Floyd Williams, *History of the San Francisco Committee of Vigilance of 1851* (Berkeley: University of California Press, 1921).

23. *Daily Picayune*, March 25, 1854.
24. *The Laws and Ordinances of the City of New Orleans* (New Orleans, 1857), 376–80.
25. Richard Tansey, "Prostitution and Politics in Antebellum New Orleans," *Southern Studies* 18 (1979): 449–79.
26. *San Francisco Municipal Reports*, 1860–1881.
27. *Annual Report of the Board of Commissioners of the Metropolitan Police*, 1867–1870; William Sanger, *The History of Prostitution: Its Extent, Causes, and Effects Throughout the World* (New York: Harper, 1859); Gilfoyle, "City of Eros," chap. 1.
28. Dennis Charles Rousey, "The New Orleans Police, 1805–1889: A Social History" (Ph.D. diss., Cornell University, 1978), 247.
29. *San Francisco Municipal Report, 1865–66* (San Francisco, 1866), 126; on Chinese prostitution in San Francisco, see Lucie Cheng Hirata, "Free, Indentured, Enslaved: Chinese Prostitutes in Nineteenth-Century America," *Signs* 5 (1979): 3–29.
30. *San Francisco Municipal Report, 1865–66*, 139.
31. George W. Walling, *Recollections of a New York City Chief of Police* (New York, 1887), 579 passim.
32. Sanger, *History of Prostitution*, 629, 643.
33. *Annual Report of the Metropolitan Board of Health* (Albany, 1867), 300–307; *New York Herald*, February 1, 1867; Sanger, *History of Prostitution*, 647.
34. *New York Times*, February 5, 1867; *New York Herald*, February 1, 1867.
35. *San Francisco Chronicle*, December 5, 1869.
36. *Daily Alta California*, April 21, 1874.
37. Timothy Gilfoyle, "The Moral Origins of Political Surveillance: The Preventive Society in New York City, 1867–1918," *American Quarterly* 38 (1986): 637–52; *Fourth Annual Report of the New York Society for the Suppression of Vice* (New York, 1878), 9.
38. *First Annual Report of the New York Society for the Suppression of Vice* (New York, 1874), 1–6.
39. *Annual Report of the New York City Five Points House of Industry* (New York, 1857–1909), 17.
40. *Annual Report of Five Points*, 20, 16.
41. Mayor's Approved Papers, 1878, Municipal Archive, City of New York.
42. Mayor's Approved Papers, New York.
43. *First Annual Report of the Midnight Mission* (New York, 1866), 10–11, 24.
44. See Alexander Saxton, *Indispensable Enemy: A Study of the Anti-Chinese Movement in California* (Berkeley: University of California Press, 1971) on the campaign against the Chinese in California.
45. Peggy A. Pascoe, "The Search for Female Moral Authority: Protestant Women and Rescue Homes in the American West, 1874–1939" (Ph.D. diss., Stanford University, 1986), 46–48, 106–32.
46. Ibid., 135–65.
47. Aaron M. Powell, *State Regulation of Vice* (New York, 1878), 39; Aileen S.

Kraditor, ed., *Up from the Pedestal: Selected Writings in the History of American Feminism* (Chicago: Quadrangle Books, 1968), 159–67.

48. Mrs C.[aroline] M. Churchill, "The Social Evil: Which Do You Prefer?" Broadside, Bancroft Library.

49. *San Francisco Call,* October 17, 1871.

50. Nanette B. Paul, *The Great Woman Statesman:* An Abstract of "The Life and Labor of Susan B. Anthony," by Ida Harper (New York, 1925).

51. Sarah Hopper Emerson, ed., *Life of Abby Hopper Gibbons* (New York: Putnam's, 1897), 180.

52. Rachel Amelia Bernstein, "Boarding-House Keepers and Brothel Keepers in New York City, 1880–1910" (Ph.D. diss., Rutgers University, 1984); Gilfoyle, "City of Eros," 378; "A Citizen" to Henry Ellis, Chief of Police, February 26, 1876, Henry Hiram Ellis Papers, MS 3012/6 Letters, California Historical Society.

53. *Daily Alta California,* March 10, 1857; *Annual Report of Five Points,* 19; Phil Johnson, "Good Time Town," in *The Past as Prelude: New Orleans, 1718–1968,* ed. Hodding Carter (New Orleans: Tulane University Press, 1968), 236–37.

54. Judith Walkowitz, "Male Vice and Feminist Virtue: Feminism and the Politics of Prostitution in Nineteenth-Century Britain," *History Workshop Journal* 13 (Spring 1982): 79–93.

4. The Public Sphere: Of Handkerchiefs, Brickbats, and Women's Rights

1. Ronald P. Formisano, "Toward a Reorientation of Jacksonian Politics: A Review of the Literature, 1959–1975," *Journal of American History* 63 (1976): 42–65; Richard L. McCormick, *The Party Period and Public Policy: American Politics from the Age of Jackson to the Progressive Era* (New York: Oxford University Press, 1986); Michael E. McGerr, *The Decline of Popular Politics: The American North, 1865–1928* (New York: Oxford University Press, 1986); Morton Keller, *Affairs of State: Public Life in Late Nineteenth-Century America* (Cambridge: Harvard University Press, 1977).

2. Paula Baker, "The Domestication of Politics: Women and American Political Society, 1780–1920," *American Historical Review* 89 (1984): 620–47; Carl N. Degler, *At Odds: Women and the Family in America from the Revolution to the Present* (New York: Oxford University Press, 1980), chap. 14.

3. *Working-man's Advocate,* May 22, 1830; *New York Evening Post,* July 2, 1827, March 28, April 5, 1834; *Daily Alta California,* February 15, 1849; *New Orleans Tribune,* May 31, June 2, November 29, 1867.

4. *Evening Post,* February 3, August 26, 1835; *Daily Picayune,* November 22, 27, 1837.

5. *Evening Post,* October 30, 1835.

6. *L'Abeille de la Nouvelle Orleans [New Orleans Bee],* February 23, 1845.

7. Celia Morris Eckhardt, *Fanny Wright, Rebel In America* (Cambridge: Harvard University Press, 1984), 258–67.

8. Cited in Leonard Richards, *"Gentlemen of Property and Standing": Anti-Abolition Mobs in Jacksonian America* (New York: Oxford University Press, 1970), 115.

9. Robert Gray Gunderson, *The Log-Cabin Campaign* (Lexington: University of Kentucky Press, 1957), 135, 190, 245.

10. *Daily Picayune,* January 9, July 4, 1840, January 9, 1847; *New York Herald,* January 11, 1848.

11. *Daily Picayune,* December 4, 1847, November 1, 1851, November 1, 1849.

12. *Daily Picayune,* July 4, 1844; *New York Tribune,* January 27, March 25, 1847.

13. *New York Herald,* March 25, 1847.

14. *New York Tribune,* March 19, 1850; *New York Times,* November 11, 1854; *New York Herald,* November 24, 1857.

15. Robert W. Cherney and William Issel, *San Francisco, Presidio, Port, and Pacific Metropolis* (San Francisco: Boyd and Fraser, 1981); Richard Tansey, "Prostitution and Politics in Antebellum New Orleans," *Southern Studies* 18 (1979): 449–79; R. A. Burchell, *The San Francisco Irish, 1848–1880* (Berkeley: University of California Press, 1980), 117–32; *Daily Alta California,* May 24, 1855; *Irish American Weekly,* December 2, 1854.

16. Lee Benson, *The Concept of Jacksonian Democracy: New York as a Test Case* (Princeton: Princeton University Press, 1961); Amy Bridges, *A City in the Republic: Antebellum New York and the Origins of Machine Politics* (Cambridge: Cambridge University Press, 1980).

17. *New York Tribune,* July 16, 1862.

18. *Daily Picayune,* February 20, 1861; *New York Times,* April 20, 1861; *Daily Picayune,* February 22, 1861.

19. *New York Herald,* April 30, 1861.

20. Benjamin F. Butler, *Autobiography and Personal Reminiscences of Major-General Benjamin F. Butler: Butler's Book* (Boston: Thayer, 1892), 414–18.

21. Butler, *Autobiography,* 418–19; Sarah Morgan Dawson, *A Confederate Girl's Diary* (London: Heinemann, 1913), 29–32.

22. Marion Southwood, *"Beauty and Booty": The Watchword of New Orleans* (New York, 1867), 112, 280.

23. Marcus Bruce Christian, "A Black History of Louisiana," Manuscript, Archives of the University of New Orleans, chap. 11, pp. 17–19.

24. Ibid.

25. *New York Tribune,* April 8, 1863; *Daily Alta California,* August 27, 1867.

26. *New York Times,* April 8, 1863; *New York Herald,* July 4, 14, 1863.

27. *New York Herald,* July 14, 17, 1863.

28. *New York Herald,* July 16, 1863; *New York Tribune,* April 8, 1863.

29. Quoted in the *New York Tribune,* July 15, 1863; Christine Stansell, *City of Women: Sex and Class in New York, 1789–1860* (New York: Knopf, 1986).

30. Adrian Cook, *The Armies of the Streets: The New York Draft Riots of 1863* (Lexington: University of Kentucky Press, 1974); see appendix for the list of rioters.

31. *New York Tribune* and *New York Herald,* July 12–19, 1863; Cook, *Armies of the Streets,* 118–19.

32. Lori D. Ginzberg, " 'Moral Suasion Is Moral Balderdash': Women, Politics, and Social Activism in the 1850s," *Journal of American History* 73 (1986): 601–22.

33. *New York Times, New York Tribune,* and *New York Herald,* May 14, 1863; Nanette Paul, *The Great Woman Statesman* (New York, 1925), 48–57.

34. *New York Times, New York Tribune,* and *New York Herald,* May 14, 1863.

35. *New York Times,* May 14, 1863.
36. Elizabeth Griffith, *In Her Own Right: The Life of Elizabeth Cady Stanton* (New York: Oxford University Press, 1984).
37. *New Orleans Tribune,* May 11, 1867; *New York Tribune,* April 9, 1877; *Daily Alta California,* August 29, 1867.
38. *Daily Alta California,* September 1, 1867; *Daily Picayune,* January 7, 1877.
39. *Daily Picayune,* November 2, 1880.
40. *New York Tribune, New York Herald,* and *New York Times,* July 11–14, 1870, 1871.
41. *Daily Alta California,* January 14, September 22, November 30, 1877; *San Francisco Call,* July 9, 1870, July 4, 1877.
42. *New York Tribune,* October 11, 20, 23, December 3, 1877; *New York Times,* October 31, 1877.
43. *San Francisco Call,* February 15, 18, March 22, September 6, 1880.
44. Michael Kazin, "Prelude to Kearneyism: The July Days in San Francisco, 1877," *New Labor Review,* no. 3 (Fall 1980), 18, 19; *San Francisco Call,* February 17, 1880; *New York Tribune,* July 24, 1877.
45. *L'Abeille de la Nouvelle Orleans,* November 5, 1866; *New Orleans Tribune,* December 3, 1867.
46. *Daily Picayune,* December 16, 1874; *New Orleans Tribune,* December 15–16, 1874; *New Orleans Republican,* December 15–17, 1874; Alcée Fortier, *A History of Louisiana,* vol. 3 (New York: Goupil Co., 1904), 139–57.
47. *New York Herald,* May 12, 1872; *San Francisco Morning Call,* February 14, 1870, February 12, 1880.
48. Ellen Carol DuBois, *Feminism and Suffrage: The Emergence of an Independent Women's Movement in America, 1848–1869* (Ithaca: Cornell University Press, 1978); Paul, *Great Woman Statesman,* 58–63.
49. Ellen Carol DuBois, "Outgrowing the Compact of the Fathers: Equal Rights, Woman Suffrage, and the United States Constitution, 1820–1878," *Journal of American History* 74, no. 3 (1987): 836–56.
50. *San Francisco Morning Call,* February 23, 1871, February 12, 1880; DuBois, *Feminism and Suffrage,* chap. 5.
51. DuBois, *Feminism and Suffrage;* Paul, *Great Woman Statesman,* 63–64; Baker, "Domestication of Politics."
52. Linda K. Kerber, *Women of the Republic: Intellect and Ideology in Revolutionary America* (Chapel Hill: University of North Carolina Press, 1980); Ruth Bloch, "The Gendered Meaning of Virtue in Revolutionary America," *Signs* 13, no. 1 (1987): 37–58.
53. Paula Baker, *Gender and the Transformation of Politics: Public and Private Life in New York, 1870–1930* (Boston: Free Press, 1990).
54. Nancy Fraser, "What's Critical about Critical Theory? The Case of Habermas and Gender," *New German Critique* 35 (Spring/Summer 1985): 97–133; Hanna Fenichel Pitkin, "Justice: On Relating Private and Public," *Political Theory* 9, no. 3 (1981): 327–52.
55. Pitkin, "Justice."

Epilogue

1. Linda K. Kerber, *Women of the Republic: Intellect and Ideology in Revolutionary America* (Chapel Hill: University of North Carolina Press, 1980).
2. Judith Walkowitz, "Male Vice and Feminist Virtue: Feminism and the Politics of Prostitution in Nineteenth-Century Britain," *History Workshop Journal* 13 (Spring 1982): 79-93.
3. Linda Alcoff, "Cultural Feminism versus Post-Structuralism: The Identity Crisis in Feminist Theory," *Signs* 13, no. 3 (1988): 405-36. Derrida is quoted here.

Index

Designed by Martha Farlow

Composed by BG Composition, in Garth Graphic

Printed by R. R. Donnelley, Inc., on 50-lb S. D. Warren's Sebago
Cream White and bound in Holliston Aqualite